CCCC STUDIES IN WRITI

Edited by Steve Parks, Uni

The aim of the CCCC Studies in Writing & Rhetoric (SWR) Series is to influence how we think about language in action and especially how writing gets taught at the college level. The methods of studies vary from the critical to historical to linguistic to ethnographic, and their authors draw on work in various fields that inform composition—including rhetoric, communication, education, discourse analysis, psychology, cultural studies, and literature. Their focuses are similarly diverse—ranging from individual writers and teachers, to work on classrooms and communities and curricula, to analyses of the social, political, and material contexts of writing and its teaching.

SWR was one of the first scholarly book series to focus on the teaching of writing. It was established in 1980 by the Conference on College Composition and Communication (CCCC) in order to promote research in the emerging field of writing studies. As our field has grown, the research sponsored by SWR has continued to articulate the commitment of CCCC to supporting the work of writing teachers as reflective practitioners and intellectuals.

We are eager to identify influential work in writing and rhetoric as it emerges. We thus ask authors to send us project proposals that clearly situate their work in the field and show how they aim to redirect our ongoing conversations about writing and its teaching. Proposals should include an overview of the project, a brief annotated table of contents, and a sample chapter. They should not exceed 10,000 words.

To submit a proposal, please register as an author at www.editorialmanager.com/nctebp. Once registered, follow the steps to submit a proposal (be sure to choose SWR Book Proposal from the drop-down list of article submission types).

Rhetorics Elsewhere and Otherwise

Contested Modernities, Decolonial Visions

Edited by
Romeo García
University of Utah
and
Damián Baca
University of Arizona

Staff Editor: Bonny Graham
Manuscript Editor: Lee Erwin
Series Editor: Steve Parks
Interior Design: Mary Rohrer
Cover Design: Pat Mayer
Cover Image: iStockphoto.com/baona

NCTE Stock Number: 41410; eStock Number: 41427
ISBN 978-0-8141-4141-0; eISBN 978-0-8141-4142-7

It is the policy of NCTE in its journals and other publications to provide a forum for the open discussion of ideas concerning the content and the teaching of English and the language arts. Publicity accorded to any particular point of view does not imply endorsement by the Executive Committee, the Board of Directors, or the membership at large, except in announcements of policy, where such endorsement is clearly specified.

NCTE provides equal employment opportunity (EEO) to all staff members and applicants for employment without regard to race, color, religion, sex, national origin, age, physical, mental or perceived handicap/disability, sexual orientation including gender identity or expression, ancestry, genetic information, marital status, military status, unfavorable discharge from military service, pregnancy, citizenship status, personal appearance, matriculation or political affiliation, or any other protected status under applicable federal, state, and local laws.

Every effort has been made to provide current URLs and email addresses, but because of the rapidly changing nature of the web, some sites and addresses may no longer be accessible.

Library of Congress Cataloging-in-Publication Data

Names: García, Romeo, 1987–, editor. | Baca, Damián, 1974–, editor.
Title: Rhetorics elsewhere and otherwise : contested modernities, decolonial visions / edited by Romeo García, University of Utah, and Damián Baca, University of Arizona.
Description: Urbana, Illinois : National Council of Teachers of English, [2019] | Series: CCCC studies in writing & rhetoric | Includes bibliographical references and index.
Identifiers: LCCN 2019000313 (print) | LCCN 2019013394 (ebook) | ISBN 9780814141427 (ebook) | ISBN 9780814141410 (pbk) | ISBN 9780814141427 (ebook)
Subjects: LCSH: Rhetoric—Political aspects. | Decolonization—Social aspects.
Classification: LCC P301.5.P67 (ebook) | LCC P301.5P67 R495 2019 (print) | DDC 808—dc23
LC record available at https://lccn.loc.gov/2019000313

CONTENTS

FOREWORD

The stories told within these pages ask for the listener to bear witness to and share the obligation of challenging the imperial legacies of power and knowledge that have continued to structure the relationships we can have to place/land, history, our bodies, and one another. The book coheres around the subtle workings of power in everyday forms of epistemic obedience: those disciplining moments that have categorized, delineated, barred, tracked, devalued, and rigidly structured each and every person. At the same time, the authors illustrate the practice of epistemic disobedience—innovation, resistance and challenge, and border crossing—present within those everyday moments of disciplining.

The authors write from the self, first and foremost, as the site where we all experience the workings of epistemic obedience. Epistemic obedience manifests itself when we are placed into categories of race, gender, sex, family, and class—from the day we are born to the moment we read this book and across every educational moment in between. To some greater or lesser extent, each of us is dehumanized by the structuration demanded by epistemic obedience. No one escapes the process of being assessed, read, categorized, tracked, put into place, and positioned in educational systems. What is to be done?

The locations and positioning of the authors within these pages offer hope in their fluidity. The authors remind us that we are where we learn. We become who we are through the choices we make across everyday disciplining moments. Along the way, they demonstrate how important it is to epistemically delink during moments when we are being written and when we write others. They illustrate how important it is to cross borders of difference and division in an effort to find more capacious ways of being in this world. The authors all demonstrate how important it is to tolerate ambiguity and create liminality when learning, if we hope to achieve alliance building.

Importantly, this collection offers ways to identify local, everyday, "vernacular" knowledges as the first indicators of the legacy of empire. These knowledges and linguistic strivings mark the place where epistemic obedience has failed to take hold, the site where epistemic disobedience begins. They demonstrate the linguistic strivings necessary in the struggle to re-place and re-locate ourselves. They provide ways to challenge the workings of power in the process of becoming epistemically (dis)obedient.

Perhaps most importantly, the authors in this collection offer insight into the recovery work necessary in modern society, however partial, fragmented, and piecemeal it may be. The recovery of suppressed knowledges, languages, histories, and practices always affords a mosaic image of the self, discernable as a whole from the parts only when viewed from a distance. Recovery work is implicit and explicit throughout the writing of *Rhetorics Elsewhere and Otherwise*, making it an indispensable collection of thinking and doing.

Ellen Cushman
Northeastern University

ACKNOWLEDGMENTS

We wish to acknowledge the contributors who helped shape this collection. Many thanks to Steve Parks for his editorial support, valuable advice, and encouragement. Thanks as well to the reviewers who read our manuscript carefully and provided insightful feedback. Finally, we are especially grateful to Ellen Cushman and Victor Villanueva for their compassion and unconditional support throughout this process.

INTRODUCTION
HOPES AND VISIONS: THE POSSIBILITY OF DECOLONIAL OPTIONS

Romeo García
University of Utah

Damián Baca
University of Arizona

In the late 1980s and early 1990s, postcolonial studies emerged as a field of inquiry within writing and rhetorical studies (WRS). It offered for compositionists and rhetoricians a conceptual and theoretical vocabulary for identifying the effects of colonialism and imperialism in the university. These effects could be observed in the research taught, the theory and pedagogy developed, and the classrooms that educated minoritized as well as marginalized students. Through terms and concepts such as contact zones (Pratt) and borderlands (Anzaldúa), scholars found a way to name how the colonial traffics in the normative and to develop a political model for intervening in dominant models of Western culture in WRS. As a result, scholars considered how to approach the classroom as a borderland (Lu) and how the field was failing to incorporate students' ethnic identities, cultures, and literacy skills into the curriculum (Mejía, "Bridging"). They also brought attention to the fact that colonialism was still a reality for student populations near and distant from the United States (Villanueva; Mejía, "Tejano") as well as the ways power manifested itself in discursive practices in and beyond classrooms (Olson). The collective hope was that such work would alter the classroom and open up spaces for students to gain greater cultural agency (Giroux, *Border Crossings*). Ultimately, postcolonial scholars called for disciplinary, administrative, and pedagogical reform to address the knowledges excluded by Western paradigms.

In recent years, the humanities have witnessed a decolonial turn. While acknowledging the contributions of postcolonial studies, decolonial scholars have argued for an expanded analysis of colonialism and its production of the "other." Through the work of the Modern/Colonial Group (i.e., the M/C Group),[1] scholars such as Aníbal Quijano, Walter Mignolo, and María Lugones have highlighted how postcolonialism maintained Europe and European history as the point of reference for understanding the "globe." These scholars argue that a focus on the fifteenth- and sixteenth-century Americas, rather than postcolonialism's focus on later British and other European colonialisms, offers a way to understand that "coloniality" was a precursor to colonialism; the emergence of Western civilization in the Americas during this time laid out a colonial matrix of power that would connect other forms of Western imperial and colonial expansion. Citing Quijano, these scholars question the "post" of postcolonial studies and claim that coloniality "is still the most general form of domination in the world today . . . [and] it hasn't ceased to be, for 500 years" ("Coloniality and Modernity/Rationality" 170).[2] They emphasize that coloniality was formed in the Americas and then transformed by Western imperial countries who still control it to this day. As a result, the M/C Group claims, the modern/colonial world system that emerged from the Americas continues to implement global designs as well as hegemonic models of thinking; it did so in the name of salvation and continues to do so with a rhetoric of modernity, both of which cloak logics of domination.[3] Decoloniality, to them, would be a political, epistemic, and ethical project that surfaces from local histories, elsewhere and otherwise, and speaks back to this world system that affects all aspects of society. It emerges from the hope and vision that it is possible to explore "border thinking" as the site of knowledges and epistemic alternatives that can move us beyond Western categories of epistemology, thought, and feeling. Decoloniality is a story told from a different vantage point: the possibility of decolonial options.

With an emphasis on the return of the repressed on a public stage, decolonialism has already had an impact on composition and rhetoric scholars in WRS. Drawing from (and expanding upon) the conceptual and theoretical vocabulary of decolonial discourse, such as delinking, epistemic disobedience, and border epistemology, this scholarship has led to a different set of emphases and projects. For instance, while postcolonial scholar Min-Zhan Lu would call for "alternative accounts" (909), decolonial scholars like Ellen Cushman would contend that such rhetoric does not do enough to change the terms (concepts) and contents (histories) of the colonial foundations of knowledge and knowledge production. Indeed, decolonial scholars would work to delink WRS from the colonial legacies that authorize capital [R]hetoric and lowercase [r]hetorics. That is, there would be no "colonial center" from which to imagine an "alternative account." Decolonial scholars would work to highlight the colonialist legacies that inform the management and control of knowledges and subjectivities in literacy, composition, and rhetoric curricula. The analytic component is only one aspect of the project of decoloniality; there is also the prospective concept.

Indeed, the decolonial turn in WRS works to build a foundation, a history, of local knowledges and meaning-making practices that breaks from such Western hegemonic models. When M/C Group member Mignolo speaks of pluriversality, then, he is encouraging us to see the conceptual and theoretical vocabulary provided by decolonialism as a medium that can connect stories of local histories of thought and feeling, *elsewhere* and *otherwise*. This connection would not be conceived in terms of what Quijano calls the "unequal nature of the 'other'" ("Coloniality and Modernity/Rationality" 177) nor in the terms of "values of plus and minus degree of humanity" (Mignolo, "Delinking" 499). Rather, Mignolo argues, such histories enable us to see ourselves as connected, to see and tell stories of humanity in-between cultures, times, and spaces. This is the hope and vision of decoloniality: *where the possibility of new stories exists.*

What makes the decolonial turn potentially dangerous and possibly radical, then, is that it has as its foundation the stories, epistemologies, thoughts, and feelings of the anthropoi.[4] That is, decoloniality is marked by a shift and break from the storytellers of the past—think white Western male subjectivity—to the anthropoi, the "others" themselves. Here the anthropoi's act of delinking from the "West" for an "otherwise" local epistemology works to reinscribe the geo- and body-politics of knowledge and understanding that has been repressed and oppressed or that is still colonized as a result of hegemonic models of thinking and epistemology. The anthropoi reinscribe their position as the "knowing subjects," subjects that emerge from a local history of language, memories, and political economy and not just from the colonial European center. (Delinking, then, implies epistemic disobedience.) Decoloniality is the anthropoi expressing and engaging in actions that reflect an unwillingness to accept the domains of coloniality (power, knowledge, subjectivity, sexuality) that justify violence in the name of modernity, a concept premised on the salvation of colonized populations. The overall notion is that without locating and situating structures of thought and feeling, elsewhere and otherwise, the hope of a world built on principles of pluriversality is difficult to imagine.

The anthropoi, as the voice of the decolonial turn, serve as a reminder that there has been (and continues to be) the production of a constant interruption into the supposed "smooth" flow and circulation of Western hegemony. This interruption has the potential and possibility of decentering the "grapher of the polis" as well as disrupting the normalized historical discourse that has used a rhetoric of modernity. (Below we will detail how/why the M/C Group identify modernity and coloniality as an entanglement that has and continues to allow the "West" to assume a "managerial position" globally).[5] Within these acts of disobedience are examples of the anthropoi accessing and putting to work a border epistemology, a space from which to think about, and work toward, differently, a space from which to cultivate *an-other* way of thinking, feeling, doing, and living. The sense of urgency for such decolonial work resides, then, both in a search for options other than Western hegemonic epistemologies and in the exigency to speak, research, and "haunt" such models back. For by haunting back, reappearing from the dead in structures of coloniality, within that which for so long has haunted them, the anthropoi interrupt colonial foundations of knowledge and knowledge production as well as the circulation and flow of hegemony. Here again are the hopes and vision of a decolonial option.

Today such hopes are particularly important. We live in a world where democracy and humanity are being redefined. And we teach and research in a discipline that stands at a crossroad in its pedagogical, research, and public commitments. It is important, then, to have a clear articulation of how the decolonial option can represent one strategic intervention to ensure democracy and humanity will have a positive impact upon the communities we are from, the students we serve, and the discipline in which we carry out our work. Moreover, we believe that to accomplish this goal, we must move to delink, to "contest," what today is as normative or juridical as it has also always been prejudicial and oppressive. For example, WRS scholars continue to work within Eurocentric macronarratives, continue to visit archives embedded in Western systems of thought, and continue to use terms that erase marginalized groups. We believe, however, that democracy and humanity must reside in the local histories of all people and not just some. WRS must represent not just one voice, but the voices of all people. We invoke "contested," then, to name a struggle in pursuance of a pluriversality of stories, thoughts, and feelings—a humanity "in-between" cultures, times, and spaces. We also recognize that the very project of decoloniality itself, no doubt, will come to be "contested" as well. As for us, though, we see this contestation not as an attempt to find the correct definition of decolonial work, but to keep the project of decoloniality open to possibilities both within and outside the disciplines, possibilities that are anchored by hopes and visions, elsewhere and otherwise.

Our aim in what follows is to provide a framework for those researchers, educators, and students encountering the language and practice of decoloniality for the first time. We believe it is important that as decoloniality and decolonial terminologies enter our field there is a clear account of its potential. Moreover, as decolonial work emerges, we believe it is important to pause and reflect upon the different aims of postcolonial and decolonial efforts, both in how they imagine their theoretical/pragmatic work and in how they offer different (but important) strategies for a field attempting to maintain a commitment to the students in the classroom, but increasingly imagining itself in a global context. The point here is that we are not interested in presenting ideas of incommensurability. We are not interested in creating a battle of "postcolonial" versus "decolonial" scholars. Instead, for us, what is at stake in decoloniality is cultivating work, cultivating stories, to effectively make visible a colonial imaginary that festers beneath a 2,500-year-old metanarrative, while also fostering an environment that envisions a humanity-*in*-difference (rather than a humanity-*of*-difference). For a "humanity-*of*-difference" is a metanarrative that ultimately oppresses our insights, our classrooms, and our students. In this search for a "humanity-*in*-difference," it is conceivable to imagine postcolonial and decolonial studies, working together in the hopes of a radical and transformative disruption of Eurocentric knowledge production, offering the prospective possibility of geo- and body-politics of knowledge and understanding, *elsewhere* and *otherwise*.

Indeed, we understand our collection functioning as one access point within a constellation of such work, forming an ecology of decolonial breaks and shifts. We believe, that is to say, that we share in a language and practice that is informed by (and that informs) an agenda to potentially and possibly decolonize language and literacy practices, writing and rhetoric instruction, and research practices and methods. As noted above, we believe that WRS is at a critical juncture today. In this collection of essays, this introduction, we are asking, "How can decoloniality help us reinvigorate our field and our democracy while remaining potentially dangerous and radical?" In the following pages, then, we hope to situate the value of the decolonial option within WRS, to make clear the meaning and work of some of its key terms, and, ultimately, to create a space in which critical dialogue about decoloniality can take place in our field. To do so, however, requires a brief look at what postcolonial studies brought to the table.

STORIES-SO-FAR: POSTCOLONIALISM

In the late 1980s and early 1990s, postcolonial studies emerged as a field focused on the epistemic effects of British, French, and other colonialisms during the eighteenth and nineteenth centuries, the emergence of a "subject" of all knowledge, and the creation of the "other." As such, postcolonial studies investigated the consequences of a shift from God to man as the foundation of knowledge and reason.[6] And here it might be helpful to invoke René Descartes ("I think therefore I am") or Immanuel Kant (the "thing-in-itself") as representative of eighteenth-century philosophers who represent this shift. Such philosophers, for postcolonial scholars, enabled the "Western Empire" to define the European as the bearer of rationality and the non-European as external to it.[7] As a consequence, to echo Enrique Dussel, a macrohistorical white subject (male, man of letters, rational) emerged. This was a white subject who articulated a "reflexive consciousness of world history" within the contexts of conquest and expansionism. It was also a white subject that imagined Western "values, intentions, discoveries, technology, and political institutions as its exclusive achievement" (*The Invention of the Americas* 11).

Postcolonial scholars placed the development of this subject as simultaneous with the emergence of natural history as a structure of knowledge. For instance, Mary Louise Pratt turned to Carl Linnaeus's *Systema Naturae* as an example of Europe's effort to manage and control the chaos of nature. Linnaeus's classificatory system, she argued, essentially launched the idea that nature can be unified and ordered (30).[8] *Systema Naturae* set in motion, for Pratt, the idea that Europe would be the center of "contact" and naturalize a "global presence and authority" (28). That is, the practice of systematizing nature would be consubstantial to how the European subject understood itself, first, in relation to nature, and second, in relation to others on the globe. The former took the stance that man was separate from nature, which "he" could name and control.

The latter built on this stance and took shape in the exploration of continental interiors, in the interplay between *ego cogito* and *ego conquiro,* knowledge production and colonizing practices. That is, Pratt demonstrates how the manifestation of systematizing nature led to the systematizing of some people's histories and cultures into "nature."[9] In the naming that "brings the reality of order into being" (33), Pratt observes, a discourse emerged of the anthropos and the humanitas.[10] And in this discourse, "he who can name" does so in ways that invent the "other" by taking the "other" out of history into nature, objectifying the "other" as stuck in a "precivilized" space or time, and producing images of empty landscapes from which the inhabiting bodies of the "other" have vanished.

It is this "ethics" of "Western culture," for Johannes Fabian, that creates inequality, a lack of coevalness, among individuals/populations. It is an ethics that simultaneously reduces the "other" to a singular-cyclical system (stuck in time) while defining the Western subject against its past (moving forward in time). Like Pratt, Fabian also points to Linnaeus, but he focuses on how Linnaeus inspired anthropologists, such as John Garson and Charles Read, with regard to "observation," "collection and classification," and "description" of the "other" in their *Notes and Queries on Anthropology.* He demonstrates how these anthropologists articulated temporalization, a property of historical discourse, such that the *others'* "time is not the time of civilized history" (Fabian xxiii).[11] "Time," then, became a way to build a universal history of progress, turning travel from the center to the periphery into a passage from the modern to the past. Thus, difference and distance, or allochronism, contributed to the justification of a colonial enterprise by promoting an evolutionary sequence and by constructing its object—the "other"—which needed to be "modernized." (78). Anticipating Pratt's commentary on the "West" as projecting itself as innocent and imperial, Fabian notes, "The anthropologist proclaims himself to be in the service of science, to be nothing but an executor of the laws of nature or reason" (104). Yet, as postcolonialists note, the interplay between Western epistemology and hegemonic models of thinking and feeling play out in the production of global designs of unity and order through colonialism. To echo Dussel, that is, Europe assumed a "managerial position," thinking of itself as bearer of rationality and the "other" as the "essential alterity of modernity" ("Eurocentrism" 74–75), with European rationality enacting its managerial role through its simultaneous "explorations" and "colonizations."

Postcolonial studies would emerge as an interruption to that spatial-temporal discourse on the "other." Postcolonialist scholars such as Edward Said, Homi Bhabha, and Gayatri Spivak invoked a different geo- and body-politics of knowledge and understanding than that constructed by Western Europe. They focused on the geo- and body-politics emerging from the colonized populations of India and/or the Middle East. They attempted to reframe the "other," the "other's knowledge," and the "other's voice" in relationship to Western epistemologies/colonizations. In particular, Said's *Orientalism* is understood as one of the founding "postcolonial" pieces of scholarship through its historicizing of the production of the "other." One of the book's primary contributions is its question, "How did philology, lexicography, history, biology, political and economic theory, novel-writing, and lyric poetry come to the service of Orientalism's broadly imperialist view of the world?" (15). To answer this question, he traces how narratives on and representations of the Orient were consubstantial with colonial rule (39). He points to authors such as Silvestre de Sacy, Ernest Renan, and Edward William Lane, focusing on their public speeches, travel literature/writing, anthropology, and/or philology as examples of colonial discourse. These authors and their works, he showed, represented an effort to "read" the Orient in the service of creating an artificial division between the East and the West that could produce the "other." Said shows how Orientalism is a type of science that generalized and asserted the qualities of "the East" as uncivilized and "the West" as civilized.

Orientalism, that is, reduced people to objects/races and then confined that knowledge to classifications, similar to Linnaeus's classificatory system of organisms, which naturalized Western superiority. To solidify the West as the source of knowledge (i.e., the given), the Orient would be researched, taught, and "pronounced upon in certain discrete ways" (202). In Orientalist narratives, for instance, the image of Orient was "unchanging" and "absolutely different" (96). Such narratives, revealed in the relationship between literature, ideology, and hegemony, had great "density" and "referential power." Each work, he writes, "on the Orient affiliates itself with other works, with audiences, with institutions, with the Orient itself" (20). The network of texts on the Orient, Said argues, "helped to define Europe (or the West) as its contrasting image, idea, personality, experience" (1–2). Moreover, this *latent* and *manifest* Orientalism, Said claims, would enable the West to make the transition from a passive-knowledge-of-the-Orient narrative to a more active-knowledge narrative that would focus on how the "Orientals' bodies are lazy" and how the Orient had "no conception of history, of the nation" (253), authorizing colonialist attitudes/actions. Said's contribution to postcolonialism, then, is his assertion that the "Orient is not the Orient as it is, but the Orient as it has been Orientalized" (104). This, he argues, continues to persist today in various forms and enunciations of Western thought.

In *The Location of Culture*, Homi Bhabha is interested in recovering the "other" as "otherwise than modernity" (9).[12] Central in the invention and translation of the "other," for Bhabha, is a system of representation and a regime of truth premised on differentiation and iteration (42). Differentiation, Bhabha shows, is a process by which a tradition or discourse marks out a "subject nation" by construing "the colonized as a population of degenerate types." Iteration is the "productivity and circulation of subjects and signs . . . bound in a reformed and recognizable totality" that reaffirm this differentiation (101). Thus, Bhabha writes, in the discourse between "civil address and its colonial signification," a "strategy of surveillance, subjection, and inscription" (138) is undertaken. One of the book's primary contributions is interrupting and intervening in this subjection (differentiation and iteration) by historicizing that "colonized" space and attempting to theorize an alternative one. Bhabha does this by arguing that there is not a "given community or body of the people whose inherent, radical historicity emits the right signs" (39). Indeed, the image of the West, he continues, "depends on the production of alternative or antagonistic images that are always produced side by side and in competition with each other" (42). That is, the West necessarily produces the non-West. It is the split between an appearance of originality and the imposition of authority, the constant cycle of "iteration and difference," that reminds us that the West is a colonial fantasy. The ambivalence of colonial rule, its inability to fully realize its vision of totality in the real geography of the local, provides the opportunity, according to Bhabha, to imagine a Third Space and to carve out the concept of hybridity.

Bhabha deploys the Third Space, then, as a way to reveal the impossibility of "the West." He sets out to locate culture as "living on the borderlines" of both the "realm of beyond" (prior to/adjacent to colonized space) and the "present" (colonized space) (1). "Beyond" and "present," here, are reoriented to mean an "intervening space," a space that negotiates differences (10). Working toward shifting from "narratives of originary and initial subjectivities," such as proclaimed by the "West," to a focus on "those moments or processes that are produced in the articulation of cultural differences" (2),[13] Bhabha describes the Third Space as a space of translation, a space where negotiation rather than negation takes place. The "Third Space of Enunciation," he argues, is a site that destroys "those negative polarities between knowledge and its objects" (37–38), for in this space "meaning and symbols have no primordial unity or fixity" (55). The Third Space, thus, encourages the renegotiation of the meaning of culture (37–38). This affords him the opportunity to introduce cultural hybridity, a concept expressed in the words *neither the one nor the other.* It is, as Bhabha notes, an "ambivalent 'turn' of the discriminated subject into the terrifying, exorbitant object of paranoid classification—a disturbing questioning of the images and presences of authority" (162). Terrifying as colonial mimicry might be, the strategic space of enunciation produced in the words *neither the one nor the other* ensures that the given image of the West cannot be realized in totality, that the "other" cannot be fully constituted. In this space of negotiation, non-Western knowledges cannot be fully oppressed through a singular narrative of time as progress and space as civilized/uncivilized. "Beyond" and "present," Bhabha claims, allow us to "transform our sense of what it means to live, to be, in other times and different spaces, both human and historical" (367).

If the above work historicizes the "other" and creates a "Third Space" to (we hope) block the creation of the "West," Gayatri Spivak's seminal text, "Can the Subaltern Speak?" takes up the issue of the ability of the "other" to speak, to be heard. Spivak begins by noting that there is a desire to disclose and know the "other"—to imagine an authentic speaking-subject. "Desire and its object," Spivak writes, "are a 'unity'" (68). This unity unfolds in the relationship between the intellectual who "diagnoses the episteme" (69) and the anthropos who becomes the signifier of said representation. Spivak finds it problematic that the articulation between representation (i.e., speaking for) and re-presentation (philosophical theory) occurs through an image of intellectuals who represent themselves "as transparent" (70). Spivak argues that the subaltern does indeed produce a "constant interruption for the full telos of Reason and capitalism" ("Responsibility" 55), but takes issue with the proposition that the "oppressed subjects speak, act, and know for themselves," a stance she believes enacts as an "essentialist, utopian politics" ("Can the Subaltern Speak?" 71). She asserts that the idea of a transparent representation of the oppressed only reintroduces the "individual subject through totalizing concepts of power and desire" (74). That is, the subaltern cannot speak, for the subaltern remains a subject of "desire and power," remaining re-presented as the "subject of the oppressed" (74). Spivak writes, then, that "the subaltern's inability to speak is predicated upon an attempt to speak" in which "no appropriate response" can be proffered ("Responsibility" 62). That is, the episteme that creates the "other" cannot be used to hear the "other" outside of that definition. The imagined transparency of the intellectual, then, is a dangerous belief for it denies the continued entanglement and complicity in the "persistent constitution of Other" ("Can the Subaltern Speak?" 74–75). What we too often observe, Spivak argues, are intellectuals masquerading as the "absent nonrepresenter who lets the oppressed speak for themselves" (87).

In "Can the Subaltern Speak?" Spivak also contributes to postcolonialism through interrupting and intervening in the relationship between imperial history and imperial narrative, specifically the effect British colonialism has had on India through its codifying of Hindu Law as well as the British abolition of widow sacrifices. Through reading the historical, legislative, and traditional practices surrounding widow sacrifices, Spivak historicizes the above theoretical argument about "speaking" to point out the evident role of an ideology around widow sacrifice that disseminates "two contending versions of freedom," one where "crime" and "reward" are juxtaposed (97).[14] Paradoxically, it is within this juxtaposition that Spivak is able to locate and situate the "displaced figuration of the third-world woman," a woman "caught between tradition and modernization" (102). It is also here, however, where she again argues, now historically, "There is no space from which the sexed subaltern subject can speak" (103). The question, "Can the subaltern speak?" is not a literal question, then, according to Spivak, but one situated in the state of impossibility, based on the impossibility of concepts such as understanding, transparency, translation. With Spivak, we find the impossibility of "transparency" as a tool for letting the "others" speak for themselves and, thus, an argument for a theory of ideology that would be more attentive to desire, interests, and power in narratives and representation.

As noted earlier, composition and rhetoric scholars have used postcolonialism to theorize and articulate counterstories to Western epistemology's subject/geographical categories within WRS. In such work, it is possible to hear echoes (and direct references) to historicizing the "'other," discovering the possibility of border negotiations, and theorizing about what it might mean for our students to "speak." Min-Zhan Lu, for instance, applies a borderland perspective to her study on a "new generation of compositionists and 'minority' writers," arguing that we need to critique portrayals of basic writers which imagine them as belonging "to an abnormal—traumatized or underdeveloped—mental state and which simultaneously provides accounts of . . . Basic Writers' efforts to grapple with the conflict within and among diverse discourses" (910). And in the edited collection by Andrea Lunsford and Lahoucine Ouzgane *Crossing Borderlands: Composition and Postcolonial Studies*, Gary Olson asserts, "The literature of postcolonial theory is especially relevant to our own scholarship" (89), arguing that "the trend in composition scholarship to interrogate how gender, race, ethnicity, and power relationships manifest themselves in discursive practices is in effect a move towards the ethical, toward understanding the encounter with the Other" (93). Yet Victor Villanueva reminds readers: "There is nothing post to America's colonialism." He worries that "if we hear the term without having read the substance . . . we'll stop problematizing what we do in our assimilationist teaching" (186). This stance is affirmed by Jaime Mejía, in the special issue of the *Journal of Advanced Composition* entitled "Exploring Borderlands: Postcolonial and Composition Studies," where he illuminates how in the Southwest, "the colonizers have not left; they remain and, in many parts, continue their colonial domination" (123). Postcolonialism, then, represents a "story-so-far" in our attempt to build a discipline "beyond and otherwise."

By stories-so-far, we mean to say that postcolonial studies helped scholars, educators, and students identify and name what many minoritized and racialized people have thought and felt: the colonial trafficking in the "normative," a constant invocation of a Western epistemology centered within European contexts. But as will be discussed in the next section, there are other stories to tell, *an-other* set of stories that articulate an analysis of colonialism and coloniality from a different period in time, stories that also represent the "anthropoi" speaking, researching, and "haunting," stories that seek out the possibilities within a different model of theory, praxis, and methodology. Even then, however, all we have are stories-so-far.

THE POSSIBILITY OF NEW STORIES: DECOLONIALITY

The possibility of new stories in the project of decoloniality begins with that which has been excluded: stories *elsewhere* and *otherwise*. Decolonial scholars find it a primary responsibility to hear/record such stories without reducing their irreducible quality, the local histories and human experiences that exist outside "Western" epistemologies. Indeed, the shift away from the storytellers of the past (e.g., the traveler, the colonialist, the academic) to the anthropoi themselves (local individuals within local epistemic frameworks) is a nod to the fact that all stories told have "structural underpinnings and material consequences" and that all stories are political (Rohrer 189). As a consequence, decolonial scholars work from the potential of such stories to change the terms as well as the contents of knowledge production, thus changing the epistemes in which politics occurs. Indeed, the dangerous and radical possibility of the decolonial turn is the fact of its foundation's being based on the stories, epistemologies, thoughts, and feelings of the anthropoi. To keep the project of decoloniality potentially dangerous and possibly radical, then, decolonial scholars remain committed to the options articulated in these stories.[15] The decolonial option, thus, is always in the intermediary state of a question: a decolonial option?

This decolonial framework, similar to that of the postcolonialists, begins through tracing the shift from theology to secular humanist politics (e.g., theo- and ego-politics). The M/C Group contribution, however, situates its work in the fifteenth- and sixteenth-century "discovery" and "colonization" of the Americas. This is the event,[16] they collectively argue, that initiated the formation of a modern/colonial world system framed through concepts of the "West." In "Americanity as a Concept," Aníbal Quijano and Immanuel Wallerstein refer to the Americas, thus, as an "original creation" (556) with its "newness" at the forefront of a "series of institutions and worldviews" that would ultimately emerge into an "interstate system" of associations of social interests of which the West would come to be seen as the "leader." There was, for instance, in the Americas, the establishment of "new" social identities (Spanish, Indian, Negro, Mestizo) and "new" geocultural identities (European, American, Asiatic, African). These "were premised upon the ideas of race as 'biologically structural and hierarchical'" ("Coloniality of Power and Eurocentrism," 216) and connected to a "new" understanding of capital/capitalism. This establishment of race and ethnicities as a measurement of the "human being" provided the justification for colonization as well as for specific forms of controlling labor ("Coloniality of Power, Eurocentrism" 537).

Within a historical context that is five hundred years long, coloniality would come to be defined as distinct from colonialism. Coloniality, the M/C Group encourages us to understand, is a global structure of management and control. Specifically, coloniality would be defined as:

- "[t]hat specific basic element of the new pattern of world power that was based on the idea of 'race' and in the 'racial' social classification of world population—expressed in the 'racial' distribution of work, in the imposition of new 'racial' geocultural identities, in the concentration of the control of productive resources and capital, as social relations, including salary, as a privilege of 'Whiteness'" ("Coloniality of Power and Eurocentrism" 218)
- "the appropriation of land and the exploitation of labor, . . . the control of authority, . . . the control of gender and sexuality, . . . and the control of subjectivity" ("Delinking" 478)
- "the creation of a set of states linked together within an interstate system in hierarchical layers . . . creating not only rank order but sets of rules for the interactions of states with each other" (Quijano and Wallerstein 550)
- the ideas of Western totality, "an image of society as a closed structure articulated in a hierarchic order with functional relations between its parts," which presupposes "a unique historical logic to the historical totality, and a rationality consisting in the subjection of every part to that unique total logic." This would lead to conceiving "society as a macro-historical subject, endowed with a historical rationality, with a lawfulness that permits predictions of the behavior of the whole and of all its part[s], as well as the direction and the finality of its development in time" ("Coloniality and Modernity/Rationality" 176)
- "the most general form of domination in the world today, once colonialism as an explicit political order was destroyed" ("Coloniality and Modernity/Rationality" 170)

Here the difference between coloniality and colonization is delineated along the lines of a colonial matrix of power upon which Western civilization built itself. *Colonialism* is defined as the historical period in which European powers held colonies. *Coloniality* is the establishment of world power and authority implicitly agreed upon by "core" countries about what would constitute "order," an order premised on biological/hierarchical categories, regardless of whether a territory is/has been colonized. Its sophistication, as Quijano would say, is that even if the "interstate system" of "hierarchical layers" could be dismantled, "all or some of [the states] can and will be rearticulated in some other structural pattern" ("Coloniality of Power and Eurocentrism," 220). It has and continues to do so in the name of modernity.

It should be noted, however, that coloniality is more than the creation of racial or economic identities. As noted in the above list, gender is also an element of coloniality. In "The Coloniality of Gender," María Lugones discusses how gender and sexuality were limited in possibility/potentiality during the construction of modernity/coloniality.[17] Lugones writes, "The logic of structural axes shows gender as constituted by and constituting the coloniality of power" (4). Yet, departing from Quijano, she asserts, "Quijano's framework restricts gender to the organization of sex, its resources and products and he seems to make a presupposition as to who controls access and who becomes constituted as 'resources'" (6). In tracing the discourse of "sexual dimorphism" and "sexual differences," discourses that are consubstantial in a colonial/modern gender system, Lugones arrives at a crucial moment in which she can both think of what the colonial/modern gender system "hides, or disallows from consideration" (9) as well as reimaging a reexistence of gender in precolonial societies. Lugones brings the liberation and empowerment project of decoloniality to the forefront of gender and sexuality. In doing so, she complicates and expands the scope and breadth of coloniality.

Within this expanded framework, decolonial theory provides several key conceptual transitions to/frameworks for potential research, which, while they were briefly discussed above, we now want to discuss in more detail. These conceptual transitions include: *from colonialism to coloniality; from decolonialism to decoloniality;* and *from Western epistemology to border epistemology*. For example, in "The Prospect of Harmony," Mignolo refers to *colonization* as a "specific historical moment" as opposed to *coloniality,* which refers to "the logic of domination behind the salvation rhetoric of modernity" (par. 27). For Mignolo, the significance of coloniality is that it signals the capacity of hegemony to remain without colonies. For instance, one might turn to the Lower Rio Grande Valley (LRGV), a region at the frontera of the South Texas–Mexico geopolitical border. It is a region embedded with both historical violence (i.e., colonialism) and contemporary violence (i.e., colonial management and control). The LRGV and its people are bordered to the south by the geopolitical border and to the north by internal checkpoints. We must consider what the bordering of the Lower Rio Grande Valley effectively does and how the borders and checkpoints confirm a relationship between the Lower Rio Grande Valley and the interior parts of Texas.

The condition of possibility that is a border culture in the Lower Rio Grande Valley exists because of what the border and internal checkpoints create: a *geography of exclusion*—a space discursively interpreted, monitored, and contained (Peters 666). It is no coincidence that within this space reside people considered to be some of the most impoverished, "illiterate," and undereducated in the United States. Nor is it a coincidence that this space is seen as "dangerous" and a "disruption" to national borders and identity. Thus, this space is not simply a borderland, but rather, a border(ed)land that exemplifies how the colonial traffics in the normative—US citizens as white European descendants being protected from the "other," "the Mexican," not through direct colonization but through coloniality. This border(ed)land demonstrates how a geography of exclusion is a logic of domination cloaked by a rhetoric of progress and safety. That is, a geography of exclusion interprets, monitors, and excludes "the Mexican" in the name of the United States as a "modern" nation-state. The border and internal checkpoints mark the presencing of imperial designs, effectually ensuring that denizens of the Lower Rio Grande Valley know that the colonial will traffic in the normative.

To continue, this conceptual shift, then, enables the next stage of investigation/analysis, the shift from *decolonial* to *decoloniality*. In *The Darker Side of Western Modernity*, Mignolo refers to decolonization as the nonaligned states' struggle to "detach themselves from capitalism and communism," in contrast to decoloniality, which refers to an epistemic, political, and ethical project of "unveiling the logic of coloniality and the prospective task of contributing to the effort to build a world in which many worlds coexist" (53–54). The effects of Linnaeus's system of taxonomization and the discourse of anthropos and humanitas, of who did and did not possess the ability to produce "knowledge," should come to mind here. Quijano provides some context to how European coloniality oppressed local knowledges:

> The repression fell, above all, over the modes of knowing, of producing knowledge, of producing perspectives, images and systems of images, symbols, modes of signification, over the resources, patterns, and instruments of formalized and objectivised expression, intellectual or visual. ("Coloniality and Modernity/Rationality" 169)

This repression, Quijano notes, "was followed by the imposition of the use of the rulers' own patterns of expression," which served not only to "impede the cultural productions of the dominated" but also as a "very efficient means of social and cultural control." This efficient means of management and control, that is, unfolds through the use of a paradigm of rational knowledge, i.e., the coopting of the dominated community into Western "power institutions," propriety, and knowledge systems ("Coloniality and Modernity/Rationality" 169).

Thus, in the discourse of anthropoi and humanitates, humanitates are those who possess civilization, while the anthropoi "cannot escape the status of being the object of anthropological knowledge" (Osamu 260).[18] In historical discourse, as noted above, the "other" is absolute and either absent or objectified. For the M/C Group this is an example of how a rhetoric of modernity was used to cloak the logics of coloniality. That is, in the modernity/coloniality dynamic, there is an articulation of an evolutionary continuum: from barbaric to rational and from primitive to civilized. Acknowledging the relationship between modernity and coloniality, Mignolo uses the slash "/" to signal the division and entanglement of modern/colonial and colonial/imperial. The "myth of modernity" (i.e., a crooked rhetoric of modernity), as the M/C Group refers to it, is the "most successful fiction of the European imaginary," because it created the belief that "modernity is something you have to catch up with" (Mignolo, "The Prospect," par. 38). In the process of articulating that "something" needed to be caught up with, the idea was also articulated that the "other" was not only culpable for its own victimization, but that the victimizer was innocent, for the "West" simply sought to bring liberation, progress, and development.[19]

Decoloniality represents an ongoing process of rejecting this epistemological framework that is constitutive of modernity. Therefore, in and across the United States and the globe, decolonial scholars research local efforts to encroach upon coloniality, reflecting epistemological, political, and ethical projects unwilling to concede to "domination" or a "crooked rhetoric" of modernity. These projects can range from decolonizing gender, such as the work of Lugones, to decolonizing knowledge, such as indigenous farming practices (e.g., the White Earth Land Recovery Project), to decolonizing dietary practices (Calvo and Esquibel), and decolonizing natural resources (e.g., the Standing Rock Water Protectors). These local efforts, the M/C Group would argue, are central to the creation of a pluriversality of knowledges/worlds. In naming "coloniality" and "decoloniality," then, the M/C Group sets out to engage thereafter in a multilayered critique of Western epistemology and hegemonic models of thinking that further seeks to change the terms and content of conversations.

The final transition represents the culmination of the previous two: a move from *Western epistemology* to *border epistemology*. It is a transition to a decolonial option situated within *an-other* paradigm premised on border epistemology, with an inventory of concepts such as delinking, epistemic disobedience, and border epistemology (briefly discussed earlier) to enable this process. For instance, delinking is conceived as not being performed "within the frame of the theo and the ego-logical politics of knowledge and understanding" ("Delinking" 461) of the West. Instead, delinking is a decolonial shift which requires "analysis of the making and remaking of the imperial and colonial differences" and "visions and strategies for the implementation of border thinking leading to decolonialization of knowledge and of being" (498). Mignolo refers to "an-other" paradigm as belonging to this "different space" and *an-other* "epistemic energy" (485). Herein lies the possibility of the decolonial option, which, according to the M/C Group, has been laid out by anthropoi of the past. The transition, this shift, then, plays out in an argument for *an-other* paradigm where one is either on the colonizer's or the decolonizer's side, i.e., among those who (a) "enact the 'irrational myth that justifies genocidal violence'" or (b) those that "oppose and denounce it" (458).

The M/C Group often turn to Frantz Fanon and Gloria Anzaldúa to frame the possibilities of delinking and the pursuance of decolonial options. They are seen as examples of thinking outside the frames of theo- and ego-politics of "Western" knowledge. Their work is self-aware about a break from terms and contents that "totalize *a* reality" ("Delinking" 459) and shifts towards pluriversality and *an-other* way of thinking and feeling. For instance, in *The Wretched of the Earth*, Fanon wrote: "We must remember in any case that a colonized people is not just a dominated people" (182) and that "deep down the colonized subject acknowledges no authority" (16). Similarly, Anzaldúa referred to the US-Mexico border as "una herida abierta" and as a site where both "los atravesados" live and where a "border culture" is formed (25). At these moments, they were calling attention to local histories that emanate from imperial and/or colonial wounds, the experience of being on the receiving end of coloniality, but speak to a different epistemological space. Fanon and Anzaldúa, that is, were theorizing from an-other geo- and body-politics of knowledge and understanding premised on local experiences (i.e., an-other episteme and ontology) that had been negated by the theo- and ego-politics of the West.

In recovering historical locations and loci of enunciations, Mignolo comes to define geo- and body-politics of knowledge and understanding as follows:

> Epistemic geo-politics implies a de-colonial shift and acquires its meaning, here, not in relation to an object (the earth), but in the frame of epistemic embodiments (geo-historical and body-graphical) in the spatial organization of the modern/colonial world: the geopolitics of knowledge names the historical location (space and time, the historical marks and configuration of a space and a place, etc.) and authority of loci of enunciation that had been negated by the dominance and hegemony of both the theo-logical and ego-logical politics of knowledge and understanding. ("Delinking" 460)

Mignolo argues, then, for geo- and body-politics of knowledge and understanding from *an-other* historical location that breaks up the illusion that "all knowledges are and have to originate in the imperial form of consciousness" (462). This "restores" something taken away, managed, and controlled by the logics of coloniality—the knowing subject, local histories of languages, political economies, and political theories.[20]

In essence, scholars/writers such as Anzaldúa were using the resistance of the colonized and the border as an epistemic metaphor for connecting decolonial narratives and instigating decolonial breaks and shifts from hegemonic Western abstract universals. For instance, Anzaldúa is using the border as an epistemic metaphor both to engage in epistemic disobedience—"The work of mestiza consciousness is to break down the subject-object duality" (102)—and for delinking—"a new value system with images and symbols that connect us to each other and to the planet" (103). Anzaldúa's advancement of a new mestiza consciousness, the foregrounding of an-other episteme and ontology, as well as the theorizing of the border as an epistemic metaphor, connects all those who experience the imperial and/or colonial wound. This marks the return of the anthropoi and their sense of urgency to change the terms (concepts) and contents (histories) tied to modernity/coloniality.[21]

Border thinking is grounded, then, in "colonial wounds" and "imperial subordination" (Mignolo, "Geopolitics of Sensing and Knowing" 137). It is a conceptual space where "Western knowledge and subjectivity, control of land and labor, of authority, and ways of living gender and sexuality are in contact with other languages, memories, principles of knowledge and beliefs" (Mignolo, "Delinking" 497). The border is the limit of Westernization, physically and philosophically. Thus, delinking denounces the "pretended universality of a particular ethnicity, located in a specific part of the planet" (453). And epistemic disobedience means shifting the "geography of reason [from the West] and enacting geo-politics of knowledge" based on local histories/knowledges (Mignolo, "Epistemic Disobedience" 173). Thus, decoloniality breaks from a totalizing [*a*] reality and [*a*] linear history and shifts to *an-other* set of geo- and body-politics of knowledge and understanding that encourages the conception of non-Eurocentered paradigms (Mignolo, "The Geopolitics of Knowledge" 67). Herein lies the import of decolonial work and projects, the hope and vision for *an-other* way.

One final point: Importantly, the M/C Group would argue that analysis is not enough. Delinking, epistemic disobedience, and border epistemology would not make sense if it were not also grounded in a prospective task of contributing to build a world in which many worlds could coexist. The *prospective-programmatic* vision and pursuance of a decolonial planetary critical consciousness is the spirit of pluriversality, which imagines humanity in difference, not in the sense of the "unequal nature of the 'other'" (Quijano, "Coloniality and Modernity/Rationality" 177) nor in terms of "values of plus and minus degree of humanity" (Mignolo, "Delinking" 499). Rather, the vision means incorporating *an-other* tongue, thinking, and logic "superseding the longer history of the modern/colonial world, the coloniality of power, the subalternization of knowledge and the colonial difference" (Mignolo, *Local Histories* 338). It is a vision that seeks both the possibility of coexisting geo- and body-politics of knowledge and understanding and the possibility of an "alternative" to modernity. It reflects a "planetary critical consciousness that emerged and unfolded, precisely out of the limits of abstract universal of its current manifestations and out of the dangers that, in the future, a 'new' abstract universal will attempt to replace the existing ones; or that the existing ones will renew themselves as 'new'" (Mignolo, "Delinking" 500). In all, the *prospective-programmatic* vision rejects the linear history "from Greek to contemporary North Atlantic knowledge production" (Mignolo, "The Geopolitics of Knowledge" 67) and reflects a project of unlearning to relearn, to break and shift from a process that coalesces objectification and ownership into a formula of management and control in the name of modernity.[22]

Thus a real concern expressed by decolonial scholars is how the embourgeoisement and market-economy models of academic theory might effect decolonial practice. This is why it is important for the M/C Group that we, as scholars, educators, and students, recognize and acknowledge that border thinking is not about improving the disciplines. Delinking, epistemic disobedience, and border thinking in the humanities are the actions of the anthropoi pushing the "discipline" to move beyond itself. Decoloniality is an epistemic, political, and ethical project. It provides both the analytic for a position of critique and a vision of a world that does not deny the possibility for people, *elsewhere* and *otherwise,* to participate in the production, distribution, and/or organization of knowledge. It can and should be more than disciplinary reform.

DECOLONIAL OPTIONS: LOCATING BODIES AND PRACTICES IN WRITING AND RHETORICAL STUDIES

The project of decoloniality, including its conceptual and theoretical vocabulary, is new to the humanities. However, the experience of the anthropoi is not. And within the project of decoloniality, it is important for one to speak from a specific historicized geo- and body-politics of knowledge and understanding. This is the initial move toward a decolonial practice—a stepping outside of unified space and time. For instance, one of the editors of *Rhetorics Elsewhere and Otherwise* (*REO*), Romeo García, is from the Lower Rio Grande Valley, a region which as discussed above is still situated within local settler colonial narratives, cloaked by a rhetoric of modernity and narratives of salvation, progress, and development. In "Corrido-ing State Violence," García reads the *Texas Rangers in Action* comic book, published between the 1950s and 1970s, and demonstrates an enactment of local settler colonial narratives through a corrido-ing approach. He writes that the comics' purpose is "to induce effect and affect at the level of taste and morality by presenting history," concluding, "We must then hold the comic book accountable or responsible for justifying state violence" (61) in the name of "protection" and "progress."

He also explores how in this region of South Texas, there have been and continue to be local histories of Mexican and Mexican American communities speaking to and haunting the assumed "smooth" flow and circulation of such hegemonic concepts, such as the above comic books. These histories, including the conventions of El Primer Congreso Mexicanista and the Harlingen Convention, as well as the formation of LULAC, are what helped create the foundation for what we refer to today as the Chicano/a Movement. For García, recognizing and acknowledging these histories of bodies and places, as well as experiencing how the colonial continues to traffic in the normative, has continued to provide the impetus for coming back to the Lower Rio Grande Valley as a site from which to articulate a "haunting" of Eurocentric practices, both as historical practices in the region and, from this embodied local positionality, a moving of WRS toward a future beyond its current "disciplinary" framework. Such a positionality for García remains open to historical geographies and enunciations elsewhere and otherwise and, as such, attempts to articulate decoloniality as an elsewhere and otherwise practice in WRS.

The coeditor of this collection, Damián Baca, has attempted to delink WRS from coloniality by researching the historical locations and loci of enunciations beyond Greek and Roman civilizations in WRS. Here the delinking is a project that reemerges/articulates border epistemologies into WRS. For instance, *Mestiz@ Scripts, Digital Migrations, and the Territories of Writing* is significant to our project in that it recovers *an-other* form of writing practices (pictures, symbols, and performances linked to the Valley of Mexico). Here Baca's project centers on subversion and revision of hierarchical narratives of assimilation. There is evidence of a strategic decolonial break when he writes, "The idea here is to decenter nationalist concepts of gender and race by placing them in dialogue with local regional perspectives across the borderlands" (158). By looking at the interactions between Mesoamerican and Western cultures, as well as how those exchanges of cultural materials led to "Mestiz@ inventions" of knowledge productions and meaning-making practices, Baca illuminates subversive acts of critique and translation of colonial structures of power. Mestiz@ inventions stem, Baca articulates, from the consequence of mestizaje, an expression, he states, that "consists of a dynamic spectrum of shifting and contested subjectivity," which alludes to a "larger milieu of Latinidad across the Americas and the Caribbean at large" (2). This allows a second strategic decolonial intervention, focused on pedagogical practices, later in the text: "Incorporating the perspectives of such lives into the curriculum would engage teachers and students in material history while raising their awareness of the many regions and experiences that have informed the practice of writing across North American territories" (160).

Decolonial breaks and shifts away from narratives of assimilation and normative historical thinking continue in the collection *Rhetorics of the Americas: 3114 BCE to 2012 CE*, edited by Baca and Victor Villanueva. One chapter on Inca verbal and iconic textualizations strives to argue against the narrative that Andean communication is an "alternative" communication (Quispe-Agnoli), while another chapter focuses on Hawaiian pidgin language as a rhetorical vehicle that reaffirms vernacular local identity and practices (Nordstrom). Here Baca's chapter centers the multifaceted elements of the project of decoloniality. He argues that the rhetorical tradition reinforces myopic Eurocentric perspectives with ties both to a modernity that presumes "a universal hegemony over political ideology, cultural meanings, and historical narrative" (2) and to neocolonialism. This myopic perspective–based modernity and coloniality, he argues, informs composition and rhetorical studies' own colonial imaginary.[23] Herein emerges the impetus of the chapter and edited collection, a proposition of *an-other* epistemology and ontology for the field and its classrooms. Such scholarship calls for WRS to accept, as necessary points of origin, the discursive traditions emerging from the survivors of conquest, occupation, and colonization.

These loci of enunciation for decolonial work interact within a network of options being explored in WRS. Ellen Cushman, in "Wampum, Sequoyan, and Story: Decolonizing the Digital Archive," discusses decoloniality with regard to archival work. Her focus is on the "problems" and "promises" of digital archives in the context of indigenous communities. In particular, she focuses on the need to decolonize "imperial archives" and their methods of collecting, categorizing, and isolating knowledge, which are premised on colonial concepts of linear time. Invoking terms such as *epistemic disobedience* and *delinking,* she argues that traditional archives are premised on tenets of Western imperialist thought/categories: (1) tradition, (2) collection, (3) artifacts, and (4) preservation. These tenets ensure the distance or separation of the archive from the community of origin. Cushman writes:

> Archives of indigenous artifacts came into existence in part to elevate the Western tradition through a process of othering "'primitive'" and Native traditions. Through institutions such as archives and museums, Western knowledge is enunciated, that is, brought into being, codified, legitimized, and reproduced as knowledge. Imperialist archives function as institutions of Western thought through "'training"' of new (epistemic obedient) members and control of who enters and what knowledge-making is allowed, disavowed, devalued, or celebrated. (119)

Such imperialist and colonialist structures, for Cushman, normalize knowledge, circulate knowledge productions, and reinvent the "other" either as barbaric and/or as primitive. For Cushman, *decolonial* means imagining an "alternative epistemological structure" on a "different understanding of progress" (119). In response, she provides strategies for decolonizing the archive: (1) challenge Western understanding of time as a necessary underpinning for tradition, (2) challenge Western fetishization with collecting and displaying the past and/or artifacts, (3) challenge the situatedness and strategic use of archives, and (4) resituate knowledge of the community. These moves simultaneously question imperialist and colonialist structures while also stressing the importance of epistemic enunciations and indigenous meaning-making practices. These four moves illustrate a decolonial option for decolonizing the archives.

Here Garcia's work intersects with this decolonial option when in "Decolonizing the Archives" he insists that what is missing from archival research is learning how to create presence from absence, silence from sound. Following Cushman's four strategies for decolonizing archives, he examines the rhetorics/narratives of a "local" archival box on the history of Harlingen, Texas. García brings together notions of "community listening" and "re-searching" and accounts for the "presence" and "presencing" of the living and the nonliving while "re-searching" archival materials. He argues for a more nuanced sense of responsibility and justice through a language and praxis of spectropolitical inquiry. This work continues his commitment to the Lower Rio Grande Valley, a region in which local settler colonial narratives, cloaked by rhetorics and narratives of modernity, persist. And they persist in ways that continue to tell stories of how Texas and the Lower Rio Grande Valley was either a site of wilderness/savagery or an empty landscape where the inhabiting bodies of the "other" vanish or "evaporate." They also persist as global designs of management and control and hegemonic models of thinking, which produce a discourse that delineates space and time in ways that claim a "place" and a "people" as in place/out of place or in time/cyclical time.

All this work exists within decolonial strategies that have been invoked around issues of language use in WRS classrooms. In debates over translingualism, for instance, scholars focus on the historical expectation of monolinguistic homogeneity, which created a mainstream/nonmainstream binary. This binary is then used to make different language-use patterns by students into evidence of their own deficiency and deviancy, justifying the need for assimilation. Thus, translingualism invites explorations beyond monolinguistic homogeneity, which places students "in the unenviable position of seeming to have to choose between either submitting to demands for conformity . . . [or] . . . resisting such demands" (Lu and Horner 584). Translingual scholars focus on how language is an "emergent" and "in-process activity" of becoming, wherein difference is both the "locus" of meaning and the "norm of language in-practice" (Canagarajah; Horner et al.; Leonard and Nowacek; Lu and Horner). In this sense, some have argued, all students are translingual since they are always merging and emerging into living language patterns.

Yet the argument that "[w]e are always translingual" (Bawarshi), has been critiqued by scholars such as Keith Gilyard, who warns that this "linguistic everyperson" gives the impression of "sameness of difference." By this term, Gilyard warns of the flattening of language difference and the erasure of historical as well as unresolved struggles involved in meaning-making practices and knowledge production. Here is where decolonial strategies/options become an important intervention. In her "Translingual and Decolonial Approaches to Meaning Making," Cushman problematizes the idea that English can be the only language of knowledge making and learning and continues by urging scholars and teachers to rethink their methodology and pedagogy. Cushman asks a central question:

> [T]o what extent might translingual approaches to language teaching and learning allow for pluriversal splendors of human imagination and creativity to open up? This question stems from the problems of linguistic and social hierarchy that index imperialist legacies central to the history of the United States generally and manifested into composition and rhetoric specifically. (234)

Here Cushman echoes Mignolo's argument for a pluriversality of geo- and body-politics of knowledge and understanding, for local histories, and for coexistence "elsewhere and otherwise." Cushman writes that while it is "not altogether clear the extent to which translingualism is, thus far, in a de-colonial moment rather than a post-monolinguistic moment" (236), for decolonial approaches and options to be amicable with translingualism it must challenge imperialist legacies (e.g., hierarchies of knowledges and languages) in the broader and disciplinary sense, as well as be attentive to place and difference. She writes, "The translingual approach . . . still needs to envision difference as heterogeneous, as differences, better thought of in the plural. . . . Understanding the differences within difference as the norms of all utterances can help imagine one type of epistemic delinking that invites a pluriversality of knowledges and languages" (238).

The cumulative effect of the above work has led, in more recent years, to efforts to denaturalize/decolonize terms (concepts) in writing and rhetorical studies more broadly. In *Decolonizing Rhetoric and Composition Studies: New Latinx Keywords for Theory and Pedagogy,* for instance, Latinx scholars Iris Ruiz and Raúl Sánchez take on the difficult task of denaturalizing terms in writing studies. Echoing Mignolo, they write, "Epistemic delinking helps establish a separate conceptual space for 'thinking otherwise'; that is, for thinking of writing, literacy, and discourse apart from traditional (i.e., Greco-Roman) histories and theories of rhetoric and apart from traditional (i.e., classical, liberal) notions of race and ethnicity" (xiv). Ruiz and Sánchez thus propose delinking the field's research and its pedagogy from "misused" and "appropriated" terms defined by "institutional hegemonic forces" that work against "minority students." Latinx scholars' reclaiming and reinscribing their own definitions of the terms, Ruiz and Sánchez argue, creates "a more inclusive 'official' vocabulary, to represent the perspectives of an 'outsider' group of Latinx scholars who are nonetheless familiar with the 'insider' discourses of Composition and Rhetoric and with de-colonial theory" (xv). From the delinking of "race" from its colonial framework (Ruiz) to rethinking "literacy" as social justice (Alvarez) to the work of recovering "poch@" from its colonial matrix of power (Medina) to supplanting "citizenship" from its power structure (Ribero), each author in this collection demonstrates epistemic disobedience, delinking, and decolonial aesthesis efforts.

The epistemic and political project of decoloniality has also been situated within WRS as a field. Combining their scholarly projects, in "Decolonial Options and Writing Studies," Ruiz and Baca make it clear that their "indigenous/decolonial border consciousness," which "resemble a bordertown of subject positions," informs their "decolonial imperative," enabling them to reimagine and recreate "tools, perspectives, and practices most effective in helping to heal from the colonial wounds of Western history." Moreover, they argue, "decolonial praxis" is not "new" for Latinxs. They point to Gloria Anzaldúa as part of their genealogical lineage of/for "resistance" within the context of European colonialism. Ruiz and Baca claim that Anzaldúa both "critiqued" and "superseded" the field's "hierarchy of knowledge adapted from colonial histories" (226). As Latinxs, thus, who are "always searching for decolonial options, decolonial possibilities" (228), against the backdrop of the field's "colonial unconscious," they propose the need for "reclaiming" erased histories, delinking from the canon of Western philosophy, and "dismantling" cultural hierarchies. In the process, they posit an "alternative" that "shifts" understanding and writing to align with "thinking" and "writing" otherwise, "writing no longer limited by Eurocentric foundations" (227) and a global reality "no longer determined by imperial, Eurocentric horizons" (228).

Each of the above projects deploy a decolonial lens for investigating hierarchies of knowledges, language, and rhetorical practices. Each, furthermore, works toward changing the terms (concepts) and contents (histories) in WRS that have been tied to macronarratives informed by modern/colonial world designs and *pensée unique*. Importantly, decoloniality, in this context, is not being used as a "metaphor," a project where nothing substantial changes. Instead this work represents people of the border working toward improving humanity in our classrooms, our research, and beyond. In that regard each piece of WRS scholarship needs to be understood within a constellation, an ecology, of decolonial breaks and shifts that are occurring within and beyond our field, within and beyond the United States. That is, this work demonstrates a shared language of decoloniality that attempts to radically transform coloniality of power, knowledge, and being. Such works illuminate the sentiments of James Baldwin, who wrote, "I am what time, circumstance, history, have made of me, certainly, but I am, also, much more than that. So are we all" (xii). It enacts Stuart Hall's argument that "we all speak from a particular place, out of a particular history, out of a particular experience, a particular culture, without being contained by that position" (169). What the project of decoloniality announces is that the "anthropoi" are not "stuck" there. It says that the anthropoi have histories, knowledges, and meaning-making practices that can contribute to the possibilities of new stories, to a new humanity, if only we can move beyond linear and/or normative historical thinking.

In this sense, each piece of scholarship also reflect *decolonial hopes and visions* for WRS. For the above scholarship asserts that the WRS narrative of "progress" cloaks the logics of coloniality. It reminds us that colonial imaginaries and practices are carried through "languages, [through] recording the past, and [through] charting territories" (Mignolo, *Darker Side* 5). What is "progress" when literacy and rhetorical pedagogies impose and force assimilation? What is "disciplinary content" when research paradigms continue to suppress the knowledges of "elsewhere and otherwise"? For us, then, the phrase *contested modernities* stands for the struggle of delinking our field from coloniality in pursuance of a pluriversality of thought, feeling, engagement, and humanity. For rhetoricians and compositionists *elsewhere* and *otherwise,* decoloniality is a project that emerges from the sensibilities of the racialized, minoritized, and marginalized. It is in "the space between," it is the crux between *elsewhere* and *otherwise* and the hegemonic right and the hegemonic left. It is where scholars of different skins, genealogies, and experiences speak *from* and *to* the field. It is the space of possibilities and radical and dangerous thought and engagement, "beyond" and "present," while at the same time *elsewhere* and *otherwise*. What is at stake in engaging with the project of decoloniality for WRS is an invitation to learn from all forms of knowledge and reject a totalitarian approach to knowledge. Decoloniality teaches us that the future does not rest with the West as the center, but lies fundamentally anchored in the principles of humanity-for-all.

DECOLONIAL POSSIBILITIES: OPENING (NOT CLOSING) A SPACE FOR CRITICAL DIALOGUE

Our goal is not to end debates over the meaning of decolonial work, but to support and extend such work into our field. Within such an effort, as noted briefly above, there will be concerns that decolonization is being used as a "metaphor," thus undermining the project of decoloniality as a whole. Indeed, Eve Tuck and K. Wayne Yang, in "Decolonization Is Not a Metaphor," warn the humanities to stop invoking the term *colonized* without an account of specificities or particularities. Their three primary concerns are the appropriation of decolonization to supplant critical methodologies; the negation of indigenous peoples, their struggles and intellectual contributions; and, as in Gilyard's concern about translingualism, the homogenizing of various experiences of oppression as colonization. Within this context, Tuck and Yang refer to current uses of decolonization as a "trend," a "metaphor" that kills "the very possibility of decolonization." (3). What we hear in their warning is a concern that decolonization will become a "metaphor" for a "correct academic politics" that fights over the correct boundaries of "decolonial strategies" and "legitimate decolonial experiences/practices" more than intervening in how and from where knowledge is produced—disciplinary politics trumping decolonial options.

As editors, we worried that any one collection might be perceived as territorialization, with an absence of some locations/knowledges being perceived as creating "boundaries." As editors, we must account for the specificities and particularities of the local moments that have, as discussed above, given us a certain positionality within decolonial research and the field, more broadly. And, as this collection is intended to further articulate that network across national and international locations and enunciations, we must be responsible for what is and is not included in this collection. We see this collection as one further (not final) articulation of decoloniality in WRS. We are not telling (and will not tell) people, then, who are (and continue to be) anthropoi or oppressed that part of their specific and particular history, memory, and experience is not a consequence of coloniality, simply because it falls outside the contents of this collection. If "the pluriversality of each local history and its narrative of decolonization can connect through that common experience of [coloniality/modernity]," then we hope our collection will be seen as an attempt to create new nodal points of connection. That is, we are not arguing that our instantiation of the term *colonization/decolonization* is the "correct or "best" definition, but that it is part of a larger collective effort (Mignolo, "Delinking" 497). For if we define work in the humanities or WRS through a stance focused on a singular concept of "correctness," the possibilities of decolonization are hindered. If we establish such a circle of scholars who manage and control terms, we limit the ability of others to conceive of themselves, genealogically and theoretically, within the "decolonial" project. Such a stance would recreate a framework that would in every way remind individuals and communities that their ways of being, seeing, and doing exist within a structure that continuously attempts to render them inferior and irrational. It would be decoloniality as metaphor, as sport, not as prospective-programmatic.

To this end, we repeat the call made in Baca and Villanueva's *Rhetorics of the Americas* for more indigenous scholarship in WRS. We argue for sustained recognition of indigenous struggles and for inclusion of indigenous intellectual legacies into research, teaching, and institutional and community practices. Resa Crane Bizzaro, Ellen Cushman, and Scott Lyons have had a profound impact on the field's understanding of these indigenous contributions, and we look forward to more scholars contributing to and working within these critically important conversations. We would point to Cherokee scholar Rachel Jackson's "Resisting Relocation: Placing Leadership on Decolonized Indigenous Landscapes" as an important example that assists practitioners in better understanding how decolonial theories help writing programs and departments "engage Indigenous knowledges in place and support Indigenous intellectuals to do this work *in their own places*" (505). And we would point to WRS scholars outside indigenous communities likewise working through decolonial lenses, including Courtney Rivard's contributions to indigeneity and settler archives (Adams-Campbell, Falzetti, and Rivard) and M. Amanda Moulder's historiographical work on Cherokee rhetorical traditions.

And we are attentive to research that accounts for rhetorical practices beyond Western horizons such as that of Arabella Lyon and LuMing Mao (RSA 2017), as well as forthcoming scholarship from Hui Wu and Tarez Samra Graban. Beyond the humanities and WRS, we believe research informed by decolonial options, research that focuses on the everyday, space, place, and people, has the potential to reconcile the local/global divide and disrupt the politics of duality in that (1) precommitments to resistance are "checked," (2) the global is not the scale of observation, and (3) possibility, rather than certainty, remains the impetus for inquiry. While this has implications for research practices, methods, and teaching, such research also shifts and breaks from precommitments to the "everyday" as observable and interpretable. Thus we would become attentive to what Anna Tsing refers to as *ideologies of scales* and *scale-making projects*. Ideology of scale is one analytical principle that is attentive to "cultural claims about locality, regionality, and globality," while the concept of scale-making projects focuses on the units of culture and political economy "through which we make sense of events and social processes" in particular times and places (347). Through breaking down the "certainty" of the borders of our "locals," by integrating epistemologies of elsewhere and otherwise, new collective formations, new economies, and new postdisciplinary formations, premised on expansive definitions of participation and rights, become possible.[24]

Finally, for some of us, colonization is not only within the purview of our genealogy; for some of us, colonization still takes form in our everyday; and, for some of us, the rhetoric of colonization and imperialism is just a course, professor, or book away. Thus, we need to continue efforts to decolonize the writing classroom. This would allow us to break and shift from Gilyard's concern over the reproduction of sameness-of-difference models into seeing into fruition Cushman's vision of "differences within difference." As we work toward changing the terms (concepts) and contents (histories), we do so through acts of *epistemic disobedience* and *delinking*. This occurs, concretely, when we are attentive to place, geo- and body-politics of knowledge and understanding, and local histories that recognize and acknowledge coexistence and copresence, elsewhere and otherwise. Of course, as we have pointed out elsewhere, there are limits to such work. The sphere of epistemology, thought, and feeling, regardless of where they are theorized, is fraught with the possibility of mutating too into forms of management and control. Still, we persist with hopes and visions, understanding one day we might need to decolonize those as well.

Ultimately, we speak from and invoke a decolonial perspective for investigating hierarchies of knowledges and language and rhetorical practices. The framework of decoloniality thus is not being used as a metaphor, but rather as our right to speak, research, and haunt from our own dispositions and positionalities back to hierarchies of knowledge and language and rhetorical practices that attempt to silence or render invisible bodies, local histories, and/or meaning-making practices and knowledge productions. We keep decolonization "unsettling" and "dangerous" precisely by challenging how power is carried out in views of language, historiography, and mapping, while also recovering and recentering meaning-making practices and rhetorical productions, elsewhere and otherwise. Thus, if a project of decoloniality can be described as a political and … that reveals the limits of fully colonizing a …s, and languages, this is what the concept …d *otherwise*, attempts to do.

…LLECTION: RHETORICS …HERE AND OTHERWISE

…ss a spectrum, from geo- and body-politics …rstanding to local histories situated across the glo… …ention within WRS that returns the knowledges, understandings, and local histories negated by our field to "haunt" it." Our goal is a new WRS situated within a pluriversality of knowledges, experiences, memories, languages, and political formations. Hence, the emphasis on rhetorics *elsewhere* and *otherwise*.

In this spirit of pluriversality, *REO* is composed of chapters grounded in an epistemological, political, and ethical framework that personifies a claim of contested modernities and/or decolonial visions. Chapter 1: In “Writing about Others Writing,” Kate Vieira discusses how writing has participated in the subjugation of marginalized people as she works to nuance her ethnographic enterprise between herself and the communities she calls home.” She articulates the importance of embodiment in decolonial practice. Chapter 2: Haneen Ghabra and Bernadette Calafell locate and situate a geo- and body-politics of knowledge and understanding in “Intersectional Reflexivity and Decolonial Rhetorics,” carrying on a conversation from Palestine to Aztlán that covers topics such as theorizing from the diaspora, different ways of understanding occupation, and the possibilities of decoloniality. Chapter 3: Steven Alvarez invokes the methodological approach of “rhetorical authoethnography” in his chapter, “Rhetorical Autoethnography,” arguing the importance of a relational framework of ethics and politics of location as a researcher in the pursuit of making experiences and memories shift from the marginalized to the read. Each chapter enacts the work of scholars delinking from concepts of universal/place and time, demonstrating the power of such delinking for producing new knowledge.

REO continues with local histories, *elsewhere* and *otherwise*, in Chapters 4 to 7. Chapter 4: Fatima Alaoui, in “Arabizing Vernacular Discourse,” works from an Arab subjectivity, exploring the “Arab Spring” and Tunisian revolutionary graffiti, discussing a geo- and body-politics of knowledge and understanding that they manifested. Chapter 5: In “*La Cultura Nos Cura,*” Iris Ruiz and Sonia Arellano undertake, on the one hand, a consideration of what is at stake in historical and material research methods that align with Western values by grounding their own geo- and body-politics of knowledge and understanding. On the other, they allude to how WRS classrooms can benefit from decolonial methods and methodologies that make visible silenced and/or objectified epistemologies and ontologies not for the sake of recentering, but for nuancing WRS writ large. Chapter 6: In “Beyond Colonial Hegemonies,” Shyam Sharma partly reconciles postcolonial and decolonial theories to both think about institutional and intellectual normalizations of thought and practice and to encourage disciplines to consider the

pedagogical possibilities in employing alternative rhetorical traditions such as Nyāya rhetoric. Chapter 7: Kevin Browne undertakes studying Caribbean vernacular archives in "Moving the Body," and considers what is at stake for researchers invested in the rhetorical exploration of archival contents. These essays, then, explore how a focus on local moments of enunciation can alter current disciplinary research models and institutional practices.

All of this work, these interventions, within *REO* are produced in the spirit of others before us: individuals such as Alcoff, Anzaldúa, Bizzaro, Cushman, Dussel, Fanon, Gonzales, Grosfoguel, Harjo, Hernández-Avila, hooks, Lu, Lugones, Lyons, Maldonado-Torres, Mignolo, Mohanty, Motha, Pérez, Quijano, Rabasa, Sandoval, Tamez, Smith. Beyond individuals, focusing on institutions, we want to highlight how readers familiar with *Mestiz@ Scripts* will recognize "otherwise" in our title as a concept frequently evoked by the Latin America Otherwise book series at Duke University Press, by the *Worlds and Knowledges Otherwise* journal, and by scholars formerly associated with the Latin American Subaltern Studies Group. Mexican historian José Rabasa, also a significant scholar of influence in *Mestiz@ Scripts*, analyzes sixteenth-century Mexican pictorial inscription practices in *Tell Me the Story of How I Conquered You: Elsewheres and Ethnosuicide in the Colonial Mesoamerican World*. Collectively, the voices here and above point not to linear solutions to colonial problems but toward a multitude of options and possibilities. The expressions *elsewhere* and *otherwise,* in this collection, are thus invitations to join existing networks and to envision pluriversal ways of thinking, writing, and teaching that depart from the field's Eurocentric geographies, cartographies, and chronologies.

Finally, this work, like our own earlier work, was produced in the spirit of working toward decolonial futures that are no longer determined by imperial horizons that position white settler bodies at the beginning, middle, and end of all available narratives. Though we supposedly no longer live in the colonial era, colonial relations of power continue to structure canonical understandings of Western rhetoric, its false universalism, and its imposition upon the rest of the world. The unilinear logic of development imagines "rhetoric" beginning among the archons of Athens, becoming refined with Roman empire-building, flourishing during European Enlightenment, and reaching the rest of the world thereafter. This Eurocentric understanding of rhetoric is part of a logic of imperial expansion that manages identification, knowledge making, subjectivity, and deliberation. Furthermore, this dominant narrative ignores the material realities of the immense majority of cultures and historical systems across the planet. The relationship between epistemic management and control of knowledge, thought, and being and the field of rhetoric and composition cannot be ignored. Therefore, *REO* not only challenges this relationship, but moves forward by advancing scholarship *elsewhere* and *otherwise.*

We encourage the readers of this collection to take up our call for responsibility and justice within our field. While the words *contested, alternative,* and *visions* invite readers to think about the possibilities and impossibilities of moving beyond normative historical thinking and into decolonial thinking and doing, we believe these same terms prompt us to consider how we will "build" a future marked by a "pluriversality of knowledges." Toward such ends, Chicana feminist Emma Pérez, evoking Michel Foucault, offers an enduring exhortation:

> How will we choose to describe our past, now, at this moment, as an enunciation in the present? If "history shows that everything that has been thought will be thought again by a thought that does not yet exist," then what will we choose to think again as our history, the history that we want to survive as we decolonize a historical imaginary that veils our thoughts, our words, our languages? (27)

NOTES

1. The group traces its theoretical history to the Bandung Conference in 1955 as well, where a new genealogy of thought emerged, one neither capitalist nor communist.

2. The problem with the "post," according to the M/C Group, is that it indicates origins of theory that begin with French poststructuralism.

"The 18th century is but the second phase of Western formation, expansion, and rhetoric of modernity."

3. The imaginary of the modern/colonial world system is "not only what is visible and in the 'ground' but what has been hidden from view in the 'underground' by successive layers of mapping people and territories" (Mignolo, *Local Histories* 24).

4. Mignolo provides some explanation of the discourse of anthropos and humanitas: "The enunciation doesn't name an existing entity but invents it. The enunciation needs an enunciator (agent), an institution . . . but to impose the anthropos as 'the other' in the collective imaginary, it is necessary to be in a position of managing the discourse . . . by which you name and describe an entity . . . and succeed in making believe that it exists" ("Geopolitics of Sensing" 134).

5. One could turn to Michel de Certeau's concepts of "law of the other" and "law of the present" (46) for further insight into what Johannes Fabian and Walter Mignolo refer to as the myth of modernity.

6. Edward Said writes, "The secular world is the world of history as made by human beings. Human agency is subject to investigation and analysis, which it is the mission of understanding to apprehend, criticize, influence, and judge" (xxix).

7. Within a rhetoric of modernity, Quijano notes, the "'subject' is bearer of 'reason,' while the 'object' is not only external to it, but different nature," because in fact, "it is 'nature'" ("Coloniality and Modernity/Rationality" 172–73). Historical discourse and a rhetoric of modernity produces "'objects' of study or of domination/exploitation/discrimination" ("Coloniality of Power and Eurocentrism" 221).

8. Pratt writes, "Natural history called upon human intervention . . . to compose an order. The eighteenth-century classificatory system created the task of locating every species on the planet, extracting it from its particular, arbitrary surroundings (the chaos), and placing it in its appropriate spot in the system (the order—book, collection, or garden)" (31).

9. Linnaeus also accounted for a classification of human beings *(homo sapiens)* as animals that then developed, according to Pratt, into an "explicitly comparative" categorization including Wild Man, American, European, Asiatic, and African (32). Linnaeus's work coincided, Pratt argues, with the height of the slave trade, the plantation system, and colonial genocide (36).

10. Nishitani Osamu discusses anthropos and humanitas in depth: "humans who possess 'civilization' are 'humanitas,' never 'anthropos' . . . In other words, 'anthropos' cannot escape the status of being the object

of anthropological knowledge, while 'humanitas' is never defined from without but rather expresses itself as the subject of all knowledge" (260).

11. Insightfully, Fabian offers critical commentary on time and the other: "The other is constructed as a system of coordinates (emanating of course also from a real center—the Western metropolis) in which given societies of all times and places may be plotted in terms of relative distance from the present" (26). He continues, "Time is not a mere measure, or vector, of culture; it is one of its constituents. Time contributes to the makeup of a culture because it is one of the most important means of communication" (51).

12. Bhabha writes that in some places progress is only heard and not seen, suggesting that the event and enunciation followed by the sign of modernity is itself a structure of authority (351–60).

13. Bhabha writes, "The analytic of cultural difference intervenes to transform the scenario of articulation . . . The aim of cultural difference is to rearticulate the sum of knowledge from the perspective of the signifying position of the minority that resists totalization" (232).

14. Spivak writes, "insofar as [Hindu law] can be described as a unitary system," there are four texts that "'staged' a four-part episteme defined by the subject's use of memory," which include the heard, the remembered, the learned-from-another, and the performed-in-exchange ("Can" 76).

15. Mignolo in "Epistemic Disobedience" writes, "The *anthropos* inhabiting non-European places discovered that s/he had been invented, as *anthropos,* by a locus of enunciations self-defined as *humanitas*" (161).

16. Decolonial scholars are mindful to argue that though colonialism is an "event," colonialism is an installment of a structure of logics. This understanding gives way to the import of "coloniality."

17. See also Isabel Jimenez-Lucena's essay, "Gender and Coloniality: The 'Moroccan Woman' and the 'Spanish Woman' in Spain's Sanitary Policies in Morocco" and Madina Tlostanova's essay, "The Janus-Faced Empire Distorting Orientalist Discourses: Gender, Race, and Religion in the Russian/(Post)Soviet Constructions of the 'Orient'" for more insight into decolonial feminism and their critique and response to the intersections of race, class, gender, and sexuality.

18. Henry Giroux (*Border Crossings*) also notes, "Colonizing of differences by dominant groups is expressed and sustained through representations in which the Other is seen as a deficit, in which the humanity of the Other is posited either as cynically problematic or ruthlessly denied" (130).

19. Fanon acknowledges this sophistication when he writes: "the colonial mother protects her child from itself, from its ego, and from its physiology, its biology, and its own unhappiness, which is its very essence" (37).

20. See Madina Tlostanova's *Gender Epistemologies and Eurasian Borderlands* for more insight.

21. These are two examples of the anthropoi who dwell and think in the borders and who engage in delinking.

22. See Madina Tlostanova and Walter Mignolo's *Learning to Unlearn: Decolonial Reflections from Eurasia and the Americas* for more insight into decolonial breaks and shifts.

23. Here we describe the colonial imaginary, which is similar to Mignolo's definition of the colonizer's epistemic privilege as having the characteristics of "Eurocentric categories of thought" and "[carrying] both the seed of emancipation and the seed of regulation and control ("Delinking" 459).

24. As noted in the previous section, we are also cognizant of limitations and implicit contradictions. While time does not permit a full analysis, let us consider briefly the difficulty in actually doing decolonial work. The following are some predicaments: (1) identity-term politics—often scholars of color invoke identity-term politics, which runs counter to the project of decoloniality, because, like race and ethnicity, identity terms are part of what make up Americanity (Mignolo; Quijano and Wallerstein); (2) speaking for others—often scholars of color will engage in talking about their community and their students, and it is important to remember that the practice of speaking for others is undergirded by desire, interest, and power (Alcoff; Spivak); (3) an-other paradigm—in decolonial scholarship, scholars articulate an-other paradigm, which can be problematic, because it can be read as an effort to ground an essentially exceptional identity and non-Western space that suggest inherent qualities (Cortez); and, (4) decolonial conversions—often we hear and read about scholars of color scaling up decoloniality (e.g., pedagogy and curriculum) and making arguments that such is in the best interests of students, but this can be detrimental because it can be read as an effort to replace one horizon of expectation and space of experience with another. These limits and implicit contradictions leave us in another predicament, for they suggest that even decolonization is in need of decolonizing. Nonetheless, as we noted too, this means our work is never "complete" or "total," taking all of us to task to remain political and ethical as we steer in new directions.

WORKS CITED

Adams-Campbell, Melissa, Ashley Glassburn Falzetti, and Courtney Rivard. "Introduction: Indigeneity and the Work of Settler Archives." Settler Colonial Studies, vol. 5, no. 2, 2015, pp. 109–16.

Alcoff, Linda. "The Problem of Speaking for Others." *Cultural Critique*, vol. 20, 1991, pp. 5–32.

Alvarez, Steven. "Literacy." Ruiz and Sánchez, pp. 17–30.

Anzaldúa, Gloria. *Borderlands/La Frontera: The New Mestiza.* 2nd ed., Aunt Lute Books, 1999.

Baca, Damián. *Mestiz@ Scripts, Digital Migrations, and the Territories of Writing*. Palgrave Macmillan, 2008.

———. "te-ixtli: The 'Other Face' of the Americas." Baca and Villanueva, pp. 1–14.

Baca, Damián, and Victor Villanueva, editors. *Rhetorics of the Americas: 3114 BCE to 2012 CE.* Palgrave Macmillan, 2010.

Baldwin, James. "Preface to the 1984 Edition." *Notes of a Native Son,* by James Baldwin, Beacon Press, 1984, pp. ix–xvi.

Bawarshi, Anis. "Beyond the Genre Fixation: A Translingual Perspective on Genre." *College English*, vol. 78, no. 3, 2016, pp. 243–49.

Bhabha, Homi K. *The Location of Culture*. Routledge, 1994.

Calvo, Luz, and Catrióna Rueda Esquibel. *Decolonize Your Diet: Plant-Based Mexican-American Recipes for Health and Healing*. Arsenal Pulp Press, 2015.

Canagarajah, A. Suresh. "Negotiating Translingual Literacy: An Enactment." *Research in the Teaching of English*, vol. 48, no. 1, 2013, pp. 40–67.

Certeau, Michel de. *The Writing of History*. Columbia UP, 1988.

Chilisa, Bagele. *Indigenous Research Methodologies*. SAGE, 2012.

Cortez, José. "History." Ruiz and Sánchez, pp. 49–62.

Cortez, José M. "Of Exterior and Exception: Latin American Rhetoric, Subalternity, and the Politics of Cultural Difference." *Philosophy & Rhetoric*, vol. 51, no. 2, 2018, pp. 124–50.

Cushman, Ellen. "Translingual and Decolonial Approaches to Meaning Making." *College English*, vol. 78, no. 3, 2016, pp. 234–42.

———. "Wampum, Sequoyan, and Story: Decolonizing the Digital Archive." *College English*, vol. 76, no. 2, 2013, pp. 115–35.

Dussel, Enrique. "Eurocentrism and Modernity (Introduction to the Frankfurt Lectures)." *Boundary 2*, vol. 20, no. 3, 1993, pp. 65–76.

———. *The Invention of the Americas: Eclipse of "the Other" and the Myth of Modernity*. Continuum, 1995.

Fabian, Johannes. *Time and the Other: How Anthropology Makes Its Object*. Columbia UP, 1983.

Fanon, Frantz. *The Wretched of the Earth*. Grove Press, 2007.

García, Romeo. "Corrido-ing State Violence." *The Journal of Multimodal Rhetorics,* vol. 2, no. 2, 2018, pp. 51–69.

Gilyard, Keith. "The Rhetoric of Translingualism." *College English*, vol. 78, no. 3, 2016, pp. 284–89.

Giroux, Henry A. *Border Crossings: Cultural Workers and the Politics of Education*. Routledge, 1992.

———. "Border Pedagogy in the Age of Postmodernism." *The Journal of Education*, vol. 170, no. 3, 1988, pp. 162–81.

Hall, Stuart. "New Ethnicities." *Black British Cultural Studies: A Reader,* edited by Houston A. Baker Jr., Manthia Diawara, and Ruth H. Lindeborg, U of Chicago P, 1996, pp. 163–72.

Horner, Bruce, Min-Zhan Lu, Jacqueline Jones Royster, and John Trimbur. "Opinion: Language Difference in Writing—Toward a Translingual Approach." *College English*, vol. 73, no. 3, 2011, pp. 303–21.

Jackson, Rachel C. "Resisting Relocation: Placing Leadership on Decolonized Indigenous Landscapes." *College English*, vol. 79, no. 5, 2017, pp. 495–511.

Jimenez-Lucena, Isabel. "Gender and Coloniality: The 'Moroccan Woman' and the 'Spanish Woman' in Spain's Sanitary Policies in Morocco." *Worlds and Knowledges Otherwise*, vol. 2, 2008, pp. 1–22.

Leonard, Rebecca Lorimer, and Rebecca Nowacek. "Transfer and Translingualism." *College English*, vol. 78, no. 3, 2016, pp. 258–64.

Lu, Min-Zhan. "Conflict and Struggle: The Enemies or Preconditions of Basic Writing?" *College English*, vol. 54, no. 8, 1992, pp. 887–913.

Lu, Min-Zhan, and Bruce Horner. "Translingual Literacy, Language Difference, and Matters of Agency." *College English*, vol. 75, no. 6, 2013, pp. 582–607.

Lugones, María. "The Coloniality of Gender." *Worlds and Knowledges Otherwise*, vol. 2, 2008, pp. 1–17.

Lunsford, Andrea A., and Lahoucine Ouzgane, editors. *Crossing Borderlands: Composition and Postcolonial Studies*. U of Pittsburgh P, 2004.

Lyon, Arabella, and LuMing Mao. "The Rest of the World: Recognizing Non-Western Rhetorical Traditions." Rhetoric Society of America, 25–27 May 2017, Indiana University, Bloomington, IN, workshop.

Medina, Cruz. "Poch@." Ruiz and Sánchez, pp. 93–108.

Mejía, Jaime. "Bridging Rhetoric and Composition Studies with Chicano and Chicana Studies: A Turn to Critical Pedagogy." *Latino/a Discourses: On Language, Identity, and Literacy Education*, edited by Michelle Hall Kells, Valerie Balester, and Victor Villanueva, Boynton/Cook, 2004, pp. 40–56.

Mejía, Jaime Armin. "Tejano Arts of the U.S.-Mexico Contact Zone." *JAC*, vol. 18, no. 1, 1998, pp. 123–35.

Mignolo, Walter D. *The Darker Side of Western Modernity: Global Futures, Decolonial Options*. Duke UP, 2011.

———. "Delinking." *Cultural Studies*, vol. 21, no. 2-3, 2007, pp. 449–514.

———. "Epistemic Disobedience, Independent Thought and Decolonial Freedom." *Theory, Culture and Society*, vol. 26, no. 7-8, 2009, pp. 159–81.

———. "The Geopolitics of Knowledge and the Colonial Difference." *South Atlantic Quarterly*, vol. 101, no. 1, 2002, pp. 57–96.

———. "Geopolitics of Sensing and Knowing: On (De)coloniality, Border Thinking, and Epistemic Disobedience." *Confero*, vol. 1, no. 1, 2013, pp. 129–50.

———. *Local Histories/Global Designs: Coloniality, Subaltern Knowledges, and Border Thinking*. Princeton UP, 2000.

———. "The Prospect of Harmony and the Decolonial View of the World." *waltermignolo.com*, 22 Sept. 2012, http://waltermignolo.com/the-prospect-of-harmony-and-the-decolonial-view-of-the-world/. Accessed 6 June 2016.

Moulder, M. Amanda. "Cherokee Practice, Missionary Intentions: Literacy Learning among Early Nineteenth-Century Cherokee Women." *College Composition and Communication*, vol. 63, no. 1, 2011, pp. 75–96.

Nordstrom, Georganne. "Rhetoric and Resistance in Hawai'i. How Silenced Voices Speak Out in Colonial Contexts." Baca and Villanueva, pp. 117–42.

Olson, Gary. "Encountering the Other: Postcolonial Theory and Composition Scholarship. *Crossing Borderlands: Composition and Postcolonial Studies*, edited by Andrea A. Lunsford and Lahoucine Ouzgane, U of Pittsburgh P, 2004, pp. 84–94.

Osamu, Nishitani. "Anthropos and Humanitas: Two Western Concepts of 'Human Being.'" *Translation, Biopolitics, Colonial Difference*, edited by Naoki Sakai and Jon Solomon, Hong Kong UP, 2006, pp. 259–73.

Pérez, Emma. *The Decolonial Imaginary: Writing Chicanas into History*. Indiana UP, 1999.

Peters, E. J. "Subversive Spaces: First Nations Women and the City." *Environment and Planning D: Society and Space*, vol. 16, no. 6, 1998, pp. 665–85.

Pratt, Mary Louise. *Imperial Eyes: Travel Writing and Transculturation*. Routledge, 1992.

Quijano, Aníbal. "Coloniality and Modernity/Rationality." *Cultural Studies*, vol. 21, no. 2-3, 2007, pp. 168–78.

———. "Coloniality of Power and Eurocentrism in Latin America." *International Sociology*, vol. 15, no. 2, 2000, pp. 215–32.

Quijano, Aníbal, and Michael Ennis. "Coloniality of Power, Eurocentrism, and Latin America." *Nepantla*, vol. 1, no. 3, 2000, pp. 533–80.

Quijano, Aníbal, and Immanuel Wallerstein. "Americanity as a Concept, or the Americas in the Modern World-System." *International Social Science Journal*, vol. 44, no. 134, 1992, pp. 549–57.

Quispe-Agnoli, Rocío. "Spanish Scripts Colonize the Image: Inca Visual Rhetorics." Baca and Villanueva, pp. 41–68.

Ribero, Ana Milena. "Citizenship." Ruiz and Sánchez, pp. 31–46.

Rohrer, Judy. *Staking Claim: Settler Colonialism and Racialization in Hawai'i*. U of Arizona P, 2016.

Ruiz, Iris D. "Race." Ruiz and Sánchez, pp. 3–16.

Ruiz, Iris, and Damián Baca. "Decolonial Options and Writing Studies." *Composition Studies*, vol. 45, no. 2, 2017, pp. 226–29.

Ruiz, Iris D., and Raúl Sánchez, editors. *Decolonizing Rhetoric and Composition Studies: New Latinx Keywords for Theory and Pedagogy*. Palgrave Macmillan, 2016.

Said, Edward W. *Orientalism*. Vintage Books, 1979.

Smith, Linda Tuhiwai. *Decolonizing Methodologies: Research and Indigenous Peoples*. 2nd ed., Zed Books, 2012.

Spivak, Gayatri Chakravorty. "Can the Subaltern Speak?" *Colonial Discourse and Post-Colonial Theory: A Reader*, edited by Patrick Williams and Laura Chrisman, Columbia UP, 1994, pp. 66–111.

———. "Responsibility." *Boundary 2*, vol. 2, no. 3, 1994, pp. 19–64.

Tlostanova, Madina. *Gender Epistemologies and Eurasian Borderlands*. Palgrave Macmillan, 2010.

———. "The Janus-Faced Empire Distorting Orientalist Discourses: Gender, Race, and Religion in the Russian/(Post)Soviet Constructions of the 'Orient.'" *Worlds and Knowledges Otherwise*, vol. 2, 2008, pp. 1–11.

Tlostanova, Madina V., and Walter Mignolo. *Learning to Unlearn: Decolonial Reflections from Eurasia and the Americas*. Ohio State UP, 2012.

Tsing, Anna. "The Global Situation." *Cultural Anthropology*, vol. 15, no. 3, 2000, pp. 327–60.

Tuck, Eve, and K. Wayne Yang. "Decolonization Is Not a Metaphor." *Decolonization: Indigeneity, Education & Society*, vol. 1, no. 1, 2012, pp. 1–40.

Villanueva, Victor, Jr. "Maybe a Colony: And Still Another Critique of the Comp Community." *JAC*, vol. 17, no. 2, 1997, pp. 183–90.

1

Writing about Others Writing: Some Field Notes

Kate Vieira
University of Wisconsin, Madison

WRITING HAS LONG PARTICIPATED IN THE SUBJUGATION of marginalized peoples. It has been used as a tool to: create borders, define who belongs (and who does not), enforce religious compliance, mete out punishment, and secure bureaucratic dominion over land and people (see, e.g., Patel, Chapter 1; Cornelius; Mignolo; Vieira, *'American'*). Claude Lévi-Strauss, that early ethnographer of writing, partly acknowledged as much in 1966. And Maria Carolina de Jesus, the Afro-Brazilian literacy ethnographer of life in the favela, experienced it firsthand during the same time period (de Jesus; Vieira, "Literacy Studies"). Many scholars have grappled with this legacy by developing a range of explicitly decolonizing methodological approaches to qualitative research in literacy, education, and other areas.[1]

As an ethnographer of literacy, I examine here the implication of my own ethnographic work in the use of writing as a technology of oppression. I take on this analysis as someone who believes deeply in the transformative work of research and in the liberatory potential of writing, but also as someone dedicated to understanding the ways that, when I engage in the work of writing about others, I am also invoking, and potentially participating in, a history of abuse. Specifically, I tell the story of my methodological education as I

I am grateful to the students of English 201, "Fast Writing in Fast Times," and English 304, "Why Is Writing Hard?," for workshopping parts of this essay, to Mary Fiorenza, Damián Baca, and Romeo García for crucial feedback, and to Calley Marotta for research assistance.

learned to write about others, focusing on points of rupture and on moments of potential harm. In order to explore these themes, I draw on theories developed by scholars of indigenous rhetoric, literacy, and methodology.[2] History accumulates in the now, these scholars teach. It pools in contemporary sites of literacy practice.[3] And it is active in present-day research and present-day politics. Writing's troubling history resonates, named or unnamed, any time we, *I,* write about others.[4] I hope that this sociohistorical perspective, refracted through my fieldwork experiences, can shed a critical light on the ethnography of literacy, a site in which both the object and means of study, *writing,* reverberates with past and present misuses, and thus merits heightened scholarly, writerly, and social attention.

ON PRONOUNS

I wrote my dissertation about the literacy practices of documented and undocumented Portuguese-speaking immigrants in my home town. Having grown up away from the language, I had to start at the beginning, taking a Portuguese class to teach me the grammar of my heritage language. And then, equipped with language, a digital recorder, a little bit of research money and, it is worth mentioning here, a pregnant belly, I went back home. I stayed at the house of my Aunt Maria, who nourished me with the chouriço and potatoes of my childhood. She and my uncle lived on the first floor, a group of nuns on the second, a former obstetrician from Brazil on the third. It was a peaceful womb-like space from which to collect the literacy histories of people from within and outside my community.

I spoke with over fifty people, from the Azores, like my family, and from Brazil, like my then husband's. I witnessed people writing sermons to give solace to those who had travelled far away from their families. I heard of the creative uses of language to forge immigration documents. People shared with me their poems, their letters, and even recipes that they had written out on notecards, lent to others, and asked for back. They invited me in, gave me a glass of water, asked about my pregnancy, and talked. I was home.

And yet, during these conversations, my digital recorder was on, blinking red to show me it was alive, a third party to my homecoming. In fact, so important was it that I turn these conversations into data that I had two recorders in case one lost power. There were also consent forms in Portuguese and English. There was also a large plastic file folder within which I housed smaller manila folders, inked with pseudonyms, dates, sometimes family trees.

And yet, when I went to church, sometimes I prayed, but mostly I took notes, my fingers flying over the page as those next to me clapped or swayed or wept or knelt.

And yet, I had been away for so long, that I wasn't understood as local. My accent was different, stilted, some kind of strange mix of white Midwestern, local ethnic, and school-taught Portuguese. Who was I, anyway? I would explain that I was Maria's niece, *(you know, Maria, who lives on High Street, who married David? Who used to clean houses and now works at the hospital? Yeah, she's doing good),* and that I was a university researcher.

In some ways, I read as local: pregnant, petite, dark hair, white skin, easily dropping my *r*'s in English, easily rolling or hardening or gutturalizing them in Portuguese, easily translanguaging between the two. Like most everyone else in the town I called "South Mills" in my book, I drove aggressively. I cheek-kissed friends in greeting. I got my coffee-syrup milkshakes at the Newport Creamery and my sweet bread at the bakery down the street. Unlike the city where I was getting my PhD, where I had had to learn not to stand too close to others in lines, to read people's faces for the words they did not say, to wear a coat that looked like a sleeping bag, this was a place, I felt, that didn't take any kind of special knowing to know how to be.

And yet, one participant, whom I will call Cristina, kept referring to me as the lady. She was very polite about it. She was glad to see me, because she was trying to write a letter to immigration services and she was having trouble. She kept crossing words out, throwing away the paper, starting over. And she was relieved that this lady, this writing lady, could help her improve her letter. Well, I wasn't the Man, at least not yet, but for Cristina, I was the lady. The one who was writing a book, an act that seemed to set me irrevocably apart from the people to whom I hoped I belonged.

Back in graduate school in Wisconsin, where I had my baby—my bouncing bilingual baby (I was determined, you see, to bring her up in community, in that beautiful *usness* that was daily slipping further from my grasp)—I sat in a coffee shop staffed by smiling Midwestern baristas. In my hallucinatory sleep-deprived state, I wrote my dissertation for three hours a day for a year and a half. (This was not some kind of macho time-management stunt. Despite teaching at nights, it was all the daycare I could afford.) I stayed with the stories I was told, listened to them again and again. Sometimes I cried a little over my latte during particularly poignant moments, a sure sign of my privileged distance, of the whiteness that was encroaching or perhaps that I had long since embodied, my ethnicity ethnic to no one else but me.

I was lucky at this time to have an advisor who kept it real. "There are women actually working in fields," Deborah Brandt told me once, speaking, as was typical, in koan. "With children strapped to their backs." She meant that our kind of fieldwork was a responsibility and a privilege, work that should only be undertaken for the wider social good. She was, of course, right. But what I didn't say as I pushed back my chair from the kitchen table she had lodged in her small office to make conversation flow a little easier in that stark white space, what I didn't say, perhaps out of shame or perhaps because I had a child to pick up somewhere else in town, was that for me, part of the appeal of research, particularly research with my own community, was not just public. It was also personal.

The social aim of my research was to humanize discourses about immigrant literacy. But the deeper I delved into my research, the more I realized that my research was also about humanizing myself. In the process of fieldwork, the ethnographer *"I"* and the ethnographic subject, *"they,"* began to Venn-diagram themselves, at least temporarily, into a *"we."* I liked to float there in that inner circle for a while, while my daughter was encased in my womb or later while she was cared for at school. In that space I felt that the rupture between scholar Kate and, well, *Kate* Kate was temporarily sutured.

But as Cristina reminded me—Cristina, who shared so many demographic characteristics with me that to list them here would compromise her identity—my privilege made this *"we"* an unsustainable fiction. In the act of writing, I was already engaging in an objectifying act, no matter what kind of solidarity I imagined or experienced or enacted, no matter how sensitively I witnessed peoples' experiences, no matter how many participants sought me out expressly to be heard. In the writing of research, I wrenched our identification out of the communal moment in which it otherwise may or may not have existed. I examined it. I labeled it. I annotated it with footnotes. And this, I am convinced, especially from the purview of a community that many have regarded as "illiterate" or "underachieving" or whatever euphemism for *not quite like us* happens to be in vogue at any given raciohistorical moment—it was this act of writing that ultimately made me the lady.

ON ETHNOGRAPHIC HARM

In the fall of my last semester as a graduate student, when I was on the job market, I got the thrilling news that an article pulled from my dissertation was accepted in *College English.* What a win. I had a family to support, and the publication would mean employers would at least give my CV a look.

"That's great," and "This won't happen again," said Deb, always encouraging and realistic in just the right proportions. For this reason, six months later, as I was sending in the page proofs and was seized around the tender ligaments of my ever-sore neck by a sharp crisis of faith in the academic undertaking as a whole, I called Deb for some real talk. Who was I to write about others? What if what I said about Jessica, the immigration worker, was wrong? What if, worse, what I wrote about Cristina was wrong? She said herself she had trouble reading and writing. She would have no recourse. There would be no rebuttal. I would be consigning her to a print world of which I was a part and from which she was largely excluded. I had, of course, discussed with her my interpretation, asked for feedback, and involved her and others in the community in the project in other ways. But there was surely more I could have done.[5] Jacqueline Jones Royster's incisive essay about those infiltrating voices of others rang through my dreams.

If one builds one's philosophy of writing, as I do, from liberatory writing theorists Paulo Freire and Audre Lorde, writing not only says. It also does. This essay, for example, seeks to engage readers in the crucible of personal experience to illuminate the seemingly quotidian and also problematic ethnographic act of writing about others. *Praxis,* says Freire. *Action,* says Lorde. If one further builds one's epistemology of literacy from qualitative work in writing studies, as I also do, then one knows that in any instance of writing, one is enacting a complex web of social relations and histories.[6] While Freire and Lorde had their sights set on literacy's liberatory potential, and while enacting social relations through writing can be empowering, writing often acts in ways that have negative consequences for those written about, especially when the writees are from marginalized groups.[7] To repeat (because it bears repeating): Writing not only says. It also does.

My dissertation research, and ultimately my book, attempted to make this point. It described how the government wrote visas or passports or labeled people aliens. It detailed how such writing was used to restrict people's movement across borders, to arrest them in their cars, to rip them away from their families. I was pointing to the injustice inflicted through uses of literacy by the powerful, and to how people took up writing in response.

Yet as much as I incorporated participants' words and perspectives and edits into my text, wasn't I, as an ethnographer, also inflicting something on someone through my writing? I did not use guns or walls or handcuffs or detention centers to enforce my representations. But I too, like the government, was writing others. Writing wields immense social authority, I wrote in my book. It has consequences, I insisted. To take my own findings seriously, then, meant acknowledging that no matter how "local" or how "insider" or how collaborative or how on the right side of history I believed myself to be, my writing about others, from the privileged position of the lady no less, had the potential for harm.

"You always do harm in research," said Deb, never one to mince words.

ON ETHNOGRAPHIC RIGOR

As a new assistant professor in Urbana-Champaign, Illinois, when I was attempting to publish another article on my ethnographic research with undocumented immigrants, I took some high-potency methodological advice administered by one of the most rigorous and obsessed qualitative writing researchers I know, Christina Haas, who was then the editor of *Written Communication,* where, the tenure clock ticking in my ear, I was desperate to prove my mettle. Being mentored by Chris was bracing. She sent me a pdf of the brilliant Smagorinsky article with the tectonic title, "The Methods Section as Epicenter of the Social Science Research Report," and when my methods section still couldn't live up to its role as epicenter of the natural disaster that I was beginning to believe that ill-conceived article to be, she called me on the phone. "Methods sections," she said, "must often sacrifice grace for specificity."

I wasn't sure how much grace I still had left to sacrifice. It was the summer of 2011, and I was the mother of a two-year-old, whom I dropped screaming at day care each morning (always verbal, my daughter reassured the daycare providers all day long that her mommy would be back in ten minutes), so I could retreat to a coffee shop with battered wood tables on the far end of the Urbana-Champaign campus to code and recode my data until, one day, I looked up and noticed that all of my fingers were tingling, except for both pinkies and my right thumb, which I could not feel at all. In fact, so busy was I tensing my neck, hacking apart participants' personal stories, and splaying them into charts, that I also hadn't noticed the intensity of my husband's dalliances—an oversight that I believe delayed my eventual divorce by at least a year. In my final reckoning, did I cross-check his version of events with phone records and incriminating texts? Yes I did. In my ultimate analysis, did I triangulate participant interviews with ethnographic observations? You bet. Was grace sacrificed? Undoubtedly.

That summer, I learned two things about the ethnography of writing: First, there is an honesty in technical discussions of methodological analysis. A respect. There are, as decolonizing researchers Tuck and Yang have argued, some stories the academy doesn't deserve ("R-words"). But if one is to produce or coproduce knowledge within the academy about other people, if one is, in my case, to publish an article about people who are not only disenfranchised, but who are in fact also systematically persecuted by the state, one best be as clear as possible about precisely how one got to the particular representation that one is committing to print and disseminating to the public. Methodology sections at their best reveal the constructedness of ethnographic representations, highlighting the multiplicity of potential truths, even if, in the end, they make a case for one.

The other thing I learned is that part of methodological analysis comes in the form of the researcher's own writing of a story (Fiorenza). Which is why after dissecting participants' stories and my notes into axial codes, I attempted to stitch what had become pieces of data into a narrative whole. I wanted participants' stories—recounted to me over worn laminate kitchen tables, in the dank cellars of churches, once in a car in the rain, often in rooms with cigarette smoke wafting in through an open window—I wanted those stories to sing together. I wanted to see what kind of truth or action might arise from harmonizing these distinct voices, the voices that coursed over and over again through my headphones, into my transcripts, into my analysis, and then out again into my manuscript. I can hear them now, nearly a decade later, singing.

It is right to be suspicious of master narratives. In my writing, I attempted to shine light on places where the mess of reality, as Ralph Cintrón has described, befuddled my attempts at narrative order, revealing its constructed nature. And it is right to avoid constructing a narrative that fetishizes the pain of marginalized peoples, as does much "damage-centered" research (Tuck).[8] But it is also right to use the tools of story to bring to light injustice, struggle, beauty, strength.[9] On good days, I believe I used narrative as a kind of historically situated, empirically grounded, aesthetic reckoning with power. Other days I'm not so sure. What I do know is that my eventual analysis was a close, if neurotic, kind of listening that to me felt something like love.

And at that, I let the book out in the world to do its damage and its good. And there it lives. Perhaps subjugating someone or perhaps liberating someone. Or perhaps the book remains on Cristina's doorstep, where I left it when, despite her neighbor's insistence that she was home, she didn't answer the door at my knocks. In the end, though, *"or"* is the wrong conjunction. To be conscious of the potential harm of ethnographic writing means knowing that all of these outcomes can simultaneously be true.

My idealistic hope for the book was that it would teach, accompany, and otherwise speak to readers, and thereby contribute to positive humanizing change in policy, pedagogy, understanding. As I let the book go on its way, to do what it would do or not do, it was also important for me to remember that there are many avenues to such change, avenues that exceed the discursive realm of the academic. There are classrooms, community centers, poetry, streets. There are other ways, powerful ways, ways that vibrate with potential and heart, to show up in the world.[10]

ON WRITING

I always assign the article given to me by Christina Haas in my graduate seminars on methods. It doesn't on its surface appear to be a politically radical article. It is concerned with making one's research question line up with one's data collection and one's data analysis and findings. But I see it as a call to action. Methods *are* epicentric. Geologic. They are the molten core. They make plates shift, crevices gape. They are at the ethical, social, political, and relational heart of what we think we are doing when we write about others.[11] And this, this writing about others, demands the integrity of purposeful design, as well as awareness of potential outcomes.

Writing about others is a consequential act. This is perhaps why so many forward-thinking qualitative studies of other people's literacies end with a call to action—for increased awareness, a new pedagogy, a revision of policy, an out-and-out revolution. In recognition of the consequential nature of research, many scholars have developed robust frameworks for "humanizing" research agendas (Paris and Winn) that emphasize, for example, desire over damage (Tuck) and relationality over objectivity (Patel). Such models are my guide.

They have to be. Because I believe in research about writing. I believe in this activity dedicated to curiosity, learning, knowing. Ethnographic research about writing at its best directs us to look closely and with compassion to the poetry that arises in supposedly unlikely places, and to be changed, opened, and challenged by what we encounter. At its best, ethnographic research about writing persuades researchers, educators, administrators, policymakers, humans in the world, that our ways of knowing and doing literacy are incomplete if we are not taking into account particular sets of practices innovated by particular groups of people, who are positioned in particular matrices of power relationships, who find themselves swimming in particular geographic and temporal contexts. Without this kind of systematic examination of the everyday practices of people, in all of their sociohistorically situated glory, we can't know very much about literacy at all.[12] Writing about others writing, then, is necessary to the project of socially just literacy education. At its most noble, it is brave and beautiful and true and transformative. Imperfect researcher that I am, I plan to keep working toward these ideals.

My point here, then, has not been to suggest abandoning the ethnographic enterprise. Rather, I have hoped to show that to neglect writing's potential to objectify and harm those written about, especially in sites of ethnographic activity in which unequal power relationships are often reified by writing itself, is irresponsible. It neglects the lessons of history. Amidst this still urgent call to document, theorize from, and develop composition pedagogy based on communities' emic experiences of literacy, how might researchers of writing understand our own implication in writing's legacy of abuse? My answer here has been a reflective, narrative one, one of my dawning awareness of the potential for ethnographic harm, as it blistered to the surface in encounters between me and the communities that I continue to call home.

NOTES

1. See, for example, Chilisa; Paris and Winn; Patel; Smith; Tuck.

2. To be clear, neither I nor most of those in the communities with whom I research identify as Native, and so I choose to not use the terms *decolonizing* or *colonizing* to describe my ethnographic work. I am wary here of using the term *decolonizing* as a "metaphor." As Tuck and Yang write, "Decolonize (a verb) and decolonization (a noun) cannot easily be grafted onto pre-existing discourses/frameworks, even if they are critical, even if they are anti-racist, even if they are justice frameworks. The easy absorption, adoption, and transposing of decolonization is yet another form of settler appropriation." ("Decolonization" 3).

3. For how rhetorical legacies act on contemporary sites of writing and discourse, see Cushman's *Cherokee Syllabary* and Baca's *Mestiz@ Scripts*.

4. Such resonances are especially potent under the conditions of white supremacy that continue to structure so many literate ways of knowing.

5. Ten years out from data collection as of this writing, and having benefited from working with community-engaged researchers since, I know now that yes, there was more that I could have done.

6. See for example Paul Prior, *Writing/Disciplinarity*, and Kris Gutiérrez, "Developing a Sociocritical Literacy in the Third Space."

7. For Native peoples, for example, ethnography has historically participated in "a form of politics that is more than representational, as this was a governmental and disciplinary possession of bodies *and* territories" (Simpson 67).

8. According to Tuck, "the danger in damage-centered research is that it is a pathologizing approach in which the oppression singularly defines a community. Here's a more applied definition of damage-centered research: research that operates, even benevolently, from a theory of change that establishes harm or injury in order to achieve reparation" (413). She argues for a "desire-based framework" as an "antidote to damage-centered research" (416).

9. Chilisa points to the power of stories and counterstories in indigenous research contexts to challenge perceived wisdom and to embody memory, among other functions.

10. As Tuck and Yang write, research is "just one way of knowing" ("R-Words" 237).

11. See Patel on relational research in education.

12. This was the fundamental argument of New Literacy Studies scholars.

WORKS CITED

Baca, Damián. *Mestiz@ Scripts, Digital Migrations, and the Territories of Writing.* Palgrave Macmillan, 2008.

Brandt, Deborah. "Protecting the Personal." *College English*, vol. 64, no. 1, 2001, pp. 42–44.

Chilisa, Bagele. *Indigenous Research Methodologies.* SAGE, 2012.

Cintron, Ralph. *Angels' Town:* Chero *Ways, Gang Life, and the Rhetoric of the Everyday.* Beacon Press, 1997.

Cornelius, Janet Duitsman. *"When I Can Read My Title Clear": Literacy, Slavery, and Religion in the Antebellum South.* U of South Carolina P, 1991.

Cushman, Ellen. *The Cherokee Syllabary: Writing the People's Perseverance.* U of Oklahoma P, 2011.

Fiorenza, Mary. *Methods and Models of Writing and Living: Composing Brenda Ueland's Writing Life.* 2009. U of Wisconsin-Madison, PhD dissertation.

Freire, Paulo. *Pedagogy of the Oppressed.* Seabury Press, 1974.

Gutiérrez, Kris D. "Developing a Sociocritical Literacy in the Third Space." *Reading Research Quarterly*, vol. 43, no. 2, 2008, pp. 148–64.

de Jesus, Carolina Maria. *Child of the Dark: The Diary of Carolina Maria de Jesus.* Translated by David St. Clair, Signet, 1962.

Lévi-Strauss, Claude. "Anthropology: Its Achievements and Future." *Current Anthropology*, vol. 7, no. 2, 1966, pp. 124–27.

Lorde, Audre. "The Transformation of Silence into Language and Action." Paper delivered at the Modern Language Association's Lesbians and Literature Panel, Chicago, Illinois, 28 Dec. 1977.

Mignolo, Walter D. *The Darker Side of the Renaissance: Literacy, Territoriality, and Colonization.* U of Michigan P, 1995.

Paris, Django, and Maisha T. Winn, editors. *Humanizing Research: Decolonizing Qualitative Inquiry with Youth and Communities.* SAGE, 2013.

Patel, Leigh. *Decolonizing Educational Research: From Ownership to Answerability.* Routledge, 2016.

Prior, Paul A. *Writing/Disciplinarity: A Sociohistoric Account of Literate Activity in the Academy.* L. Erlbaum Associates, 1998.

Royster, Jacqueline Jones. "When the First Voice You Hear Is Not Your Own." *College Composition and Communication*, vol. 47, no. 1, 1996, pp. 29–40.

Simpson, Audra. "On Ethnographic Refusal: Indigeneity, 'Voice,' and Colonial Citizenship." *Junctures*, vol. 9, 2007, pp. 67–80.

Smagorinsky, Peter. "The Methods Section as Epicenter in Constructing Social Science Research Reports." *Written Communication*, vol. 25, no. 3, 2008, pp. 389–411.

Smith, Linda Tuhiwai. *Decolonizing Methodologies: Research and Indigenous Peoples.* Zed Books, 1999.

Tuck, Eve. "Suspending Damage: A Letter to Communities." *Harvard Educational Review*, vol. 79, no. 3, 2009, pp. 409–27.

Tuck, Eve, and K. Wayne Yang. "Decolonization Is Not a Metaphor." *Decolonization: Indigeneity, Education & Society*, vol. 1, no. 1, 2012, pp. 1–40.

———. "R-Words: Refusing Research." *Humanizing Research: Decolonizing Qualitative Inquiry with Youth and Communities*, edited by Django Paris and Maisha T. Winn, SAGE, 2014, pp. 223–48.

Vieira, Kate. *American by Paper: How Documents Matter in Immigrant Literacies.* U of Minnesota P, 2016.

———. "Literacy Studies in the 1990s: Moving through Space, Moving with Time." *College Composition and Communication,* vol. 69, no. 3, pp. 510–19.

2

Intersectional Reflexivity and Decolonial Rhetorics: From Palestine to Aztlán

Haneen Shafeeq Ghabra
Kuwait University

Bernadette Marie Calafell
University of Denver

> Is the *colonial difference* a space for oppressed people to share the experience of coloniality with other oppressed people who come from different experiences of coloniality?
>
> —Gabriella Veronelli

MOVING AWAY FROM EUROCENTRIC RHETORIC, we are guided by the theoretical contributions of women of color and transnational feminisms. Scholars such as Kimberlé Crenshaw argue that the experiences of women of color are shaped at the intersections of racism, classism, and sexism. Building on Crenshaw's work, Patricia Hill Collins suggests that the matrix of domination structures relations of power through the interpersonal, economic, political, and ideological domains. In response, Collins, along with others, such as María Lugones, Chandra Mohanty, and Angela Davis, have argued for the importance of thinking transnationally about feminism and coalition building. As women of color within the United States are building their own foundations for feminism, third-world women's voices remain obscured (Mohanty 4). Of this context Nadine Naber writes, "In the 1990s, as women of color feminisms were institutionalized in US academia, identitarian approaches that privileged 'domestic' politics over international alliances dominated feminisms" (119). In the racist, sexist, and imperialist US imaginary, third-world women are read as ignorant, poor, and subservient. Their stories often remain untold or filtered through hegemonic narratives of needing to be saved. Therefore, work is needed to bridge the gap between US and transnational women of color. This chapter is a step toward doing this as we engage together in dialogue.

Black and Latina feminists, such as Linda Martín Alcoff, Gloria Anzaldúa, and bell hooks, have created space for intersectional feminism and activism to emerge, as have Muslim women transnationally (Abu-Lughod; Ahmed; Ghabra). We write in conversation with these scholars as we attempt to build bridges transnationally that explore the relational and rhetorical possibilities between our respective homelands of Palestine and Aztlán. We articulate our positionalities as decolonial subjects, which allow us to deconstruct hegemonic rhetorics in the name of resistance. Like Lugones we see "the possibility of overcoming the coloniality of gender" as "decolonial feminism" ("Toward" 747). We desire "complex communication" and "deep coalition" that recognizes the "intersectionality of oppressions as real and important for struggle" and "requires a movement outward toward other affiliative groups recognized as resistant" ("On Complex" 76). When we call for a "decolonial feminism," we are calling for a feminism that dismantles the intersectional pervasiveness of power and privilege. A decolonial feminism is one attempt to dismantle power intersectionally instead of privileging one identity over the other, for example, race over gender.

As hegemonic rhetorics circulate into domains of power it is important to develop decolonial tools to dismantle them. We define hegemonic rhetoric as dominant narratives that circulate in the media and popular culture and favor the privileged point of view. This could include privileges such as white, heterosexual, upper-class, able-bodied, and so forth. Decolonization challenges this hegemonic system in an attempt to reverse the existing order (Fanon 2).

Scholars have suggested that sometimes it is difficult to identify which approach works best for decolonization. Do we focus on the indigenous, stressing their struggles, or do we study the power dimensions of colonialism and what effects it has had (Hasian 2)? We understand these tensions and assert that there is a need to be critical of power structures while also not dismissing the voices of the subaltern. Within decolonial rhetoric, it is important to also work against Eurocentric rhetorics that have muffled the voices of marginalized identities. This is not to say that Eurocentric rhetorics or the white canon should be avoided; however, when the white canon is used to study a Latina/o/x or Arab community, the message and results of the analysis become distorted. For this reason, speaking for the Other becomes an ethical dilemma within representation and communication. Thus, we follow Bernadette Calafell and Fernando Delgado's call to understand texts and narratives produced by historically marginalized communities on their own terms rather than force inorganic Eurocentric lenses upon them. This is important for critical scholars to keep in mind when engaging with and performing decolonial rhetorics.

As we begin to dismantle power structures, valorize the voices of the marginalized, and introduce methods of being critical, we must also reflect on our positionalities. For instance, many women of color face the sense of betrayal when critiquing oppressive elements within their cultures (Holling and Calafell, "Tracing" 24). This is extremely critical because it demonstrates the intersections of privilege and oppression and the axiological dilemmas that researchers face. As we begin to critique systems of domination they will change from country to country and region to region. For example, what is oppressive in the United States will manifest itself differently in Kuwait, Palestine, or Mexico. As we critique our own systems against global white Western systems, it is important to keep this in mind. More important, as we bridge the transnational and the local, it is important to keep in mind that the transnational experiences of women of color will shift geopolitically based on their locations. This becomes crucial when creating alliances with US women of color. We seek a decolonial feminist rhetoric that allows us "learn about each other as resisters to the coloniality of gender at the colonial difference" (Lugones, "Toward" 753). We take up Lugones's call by exploring our own experiences with decoloniality to consider points of symmetry and difference.

Calafell ("Performance") argues that performance studies can keep rhetoric "honest" and accountable to the body. The necessary turn to performance and the body is echoed by Lisa Flores, who suggests that performance allows critical rhetoric scholars to "undo the realness of the raced body" while also being able to "claim and proclaim its possibilities" ("The Rhetorical" 95). This move to center the body in critical rhetoric echoes aspects of what Holling and Calafell ("Tracing") term *Latina/o/x vernacular discourse.* In a departure from studying a community by focusing on "exceptional" rhetors or the rhetoric of an oppressor, a critique of vernacular discourse is focused on discourse created by historically marginalized communities, which can range from textual to performative discourse (Ono and Sloop). Embodiment is a central aspect of a performative vernacular discourse (Calafell and McIntosh; Holling and Calafell, "Identities"). Furthermore, a focus on the body is also tied to decoloniality as it centers Other ways of knowing rather than simply those produced as written texts (Holling and Calafell, "Tracing"; Calafell and McIntosh). We engage in a dialogue that reflects the embodied and vernacular performances we engage in as women engaging in decolonial struggles.

While mainstream rhetoricians have latched onto "rhetorical field methods" as a "new" methodological paradigm, scholars such as Bernadette Marie Calafell ("Rhetorics of Possibility," *Latina/o Communication*, "Love, Loss," and *Monstrosity*) and Darrel Wanzer-Serrano have long argued for bringing together rhetorical, qualitative, and performance methodologies. Furthermore, women of color feminists have privileged the telling of our stories, whether through the language of *testimonio* or personal narrative, particularly as many women of color have historically been denied access to education, literacy, and the ability to produce written texts. Cherríe Moraga and Gloria Anzaldúa advocate for theories in the flesh, which attest to the knowledge we gain from our embodied experiences. This type of knowledge disrupts dominant narratives that privilege the mind as the site of knowing and the body as a space of excess and waste. Moraga's and Anzaldúa's theories in the flesh inform our approach to personal narrative, as they speak against and challenge master narratives that structure society, reflecting hegemonic interests (Corey).

Thus a central aspect of personal narrative is the way it uses individual stories to speak in relation to and talk back to larger histories of domination and power. Furthermore, the performative and personal narrative perspective we advocate understands the importance of seeing everyday acts as connected to coloniality, particularly the coloniality of gender (Lugones, "Toward"). This approach mirrors Lugones's move from women of color feminisms to decolonial feminism, which has "a strong emphasis on ground, on a historicized incarnate intersubjectivity" ("Toward" 746).

As we situate ourselves in this decolonial system, a decolonial feminist rhetoric with performative dimensions allows us to explore the (im)possibilities of our own positionalities. Our different identities bring forth a wide spectrum of privilege and oppression. Through intersectional failure and possibility, we situate ourselves in this system and realize the possibilities for a decolonial rhetoric. First, performance studies allows the researcher to theorize through the flesh and through the personal in comparison to hegemonic rhetoric. Second, rhetoric has played a significant role in marginalizing and oppressing identities; therefore, a decolonial rhetoric is a method that can dismantle these overarching narratives that muffled the voices of many for centuries. Third, we use Anzaldúa's concept of borderlands as being in a constant liminal state (*Borderlands* 95). This borderland is important for the study of rhetoric because it allows us to recognize that we do not fully belong somewhere and this in turn opens up a space for one to come to peace with oneself that it is okay to live in an in-between space.

Our turn to personal narrative is also driven by an intersectional reflexivity (Jones; Jones and Calafell) that asks us to be attentive to the ways in which we are not only marginalized, but also privileged. Therefore, this chapter offers our intersectional personal narratives in relationship to larger cultural histories of our respective homelands to consider shared possibilities for decolonial coalitional spaces or rhetorics. Our commitments are similar to those of Angela Davis, who frames her approach to intersectionality as "reflecting not an individual analysis, but rather a sense within movements and collectives that it was not possible to separate issues of race from issues of class and issues of gender" (18). Davis further calls for the development of activist knowledges between US women of color and Palestinians to broaden US understandings of intersectionality. With this chapter, we hope to take steps toward Davis's call by drawing on our histories, rhetorics, and personal narratives as a queer cisgender Chicana from Aztlán and a heterosexual cisgender Kuwaiti-Palestinian to engage in intracultural dialogue as people with "shared knowledge of coloniality" (Veronelli 407). This is our joint step toward decoloniality.

PART ONE: THEORIZING THE OCCUPATION, HOMELANDS, AND THE BODY

Navigating My Kuwaitiness: A Transnational Dilemma (Ghabra)

In 1895 Theodore Herzl, the founder of Zionism, speculated that by removing the Palestinians and displacing them, Zionists would be able to create a Jewish state (Said 13). In 1917, the Balfour Declaration granted Palestine as the homeland for the Jewish population. This project, which grew over time, eventually, in 1948, displaced over 780,000 Palestinians during a catastrophe called "Al Naqba." Today, Palestinians inside present-day occupied Palestine (the West Bank and Gaza) number approximately nine million. However, the diasporic population outside Palestine has reached an approximate eleven million ("Palestinian Central Bureau of Statistics"). For this reason, the Palestinians are divided between those who are outside Palestine, those who have become Israeli citizens, and those in the West Bank and Gaza.

The events of 1948 displaced my grandfather from his home in Haifa. Even as he became Kuwaiti in the 1950s after moving to Kuwait, he hung onto his Palestinian accent until his death. As I navigate between two dialects, Kuwaiti and Palestinian, I am often haunted by the guilt of abandoning my accent. Won't that erase the Palestinian cause? Am I a traitor? But if I am Kuwaiti and I speak Kuwaiti (depending on who is speaking to me and in what accent), why am I feeling so guilty? I am a third-generation Kuwaiti, and most third-generation Kuwaitis have completely erased their accents of origin. However, I still navigate back and forth, adapting and changing depending on which accent is more feasible or will protect me more.

> For Falasteen is a society with no home
> a land with no people . . .
> Ripped from their homes . . .   Torn from their families.
> Palestine is that place,   of pain and belonging   of suffering and hope . . .
> Of endings and beginnings . . . Of Diasporic imaginations . . .

For most of my life I have been trying to grapple with my identity. For identity is what gives us a sense of completeness but also haunts us with a sense of confusion. As I grapple with my ethnicity, I occupy a space that is between two cultures (Anzaldúa, *Borderlands* 100). The more Kuwaiti I become, the more I am reminded that I am originally Palestinian. I am the *Muhujana woman* (Ghabra 5), two ethnicities blended into one (Anzaldúa, *Borderlands* 99). I am not reminded because I am neither pure Palestinian nor pure Kuwaiti. I am reminded because power structures and racial privilege and purity do so. These are the rhetorics of colonization, whiteness, and purity. They seep into the systems of privilege from country to country, system to system. I am neither pure Kuwaiti nor pure Palestinian. In the West I am too brown to be privileged. This is what it means to be Palestinian, to be part of a diasporic community. To see one side of my family become Kuwaiti, while the other becomes Jordanian. To have to be able to provide a label for people because they can't tell if my accent is Kuwaiti or Palestinian. Why does it matter so much to them? Privileges are manifested through rhetorics of colonization to control and put us down, to remind us that we have oppressions.

As I battle my identity as a Kuwaiti, who is often reminded I am Palestinian, I enter the West, where I am reminded of my brownness. Whereas I am reminded of my hybridity in the Middle East, I am tainted with Palestinianness in the West. As Palestinians make the bottom of the list, I am constantly reminded of this through pro-Israeli rhetorics and through rejections of academic journal articles I write that support the Palestinian cause. Having Palestinian blood means your hybridity is never static. Being a transnational woman who has lived all my life between the United States and Kuwait constantly alters my identity geopolitically.

I write this narrative because there needs to be ways to theorize the diasporic, in order to recognize the complexities between different ways of occupation. As I theorize through my flesh, I offer a way in which my body and identity have made sense of the occupation.

Seeking Aztlán: Decolonizing Belonging . . . (Calafell)

You mention 1948. A hundred years earlier, in 1848, our borders shifted, and I don't think we've ever recovered. The Treaty of Guadalupe Hidalgo and the end of the Mexican-American War made parts of Mexico into US states. Among them was the land I grew up on, what is now called Arizona, but is forever Aztlán, the mythical homeland of the Aztecs. Davis writes about the painful history of Palestinians in Palestine "who have been transformed into immigrants against their will, indeed into undocumented immigrants on their own ancestral lands" (58). Nadim N. Rouhana and Areej Sabbagh-Khoury frame "Israel's relationship with its Palestinian citizens as a special and complex case of settler-colonial control" (1). They write of Palestinians who on the land were "perceived and treated an obstacle to achieve the state's Zionist goals" (3). Therefore, "these Palestinians were granted Israeli citizenship and Israel's Declaration of Independence referred to them as 'full and equal'" (3). However, policies "were introduced that made meaningful citizenship unattainable" (3). Rachel Busbridge argues that there is no significant discussion or theorizing of decolonialism within settler colonialism. Our spaces of convergence are starting points for decolonial rhetorics and possibilities.

This history in many ways mirrors that of Mexican and Chicanx peoples, and what has been written about Mexicans living in what became the United States after the Treaty of Guadalupe Hidalgo.

Superficial acknowledgement of citizenship,
without practiced rights,
and based on a skin color caste system that favored
those closest to
whiteness.
Is it all that different now?

Forever foreign
in one's own homeland.

The pain associated with loss of home goes much deeper and further back, starting with the Spanish colonization of Mexico and our creation as mixed-race people. The violence against indigenous women, and the one whom I love the most: Malintzin. My spiritual mother. *La llorona* who takes all our pain and hurt, crying for us all. It is a pain written into and on our bodies as mixed-race people.

> I cannot flee the United States, my land resides beneath its borders. We stand on land that was once the country of Mexico. And before any conquistadors staked out political boundaries, this was Indian land and in the deepest sense remains just that: a land sin fronteras. Chicanos with memory like our Indian counterparts recognize that we are a nation within a nation. An internal nation whose existence defies borders of language, geography, race, Chicanos are a multiracial, multilingual people, who since 1848, have been displaced from our ancestral lands or remain upon them as indentured servants to Anglo-American invaders. (Moraga 54–55)

I remember the first time I heard the word *Aztlán.* And when I read *Yo Soy Joaquin* and *El Plan Espiritual de Aztlán.* Aztlán is connected to "the sacred history of the Aztecs' peregrination from a northern homeland Aztlán, to the founding of the empire of Tenochtitlan" (Pina 38). In college I discovered Chicanx Studies, or should I say it let me discover me. I read all I could about Chicanx rhetoric. From Fernando Delgado to John C. Hammerback, Richard J. Jensen, and Jose Angel Gutierrez. Reading Lisa Flores ("Creating") brought me to tears based in the pain of recognition and realization of a longtime absence. It felt like the most beautiful thing I had ever read. Then a voice that was much more familiar emerged. Moraga's desire for queer Aztlán, "A Chicano homeland that could embrace *all* its people, including its joteria" (147). Her desire was mine too, even if at the time I wasn't ready to admit it. Moving across the country for graduate school, a privilege no doubt, caused my body and spirit to hurt for Aztlán (Calafell, *Latina/o Communication).* Aztlán isn't just a state of mind. It is the land I walk on. The desert I call home. The place where I actually feel a connection to the land. I was not myself until I returned to the Southwestern United States in 2006.

PART TWO: BORDERS AND WALLS

The Rhetoric of the Palestinian Apartheid Wall (Ghabra)

Shortly after the second intifada (uprising) in 2002, the State of Israel began construction of a "security" wall, designed to shield Israel against Palestinian terrorists. Over seven hundred kilometers long, the wall also runs through the West Bank. Designed to control movement, the wall has been a source of pain for many Palestinians. Being cut off from family members, destroying business ties, and limiting access and movement, the wall has restricted basic daily needs for the Palestinians. Even recently, Israel has also built a fence along the Egyptian-Israeli border designed to keep "illegal" immigrants from entering Israel (Kershner). President Trump has also announced he will build a wall along the Mexico-US border and has used Israel as the perfect example. Claiming that this wall has protected many against terrorism and illegal immigrants, he ensures that history will repeat itself in Mexico.

I am having coffee with my advisor, Bernadette. Throughout my PhD program I read almost all of Bernadette's work and she has read mine in order to prepare me for the publishing world.

However, I wasn't aware that I would be reading dozens of articles about Latinx feminism and the Mexico border and immigration. I also wasn't aware that her and my borders were so similar, full of apartheid, oppression, and death. I had recently taken a class with her on *Monsters in Popular Culture* in which the goal is to analyze horror films and how they manifest racism and sexism and so forth. I am stunned. The films that keep reframing Mexicans into illegal aliens also reframe Palestinians and Muslims into mindless zombies or terrorists. I tell Bernadette that I wasn't aware of the similarities between the Mexicans and Palestinians. She agrees with a sad smile.

I realize that the media have cut us off from alliance building and awareness. I had to work with a Latinx advisor to know that oppression can manifest transnationally in similar ways. The rhetoric of the wall is reframed into a security wall while it kills people on a daily basis. There are no ethics in representation when privileged power structures dictate what is said in the media. The wall is based on a rhetoric of racism and apartheid, reframed into a security wall. It is designed to oppress and normalize death. The rhetoric of security is manifested in the media and popular culture, such as in movies like *World War Z,* where Israel is the only country able to secure its country from the mindless zombies. This rhetoric of a security wall feeds into the rhetoric of fear. What if this wall comes down? Terrorists will seep into the country, haunting every Israeli citizen. They will kill as many Israelis as they can, one by one, until they have no country left. However, the rhetoric of fear and security is what is killing the Palestinians, hour by hour, day by day. This is because the rhetoric of fear causes oppression. Take for example the Palestinian towns that are starved to death and can be disposed of in any hour of the day. As the Palestinians live under terror, they also realize that death is the only power in which freedom can operate (Mbembé 186). Therefore, death escapes the occupation (184). The cycle of violence continues from both sides, one living in fear and security and another living in apartheid and death.

I ask Bernadette if I can teach a few weeks on Middle Eastern feminism in her Intersectional Feminism class, focusing one week on the Palestinian cause. Maybe I can teach a counternarrative to US students.

The Rhetoric of the Mexican/US Wall (Calafell)

On August 31, 2016, Donald Trump, then the Republican presidential candidate, spoke in Phoenix, my hometown, about Mexico and his desire to build a border wall. Claiming Mexico would pay for it, Trump stated,

> We will begin working on intangible, physical, tall, power, beautiful southern border wall. We will use the best technology, including above and below ground sensors that's the tunnels. Remember that, above and below. Above and below ground sensors. Towers, aerial surveillance and manpower to supplement the wall, find and dislocate tunnels and keep out criminal cartels. . . . (*Los Angeles Times* Staff)

He continued by talking about the "criminal aliens now inside our country" who must be removed (*Los Angeles Times* Staff). In other speeches Trump talks about "radical Islamic terrorism" as he tries to vilify yet another group of people. The bodies of Latinx and Arab peoples are "browned" through discourses that transform them into threats post-9/11 (Bloodsworth-Lugo and Lugo-Lugo). This is not the first time I have written about our people's historical connections (Calafell, "Performing," "Brownness," "Love, Loss"). I am always looking for connections. I need them to sustain me.

Trump's reign of terror is the latest in the line of hateful rhetoric and actions that thrive in Arizona. From racist former sheriff of Maricopa County Joe Arpaio, to "show me your papers laws" like SB 1070, and finally to calls to ban books that dare to teach Chicanxs our history and our connection to the land, Arizona has become an ideological and material battlefield. All of these actions work to "remind" us that we do not belong. Palestinians are killed and maimed through state-sanctioned violence, while we deal with the remnants of colonial violence every day, which now manifest themselves in xenophobic rhetorics, police brutality, and death at the border. Rhetorics of nationalism based on vilifying us prevail. However, "the nationalism I seek is one that decolonizes the brown and female body as it decolonizes the brown and female earth. It is a new nationalism in which la Chicana Indigena stands at the center, and heterosexism and homophobia are no longer cultural order of the day" (Moraga 150).

I don't go back to Phoenix very much, but when I do I am overcome with a sense of loss as I witness the gentrification of my historically Mexican American and African American community of south Phoenix. In high school some of my more affluent friends' parents wouldn't let them come to my house because of where I lived. Now these same people are buying up land in the South Phoenix desert and building their giant dream houses. We are once again being driven from our home. Davis compares the segregation of occupied Palestine to "the historical apartheid of racism in the southern United States of America" (60). I further connect this not only to the taking of Aztlán, but also to violence in the form of gentrification that is pushing Latinx and African American communities in south Phoenix to the margins.

Alongside the gentrification, violent rhetoric and scapegoating continue on multiple fronts as we are dehumanized by Trump while white people chant, "Build the wall!"

> One by one we are finding the illegal gang members, drug dealers, thieves, robbers, criminals and killers. And we are sending them the hell back home where they came from. And once they are gone, we will never let them back in. Believe me. The predators and criminal aliens who poison our communities with drugs and prey on innocent young people, these beautiful, beautiful, innocent young people will, will find no safe haven anywhere in our country. And you've seen the stories about some of these animals. They don't want to use guns, because it's too fast and it's not painful enough. So they'll take a young, beautiful girl, 16, 15, and others and they slice them and dice them with a knife because they want them to go through excruciating pain before they die. And these are the animals that we've been protecting for so long. Well, they're not being protected any longer, folks. (Latino Rebels)

As the headline reads, "It's Official: Trump's Immigration Criminal Terrorist Rhetoric Is Normalized and Nobody Cares." I know you care.

PART THREE: BORDERLANDS, PAIN, AND POSSIBILITY

Emotional Displacement: Teaching White Students (Ghabra)

I am lecturing today about the Palestinian cause and the plight of Palestinian women.

My heart is racing; I was tossing and turning in my sleep all night, afraid of what might be in store for me today. How would I teach a predominantly white class about the plight of the Palestinians? How would I teach them about the violence and rape that was carried out by the US occupation forces in Iraq (Al-Ali) or the Israeli forces in Palestine (Shalhoub-Kevorkian)? I begin my lecture. Should I say the word *genocide?*[1] No, Haneen, they might think that's a little extreme. . . . You should do research, find out how some consider it genocide. It's a catastrophe! My students are silent throughout most of the lecture—it is a heavy silence that I can't read through. I can't tell if they are silent because the content is so heavy or because I have showed them the video of a little boy being shot during the second intifada in Palestine. Or maybe it is their resistance to hearing the Palestinian narrative. Why are they so quiet? My nonverbal communication skills are completely clouded. My heart races faster and my body starts to tremble. Maybe I shouldn't have shown them the video.

During the next class, I passed out a statement by Jerusalem's Women's Coalition; it was a memo urging the international community to let Palestinian mothers bury their dead children's bodies. Were they sad or were they disengaging in the content? Only one group participated—the rest stayed silent—but this group had a lot to say. How are they managing bodies that are dead? They are torturing Palestinian women through their dead children—this is wrong. The group of girls were stunned and angry. But why were the other groups silent? Was it a fear of delving into the narrative of the Other? Teaching the weeks on Palestinians was one of the most emotional and difficult classes I would ever teach. Difficult because I was not teaching Arab students but on the contrary teaching young adults who have grown up believing the Israeli narrative. Teaching young adults who are conditioned to treat my brownness differently. Being vulnerable to a privileged group while I teach them a painful history that I once belonged to, a history that has been passed down to me from generation to generation.

However, I would soon find out that I had misread my students. As I read their weekly journals, I learned that their silence was from the shock of hearing the Other narrative. Their silence was empathy, and sadness for not ever knowing that the Palestinians were living under so much oppression. Tears streamed down my face as I read the journals. I went back to class the next day and vulnerably told them how scared I had been of their silence and how stunned I was when I read their journals. I realized that I was living in fear. Sometimes moments of opportunity, teaching, and learning can scare us from alliance building. These students taught me that the rhetoric of fear can sometimes prevent alliance building and create defenses and walls that don't need to be there. As walls can create physical displacement they can also emotionally displace us as we fear connecting with those in privileged positionalities, always fearing that they may attack us at any moment. Working through these rhetorics of fear will open up spaces of alliance and trust building.

Liminal Spaces: Healing and Connecting (Calafell)

Remembering those days you lectured, I think about how you taught me so much. I come to see more and more points of connection between our respective histories. Each of us is engaged in the Coyolxauhqui imperative, which is "a struggle to reconstruct oneself and heal the sustos resulting from woundings, traumas, racism, and other acts of violation que hechan pedazos nuestras almas, split us, scatter our energies, and haunt us" (Anzaldúa, *Light* 2). You live in the borderlands too, somewhere between Palestine and Kuwait, just as I am somewhere between Mexico and the United States. We are always in the space of *nepantla,* which allows us to sit in "constant tension" as our "missing or absent pieces can be summoned back, where transformation and healing may be possible, where wholeness is just out of reach but seems attainable" (2). You too are in a liminal space, constantly shifting, and developing a tolerance for ambiguity.

CONCLUSIONS

We've come together despite racist discourses in the United States that would prefer we remain separate, pitting us against one another. We hold our histories and stories up as mirrors to one another. In your reflection I see myself. Histories of separation. Histories of being made unintelligible or foreign in lands we call home. Driven by decolonial desires we demand something more.

As we push for decolonial rhetorics we have an opportunity to resist Eurocentric and hegemonic rhetorics. As we face triple the work of voicing the decolonial, we must be more active in theorizing through our bodies while seeking alliance building. We engage in decolonial dialogues that recognize our points of convergence *and* divergence. We have theorized together through the three sites of occupation, border/walls, and pain in the borderlands. These are our spaces of possibility for coming together in colonial differences to begin to decolonize.

Through three points of contestation we can come closer to voicing the needs of the marginalized. First, by theorizing a rhetoric of the occupation and the homeland through our bodies we are better able to create a third space where individuals are allowed to be comfortable in a hybrid identity that is constantly marked as different. It becomes possible to find calmness in the "in-between" spaces. As we theorize as hybrid individuals, we are able to open up sites of alliance building for those who have struggled with their own hybrid identities. These identities are never static, but rather in flux, changing geographically and transnationally. Therefore, theorizing through the occupation, homeland, and body allows for a place to start resolving the pain of displacement.

Second, theorizing through the body also allows us an opportunity to identify the similar physical barriers that are meant to oppress those in marginalized identities. As the media cut us off from knowing one another's similar histories, decolonial rhetoric allows us to connect again. Theorizing through the material allows us to identify the rhetoric of reframing. As these walls are framed as walls of security they in fact are walls of apartheid. Training ourselves to think critically of these rhetorics allows us to identify when the media and hegemonic rhetoric have obscured reality. Finding similarities between the material effects of displacement also allow for alliance building. Additionally, coming to terms with our privileged positionalities and when we can speak "with" and not "for" is crucial in materializing a decolonial rhetoric (Alcoff 7). As hegemonic rhetoric occupies a space of privilege and speaks "for" and not "with," we must center this when engaging in a decolonial rhetoric.

Finally, pain and living in the borderlands is a site of contestation. In moments when we felt we have failed, we risk identifying the moments when we have succeeded. We have often felt the pain of erasure and the disciplining of our voices (Ghabra and Calafell). We have often been in situations where alliances fail between those in marginalized identities. For instance, when discussing the marginalization of LGBTQ communities, the conversation is often re-centered to heterosexuality by people of color who should be building alliance instead of failing potential allies (Ghabra and Calafell). However, failure is an opportunity for alliance building. As we theorize through the fear of being erased, as when teaching a predominantly white class about the Palestinian conflict, we sometimes miss the moments when an opportunity arises. However, these instances are moments of possibility and future coalition.

As we have theorized through various forms of displacement, we envision a decolonial rhetoric as a method that dismantles and allows the critic to develop the skills needed to take apart hegemonic rhetoric. We envision this as, first, developing the skills through Collins's matrix of domination, which allows us to envision intersectionality as a map of privileges and oppressions (4). This matrix allows us to understand how power works. As the individual begins to develop the skills to critique and identify hegemonic rhetorics, the critic in turn begins to dismantle the overarching narratives. For this reason, we see decolonial rhetoric as a process and realize that by "centering" historically marginalized communities and their narratives we also risk silencing their voices by hegemonic rhetoric. We also risk ourselves when centering our own voices as this centering could have consequences in academia, institutions, government, and the media. However, we hope that the risks we take by centering marginalized communities will allow us to redefine rhetoric, borderland, and possibility.

Looking at you,
"I see Raza as a set of attitudes, expectations with no geographical limits" (Anzaldúa, *Light* 71).
And,
like Nelson Mandela,
I "know too well that our freedom is incomplete without the freedom of the Palestinians" (Davis, 53).
For sometimes the homeland is a liminal space, nonexistent, nonmaterial
And sometimes the borders and walls remind us that we are in that liminal space
Pain and possibility move us forward, toward a rhetoric of coalition
So that we can finally put the ghosts of rhetoric to rest.
Together me and you
In moments of possibility

NOTE

1. For more information on the ethnic cleansing and genocide of Palestine, see Ilan Pappe, *The Ethnic Cleansing of Palestine* (Oneworld Publications, 2006) and "Israel's Incremental Genocide in the Gaza Ghetto," *The Electronic Intifada*, 13 July 2014, electronicintifada.net/content/israels-incremental-genocide-gaza-ghetto/13562; and Edward Said, *The Question of Palestine* (Vintage Books, 1979).

WORKS CITED

Abu-Lughod, Lila. *Do Muslim Women Need Saving?* Harvard UP, 2013.

Ahmed, Leila. *A Quiet Revolution: The Veil's Resurgence, from the Middle East to America*. Yale UP, 2011.

Al-Ali, Nadje Sadig. *Iraqi Women: Untold Stories from 1948 to the Present*. Zed Books, 2007.

Alcoff, Linda. "The Problem of Speaking for Others." *Cultural Critique*, vol. 20, 1991, pp. 5–32.

Anzaldúa, Gloria. *Borderlands/La Frontera: The New Mestiza*. 4th ed., Aunt Lute, 1991.

———. *Light in the Dark/Luz en lo Oscuro: Rewriting Identity, Spirituality, Reality*. Duke UP, 2015.

Bloodsworth-Lugo, Mary, and Carmen Lugo-Lugo. "Citizenship and the Browning of Terror." *Peace Review*, vol. 20, no. 3, 2008, pp. 272–82.

Busbridge, Rachel. "Israel-Palestine and the Settler Colonial 'Turn': From Interpretation to Decolonization." *Theory, Culture & Society*, vol. 35, no. 1, 2017, pp. 91–115, http://journals.sagepub.com/doi/abs/10.1177/0263276416688544#articleCitationDownloadContainer. Accessed 27 July 2017.

Calafell, Bernadette Marie. "Brownness, Kissing, and US Imperialism: Contextualizing the Orlando Massacre." *Communication and Critical/Cultural Studies*, vol. 14, no. 2, 2017, pp. 198–202.

———. *Latina/o Communication Studies: Theorizing Performance*. Peter Lang, 2007.

———. "Love, Loss, and Immigration: Performative Reverberations between a Great-Grandmother and a Great-Granddaughter." *Border Rhetorics: Citizenship and Identity on the US-Mexico Frontier*, edited by D. Robert DeChaine, U of Alabama P, 2012, pp. 151–62.

———. *Monstrosity, Performance, and Race in Contemporary Culture*. Peter Lang, 2015.

———. "Performance: Keeping Rhetoric Honest." *Text and Performance Quarterly*, vol. 34, no. 1, 2014, pp. 115–17.

———. "Performing the Responsible Sponsor: Everything You Never Wanted to Know about Immigration Post-9/11." *Latina/o Communication Studies Today*, edited by Angharad N. Valdivia, Peter Lang, 2008, pp. 69–89.

———. "Rhetorics of Possibility: Challenging Textual Bias through the Theory of the Flesh." *Rhetorica in Motion: Feminist Rhetorical Methods and Methodologies*, edited by Eileen E. Schell and K. J. Rawson, U of Pittsburgh P, 2010, pp. 104–17.

Calafell, Bernadette Marie, and Dawn Marie D. McIntosh. "Latina/o Vernacular Discourse: Theorizing Performative Dimensions of an Other Counterpublic." *What Democracy Looks Like: The Rhetoric of Social Movements and Counterpublics*, edited by Christina R. Foust, Amy Pason, and Kate Zittlow Rogness, U of Alabama P, 2017, pp. 201–24.

Calafell, Bernadette M., and Fernando Delgado. "Reading Latina/o Images: Interrogating Americanos." *Critical Studies in Media Communication*, vol. 21, no. 1, 2004, pp. 1–24.

Collins, Patricia Hill. *Black Feminist Thought: Knowledge, Consciousness, and the Politics of Empowerment*. Rev. ed., Routledge, 2000.

Corey, Frederick. "The Personal: Against the Master Narrative." *The Future of Performance Studies: Visions and Revisions*, edited by Sheron J. Dailey, National Communication Association, 1998, pp. 249–53.

Crenshaw, Kimberlé. "Mapping the Margins: Intersectionality, Identity Politics, and Violence against Women of Color." *Stanford Law Review*, vol. 43, no. 6, 1991, pp. 1241–99.

Davis, Angela Y. *Freedom Is a Constant Struggle: Ferguson, Palestine, and the Foundations of a Movement.* Haymarket Books, 2016.

Delgado, Fernando Pedro. "Chicano Movement Rhetoric: An Ideographic Interpretation." *Communication Quarterly*, vol. 43, no. 4, 1995, pp. 446–55.

Fanon, Frantz. *The Wretched of the Earth*. Grove, 1963.

Flores, Lisa A. "Creating Discursive Space through a Rhetoric of Difference: Chicana Feminists Craft a Homeland." *The Quarterly Journal of Speech*, vol. 82, no. 2, 1996, pp. 142–56.

———. "The Rhetorical Realness of Race, or Why Critical Race Rhetoricians Need Performance Studies." *Text and Performance Quarterly*, vol. 34, no. 1, 2014, pp. 94–96.

Ghabra, Haneen. "Disrupting Privileged and Oppressed Spaces: Reflecting Ethically on My Arabness through Feminist Autoethnography." *Kaleidoscope: A Graduate Journal of Qualitative Communication Research*, vol. 14, 2015, pp. 1–16.

Ghabra, Haneen, and Bernadette Marie Calafell. "From Failure and Allyship to Feminist Solidarities: Negotiating Our Privileges and Oppressions across Borders." *Text and Performance Quarterly*, vol. 38, no. 1-2, 2018, pp. 38–54.

Hammerback, John C., Richard J. Jensen, and Jose Angel Gutierrez. *A War of Words: Chicano Protest in the 1960s and 1970s.* Greenwood Press, 1985.

Hasian, Marouf A., Jr. *Colonial Legacies in Postcolonial Contexts: A Critical Rhetorical Examination of Legal Histories.* Peter Lang, 2002.

Holling, Michelle A., and Bernadette M. Calafell. "Identities on Stage and Staging Identities: ChicanoBrujo Performances as Emancipatory Practices." *Text and Performance Quarterly*, vol. 27, no. 1, 2007, pp. 58–83.

———. "Tracing the Emergence of Latin@ Vernaculars in Studies of Latin@ Communication." *Latina/o Discourse in Vernacular Spaces: Somos de Una Voz?*, edited by Michelle A. Holling and Bernadette M. Calafell, Lexington Books, 2011, pp. 17–29.

hooks, bell. *Yearning: Race, Gender, and Cultural Politics.* South End Press, 1990.

Jones, Richard G., Jr. "Putting Privilege into Practice through 'Intersectional Reflexivity': Ruminations, Interventions, and Possibilities." *Reflections: Narratives of Professional Helping*, vol. 16, no. 1, 2010, pp. 122–25.

Jones, Richard G., Jr., and Bernadette Marie Calafell. "Contesting Neoliberalism through Critical Pedagogy, Intersectional Reflexivity, and Personal Narrative: Queer Tales of Academia." *Journal of Homosexuality*, vol. 59, no. 7, 2012, pp. 957–81.

Kershner, Isabel. "Hamas and Israel Are in a Perilous Cycle. Is War a Miscalculation Away?" *The New York Times*, 21 July 2018, https://www.nytimes.com/2018/07/21/world/middleeast/israel-gaza-hamas.html. Accessed 11 Dec. 2018.

Latino Rebels. "It's Official: Trump's Immigration Criminal Terrorist Rhetoric Is Normalized and Nobody Cares." *Latino Rebels,* 27 July 2017, http://www.latinorebels.com/2017/07/27/its-official-trumps-immigration-criminal-terrorist-rhetoric-is-normalized-and-nobody-cares-video/. Accessed 27 July 2017.

Los Angeles Times Staff. "Transcript: Donald Trump's Full Immigration Speech, Annotated." *Los Angeles Times,* 31 Aug. 2016, http://www.latimes.com/politics/la-na-pol-donald-trump-immigration-speech-transcript-20160831-snap-htmlstory.html. Accessed 18 July 2017.

Lugones, María. "On Complex Communication." *Hypatia: A Journal of Feminist Philosophy*, vol. 21, no. 3, 2006, pp. 75–85.

———. "Toward a Decolonial Feminism." *Hypatia: A Journal of Feminist Philosophy*, vol. 25, no. 4, 2010, pp. 742–59.

Mbembe, Achille. *Critique of Black Reason*. Duke UP, 2017.

Mohanty, Chandra Talpade. "Introduction: Cartographies of Struggle: Third World Women and the Politics of Feminism." *Third World Women and the Politics of Feminism*, edited by Mohanty, Ann Russo, and Lourdes Torres, Indiana UP, 1991, pp. 1–49.

Moraga, Cherríe. *The Last Generation: Prose and Poetry.* South End Press, 1993.

Naber, Nadine. "Arab and Black Feminisms: Joint Struggle and Transnational Anti-Imperialist Activities." *Departures in Critical Qualitative Research*, vol. 5, no. 3, 2016, pp. 116–25.

Ono, Kent A., and John M. Sloop. "The Critique of Vernacular Discourse." *Communication Monographs*, vol. 62, no. 1, 1995, pp. 19–46.

"Palestinian Central Bureau of Statistics." http://www.pcbs.gov.ps/site/lang__en/881/default.aspx#Population. Accessed 5 Jan. 2017.

Pina, Michael. "The Archaic, Historical and Mythicized Dimensions of Aztlán." *Aztlán: Essays on the Chicano Homeland,* edited by Rudolfo A. Anaya and Francisco A. Lomeli, Academia/El Norte, 1989, pp. 14–48.

Rouhana, Nadim N., and Areej Sabbagh-Khoury. "Settler-Colonial Citizenship: Conceptualizing the Relationship between Israel and Its Palestinian Citizens." *Settler Colonial Studies*, vol. 5, no. 3, 2015, pp. 205–25.

Said, Edward W. *The Question of Palestine*. Times Books, 1979.

Shalhoub-Kevorkian, Nadera. "Racism, Militarisation and Policing: Police Reactions to Violence against Palestinian Women in Israel." *Social Identities*, vol. 10, no. 2, 2004, pp. 171–93.

Veronelli, Gabriela. "A Coalitional Approach to Theorizing Decolonial Communication." *Hypatia: A Journal of Feminist Philosophy*, vol. 31, no. 2, 2016, pp. 404–20.

Wanzer-Serrano, Darrel. *The New York Young Lords and the Struggle for Liberation*. Temple UP, 2015.

3

Rhetorical Autoethnography: Delinking English Language Learning in a Family Oral History

Steven Alvarez
St. John's University

ALL SCHOLARLY ACCOUNTS OF LIVING CULTURES construct knowledge by parsing material conditions not only in motion but also generated by autobiographical convergences in the "web of self" of the researcher (Chang 13). This web of self, to be sure, is more like a reflexive web of scholarly selves, and the convergences of these dynamic social positionalities are the intersecting networks of plural identities, languages, and complex lived histories. This reflexive stance toward studying the self in society "utilizes the researchers' autobiographical data to analyze and interpret cultural data" (9), taking into account how observers' positionalities participate and affect their research, connecting the personal to the cultural as an individual critically studies the social self positioned within cultural webs.

In this chapter, I employ the reflexive scholarly methodology of critical autoethnography to uncover my webs of research, to situate the historical context of my researcher positionality and my interpretations of the literacy practices of immigrant families. In doing so, I turn "the ethnographic gaze inward on the self (auto), while maintaining the outward gaze of ethnography, looking at the larger context wherein self experiences occur" (Denzin 227). In *Autoethnography as Method*, Heewon Chang describes this process of rewriting the social production of self-identity via autoethnographic methods, applying qualitative research to understand the self:

> autoethnographers attempt to achieve cultural understanding through analysis and interpretation. In other words, autoethnography is not about focusing on self alone, but about searching for understanding of others (culture/society) through self. . . . autoethnographers use their personal experiences as primary data. (48–49)

Autoethnography explicitly seeks to connect the self to research/writing projects with the aim of generating insights from data accumulated about the self (for example, personal records, report cards, photograph albums, interviews, observations, diaries), but also to see how research is shaped by society, cultures, and lived experience with institutions. Such reflexivity explores personal experiences and social interactions as a method for achieving wider cultural, political, or social understanding. Critical autoethnographers—like all ethnographers—must ask: What are the limits to where research can go? Where are the spaces researchers cannot enter? What contact zones do we collaborate in shaping? What borders can we cross? How do researchers address researchers, subjects, and audiences as "outsiders" and "insiders" (Holdman Jones, Adams, and Ellis; Reed-Danahay)?

To further complicate these issues, I propose a rhetorical understanding of critical autoethnography that examines the colonizing gaze of the decontextualized researcher and the accompanying rhetoric that normalizes a "universal" viewpoint. A self-reflexive "auto" reckoning must articulate how such a rhetoric of transparency affects the situated contexts of researchers and their works. A critical autoethnography accomplishes this by localizing dominant discourses that frame, categorize, interpret, and critique the social life of the researcher, in an effort to produce an observation-based theory of self-interpretation that can give voice "to previously silenced and marginalized experiences, answer unexamined questions about the multiplicity of social identities, instigate discussions about and across difference, and explain the contradictory intersections of personal and cultural standpoints" (Boylorn and Orbe 15). This rhetorical dimension to critical autoethnography demonstrates a commitment to positionality as analysis, not just capturing what is going on in an individual life or sociocultural environment but also the sociopower dynamics that affect the possibility of a decontextualized scholarly objectivity. The epistemological thrust is an effort at decolonizing the "natural" conventions of a detached researcher.

In this chapter, I therefore contextualize my position as language researcher through a critical autoethnography of my family's Mexican immigrant history and the social roots behind the gradual loss of Spanish language in our household, researching my family's educational networks and our adaptation to English dominance in a single generation in the United States. I argue that positionality and family stories about language learning influence how language and literacy researchers approach qualitative research. With critical autoethnography, we have powerful tools to analyze oral histories with a decolonial positioning away from "subtractive schooling." In *Subtractive Schooling: U.S.-Mexican Youth and the Politics of Caring*, Angela Valenzuela argues that cultural erasure means that schooling expects immigrant and minoritized children to give up their ethnic cultures and lose this valuable support for their educational development. Subtractive schooling is one way in which the values and home language practices of students become perceived as "deficits." This chapter, based on oral history interviews conducted in 2011, explores the history of the border politics and subtractive schooling that structured my family's loss of Spanish, focusing on the early educational experiences of my parents, Robert and Anna Alvarez. Both remembered their first teachers in Bisbee, Arizona, but Robert's negative encounters with subtractive schooling contrasted greatly with Anna's positive emergent bilingual experiences, in a segregated Arizona copper-mining border town during the 1940s and 1950s. I examine further how subtractive schooling shaped my literacy education, as well as my literacy research. Uncovering these literacy histories about the subtractive schooling of my parents became a reflexive turn to decolonizing educational notions of "deficiency," a turn that has positioned me as a researcher challenging the historical, structural, and institutional conventions of subtractive schooling for Latinx students. I conclude with a discussion of decolonizing subtractive schooling practices through critical autoethnography for studying literacies that challenge these deficit orientations.

CRITICAL AUTOETHNOGRAPHY: QUALITATIVE METHOD FOR REFLEXIVE SELF-ANALYSIS

Pierre Bourdieu argues in *Sketch for a Self-Analysis* that "[t]o understand is first to understand the field with which and against which one has been formed" (4). Bourdieu's doubling of the verb "to understand" speaks to the self-reflexive and doubling sense of the self in different social contexts. The self-reflexive accordingly has its limits for accounting for complete decolonial delinking, but the importance of theorizing from the margins has significance in the undertaking to position oneself strategically. Critical autoethnography allows the marginal subject to speak of the "cultural and political center from academic margins" (Mignolo 312). In this vein of intellectual decolonization, Deborah Reed-Danahay calls for autoethnographic studies by scholars who hail from marginalized groups where "people who were formerly the subjects of ethnography [can] become the authors of studies of their own group" (2). No doubt, the lived experiences of the marginalized can be rhetorically examined to better grasp how culture inculcates ideologies and frames their interpretations of the world. The importance of critical autoethnography in this endeavor is to locate those intersections of shared oppressions across differences in lived experiences, especially among the marginalized. Nevertheless, simply writing one's story is not autoethnographic, as the method and practice of autoethnography are not a writing of the self, but, rather, a rewriting of the self from the individual to the social, potentially rewriting the self for liberatory ends. This becomes a delinking option, then, when we begin to uncover how a critical autoethnography challenges power and privilege by centering previously marginalized histories and dismantling inculcated systems of social inequality in scholarly projects in an effort "toward intellectual decolonization" (Mignolo ix).

For this project, I conducted three interviews each with Robert and Anna at their home during the late spring of 2011, totaling a combined four and a half hours and 165 pages of transcripts. Using a grounded-theory approach (Glaser and Strauss), I open-coded the interviews, identifying salient themes connected to schooling, immigration, and literacy practices. In coding the different domains, I began to see a more complete picture of the challenges encountered and the actions taken to maintain bilingualism against language loss. I justified the selection of the dialogues presented here as critical case sampling (Onwuegbuzie and Leech) to bring forward the discourse that best illustrates the strategies my family used to articulate language and literacy practices.

LANGUAGE LEGITIMACY AND LANGUAGE LOSS

In my educational history, there had been a strong discrepancy between language use in everyday life and language use in academia, between high-academic "consecration" and low social origins, a problem of awkward upward mobility discussed famously by Richard Hoggart in *The Uses of Literacy*, by Linda Brodkey in her literacy autobiography "Writing on the Bias," by Mike Rose in his best-selling *Lives on the Boundary*, and by Bourdieu, who described the problem as a "conciliation of contraries" (103). The tensions between languages I associate with academia and my life outside academia are the same that establish the grounds for what I term "school" and "home" literacies, a dichotomy that became the foundation for how I understood the language and literacy practices of communities in which I conducted ethnographic projects (Alvarez, *Brokering Tareas; Community Literacies* en Confianza). Inspired by the works of Shirley Brice Heath and Mary Louise Pratt, I theorized that the distinctions of spaces and interactions for bilingual schooling in communities structured educational opportunity in unequal ways. Subtractive English-only ideologies dynamically positioned communities' home practices as deficient, as schools policed language discrimination. These ideologies are also inherent in language policies, which, in turn, are internalized by students as assessable abilities or deficiencies.

There is a myth that immigrants "don't want to" learn English. Research demonstrates, however, that children in bilingual households who attend school in the United States learn social English within one to three years (Ovando, Combs, and Collier), often quickly losing their home languages as they become English-dominant (Rumbaut, Massey, and Bean; Portes and Rumbaut). Indeed, home language policing is clearly the exception rather than the norm in the US context. With language shift, the language loss that may follow represents a loss of "more crucial core values" and a part of one's identity that is associated with cultural and ethnic groups (Lanza and Svendsen).

The challenge to subtractive schooling became my endeavor as a college writing instructor, and this orientation toward social effects taught me to focus on the dynamics of literacy practices, of reading, speaking, and writing, and where and when they were policed. Following the influence of Freirean pedagogy, I looked to the cognitive and linguistic skills students brought to classrooms about the disciplining of languages and literacies—their lived experiences with subtractive schooling that undervalued their home languages (Farr; Santa Ana; Zentella). This entailed looking to situations of contact as content for critical scrutiny, and constant self-reflexive awareness on my part of the pedagogical potentials of any moment of discourse for decolonial liberation through uncovering the dynamics of power relations directly affecting students' educational trajectories.

As I have designed writing projects over time, I have always begun with students conducting interviews for autoethnographic projects about their communities, their homes, and their families. My participation in this unique process of learning and teaching critical autoethnography displayed to me in everyday language use the meaning of the decolonial option to subtractive schooling. In the case of oral histories, there is also the understanding that these texts are also artifacts for memory, and for families, the records of voices and stories are invaluable. This exercise of recording the voices of my parents became the honor I gave to sharing the respect for their literacy narratives as significant for the stories of future generations. That is, I performed the same project of my college writing students and began by speaking to my parents, convincing them to participate in the oral history, and honoring them with texts that will carry their voices to future generations of our family. In the next section, I explore further this element of generational narratives in depth; however, I begin with shaping the macropicture of the historical context of the Arizona borderlands during the first two successive waves of Mexican migration into the US Southwest. I connect the microhistory of my family's migration and how subtractive schooling affected my parents' views about bilingual learning. Below, I offer samples from the oral histories with Robert and Anna that highlight aspects that best illustrate important memories about language prejudice, immigrant assimilation, and subtractive schooling that affected their outlooks on education and, subsequently, that became the "English-only" normalization of my schooling.

BILINGUALISM ON THE BORDERLANDS

Charged clashes at the border between Mexico and the United States in Southern Arizona had been a constant since the Gadsden Purchase of 1853, when the United States purchased all of southern Arizona and southwestern New Mexico in a treaty with Mexico. In 1910, the Arizona Territory elected an all-male, all-Anglo state constitutional convention that debated immigration restrictions later passed by statewide vote. Eventually, these restrictions were ruled unconstitutional by federal courts. At the same time, in Mexico itself, long-smoldering resentment over the nearly fifty-year dictatorial regime of Porfirio Díaz broke into revolution. The Revolution precipitated the influx of thousands of war refugees to border cities like El Paso, Texas, and Nogales and Douglas, Arizona (Farr and Domínguez Barajas 7). These refugees were the "vanguard" in what would become the first mass migration of Mexicans to the United States (Benton-Cohen).

The first influx of immigrants during the revolution was followed by two later flows, in 1900–1929 and in 1942–1964. The flows of Mexican immigrants happened in three large movements during the twentieth century. The third of these mass migrations still continues, from 1964 into the twenty-first century. The first wave, referred to by Jorge Durand, Douglas Massey, and Chiara Capoferro in "The New Geography of Mexican Immigration" as the "Classic Era" in Mexico-US migration history (1), the first third of the twentieth century, reduced Mexico's population by 10 percent. The Great Depression ended this first wave (Alba and Nee). During this "Classic Era," the political situation in Mexico was unstable, which served as a "push factor" for many who became immigrants. At the same time, the United States was expanding its railroad system in the Western states, which led to a massive recruitment of Mexican laborers between 1929 and 1937, during which nearly a half million Mexicans were arrested and expelled from the country (Massey, Durand, and Malone).

My grandparents emigrated during the Mexican Revolution from the northern states of Durango, Sinaloa, and Sonora to Arizona because of political turbulence and the pull of rapid economic development in the mining and railroad industries in the US Southwest during the early twentieth century. Between 1900 and 1920, the southwest United States saw the greatest increases in the Mexican immigrant population. In 1910, Arizona's two major industries—railroad transportation and copper mining—used discriminatory pay scales, or a dual-wage system, to pay Mexicans less than white men, regardless of their citizenship status (Benton-Cohen). This was not a casual racism, but a formal practice illustrated in corporate wage scales with separate columns for "white/American" and "Mexican" wages. In mining towns around the border known as "white man's camps," Mexican-origin workers were hired only for unskilled, "surface" labor rather than the more lucrative mining jobs (Benton-Cohen; Horne). My maternal grandfather, Gilberto Navarro, was born in one of these "white man's camps."

My paternal grandfather, Francisco Alvarez, was part of the first mass migration of Mexicans to the United States. He emigrated initially from Tetaroba, Sinaloa, Mexico, first to the Mexican border copper mine at Cananea, Sonora, then later to Bisbee, Arizona. My father was born in Bisbee. My mother was born in Cananea, Sonora, and her family migrated to Bisbee when she was five, in 1951. Her family was part of the second mass migration of Mexicans to the United States, referred to as the "bracero" period after the bracero (Spanish for "arm-worker") agreements for the importation of temporary laborers from Mexico into the United States.

Though I grew up just a few hours north of the Mexican border in southeastern Arizona decades after my family's initial migration, I had never considered how border politics created contact zones for my family's home language loss and turn to English-dominant monolingualism. Higher education was out of reach economically for my parents, but also for my elder siblings. My parents had five children over fifteen years, 1967–1982. Between my oldest sibling and me, the second youngest, there was a gap of eleven years. There was also a gap of seven years between my next oldest sibling, my older sister, born in 1972, and me, born in 1979. My younger sister arrived in 1982. By the time my three older siblings had come of age, my parents had increased economic security, helped in part by the older children assisting in child care duties for the two younger siblings, freeing my mother to work outside the home, which she did, increasing our family income. The increased income earned by my parents when I was a child as well as the mentoring provided by my older siblings had positive outcomes for my educational trajectory, including knowing how to read before beginning kindergarten.

A generation earlier, when they were children, my parents, Robert and Anna, learned English in elementary school in Bisbee, Arizona, where both grew up in blue-collar working families. My father, Robert, told the strange and cruel—but not uncommon—story of being punished into learning English by forced standing behind the classroom door. As an educator, I listen to these stories knowing full well that they shape my story, and also my views toward decolonizing language ideologies that dehumanize immigrant communities and subtract the educational potential of emergent bilingual students. In the following sections, I delve further into my parents' oral history narratives.

Robert Alvarez

My father and I have had only a few serious conversations with each other in my life. One conversation we shared before my research for this study took place several years previously. As an undergraduate, I interviewed him for an ethnography project about a large copper strike in Morenci, Arizona, which he witnessed firsthand. Another conversation we shared was when we traveled to Sinaloa, Mexico, together to search for his father's home and meet extended family he had found through genealogical research. The following conversation, on May 29, 2011, was one more rare occasion when I could sit with him alone and speak candidly. Just before the interview, our family suffered a health scare on his part. We were all thankful when everything turned out fine, but during the time of this interview we were both slightly tense.

Robert Alvarez was born in Bisbee, Arizona, in 1943. His parents were immigrants from Mexico who had crossed the border in the same year, 1915: his father from Sinaloa, his mother from Durango. Five years of the bloody Mexican Revolution had passed. Robert's father, Francisco, was twenty-seven years old when he emigrated with his second wife, Gloria, a Basque immigrant. He had abandoned his first wife, Rosario Quintero, and three children back in Sinaloa.

Robert's mother, María, was eight years old when her family immigrated. She grew up down the street from Francisco in Bisbee. In 1942, a year after his second wife of twenty-seven years, Gloria, passed away, Francisco married María. They had three children together before Francisco died in 1955. María died in 1970.

Robert completed eleven years of schooling, earned his GED diploma, and joined the military at seventeen. He was sent to Korea directly after boot camp in 1960. According to Robert, his mother completed the eighth grade in the United States: "My mother went to a Mexican school. It was called Lincoln School. It was only Mexicans up to the eighth grade. All the way through it was for Mexicans. It wasn't around when I started. It was disbanded." Robert said his mother learned the basics of English at school, but learned mostly on her own since she read a great deal: "My mother used to read a lot. Anything. Fiction . . . almost any kind of novel, she read. In English. Most women didn't read as much her, or most men either."

"How would you describe my grandparents' spoken English?" I asked Robert as we sat on the sofa in the living room of his home drinking coffee with my digital recorder resting on a book between us.

"My mother spoke it. She spoke good English."

"What do you mean that your mother spoke good English?"

"As normal people do here in the United States," he answered. "No accent."

Robert looked at me skeptically. As if I did not know what it meant to speak "good English" with "no accent." I assured him that I was asking questions as a researcher.

"Put it this way, compared to my father, she sounded American. My father spoke broken English. People understood him, but he had . . . well, he would say the words with an accent. My father had a Spanish accent with some words. Once in a while, if [he] went to an office or something, he would communicate with the people there, but he had an accent. He could do what he needed to do. They didn't have none of these Spanish signs and stuff like that. The person you went to always spoke English."

"Did he ever have to speak English?"

"Well, then, I guess the only time he spoke English was when he was at work. He would speak Spanish at home all the time. My mother was always in Spanish until before I went to school. When I started school, everybody was speaking Spanish at home."

Robert had two younger brothers. The elder was a year younger, and youngest seven years distant. When Robert began school, he spoke only Spanish. Though his mother had command over English, or she spoke "normal" as Robert put it, she maintained her home language in her gendered domestic duty of raising her sons.

"Was Spanish used at your school?" I was expecting to hear how Spanish was discouraged, as I had read in various anthropological studies of English and Spanish on the borderlands during this period. He verified this, but Robert's experience moved me in ways that forever affected how I understood the colonizing power of English-only ideologies in my family history, and why I chose to study the language and literacy practices of immigrant families.

"Everything was taught in English. No bilingual or anything like that. When they would give me directions sometimes the teacher would get madder than heck because I didn't know—I couldn't do what she told me to do because I didn't know what it was. So she'd get the ruler and hit me all over, on the head . . . and I guess she finally got tired of me, of hitting me. So then she put me behind the closet door every day."

"Now what grade was this?" I asked.

"My first year," he said.

"Kindergarten?"

"We didn't have no kindergarten then. First grade. But that closet—" he continued where he left off before I interrupted him. By this time in our discussion, I think I lost some of my own composure hearing my father's recollection.

"—well, a closet, but really just a corner. You know where a door opens against a corner? And you know how when you open the door all the way, there's a little triangle space behind it? Well it was that way in the hallway—between the classroom and the hallway. The part of the classroom where the kids hung up their coats and stuff. So she would open up that door and put me behind there. And I'd stay there all day until lunch. At lunchtime, go eat lunch, then come back, and go behind there again. I could look through the crack of the door when it was open—in the crack between the hinges and the door. She only did that with me, that I remember."

I asked why he thought she did that to him.

"Because I couldn't speak English at all. After a while, you know, she wouldn't even take me back there anymore. I would come in, take my coat off, put my lunch away, and I'd go straight behind the door. That probably went on for about five months or somewhere around there."

"Five months?" I asked. I was incredulous. "Half the school year you were standing behind the door?"

"Yeah," he said. "After my mother found out I was having lots of trouble, she told my father to start speaking English at home too. She saw my report cards, and she talked to the teacher. My mother was upset."

"With the teachers or with you?"

"Well, with herself mostly," he said.

"What do you mean?"

"She kept saying that she should have taught me English a long time before I went to school. She thought it was her fault."

Robert's negative views of schooling seemed in part to reflect a disconnection between his family's familiarity with the US system of schooling and what María deemed as her own deficiency. She internalized a misrecognition of racism against her own tongue as a lack of linguistic capital. Even though her son was the victim of a bigoted teacher, María regretted not providing her son with sufficient mainstream English learning. The English-only ideology of Robert's school structured failure so that María turned this failure into her own, and not failure on the part of the school to implement subtractive policies for emergent bilingual children.

According to Robert, María felt as if she had failed her son by not teaching him English, thereby preparing him only for failure at school. In one way, we would expect that such racialized, terrible teaching practices would be countered by the safety of the home. Of course families are situated within an educational nexus of power, and they mediate home languages and attitudes toward learning to institutional language and school notions of linguistic propriety. For children it is their everyday experiences in their relations to social institutions—most especially schools—that particularly challenge attitudes about schooling and one's sense of place and self.

In contrast to Robert's experience, I present my mother Anna's more positive bilingual experiences in Bisbee schools.

Anna Alvarez

My earliest memories of hearing Spanish spoken by my parents happened when they conversed with my maternal grandparents. Gilberto and Rosaura Navarro spoke Spanish, and very little English.

I remember my grandmother Rosaura pronouncing shoes as "chú-ses,"—"Estévie, pood on ĵour chú-ses" (Stevie, put on your shoes). My grandfather said few words I remember, aside from "that's good," "yes," and "very nice." With such few words in his English vocabulary, he could not have been anything but a kind man. I remember communicating with him mostly in gestures, but nearly always smiles.

My grandparents and I never truly communicated without translators, typically my parents. I still regret thinking about all the stories and family histories I never heard from them because I did not have a sufficient command of Spanish then. I had heard some of these translated stories from my mother and also from relatives in Mexico and Arizona, but even with direct access to Rosaura and Gilberto, there was much about them I did not know. Rosaura died in 1992 and Gilberto in 2007.

Whatever connection to Mexican culture I have maintained from childhood and nurtured now as an adult has come from my mother. Anna Navarro was born in Cananea, Sonora, Mexico, approximately thirty miles south of the US-Mexico border. She was seven years old when her family migrated to Bisbee, Arizona, in 1953. Her brother was ten, her sister thirteen. Regarding her family's migration, Anna said of her parents, "They wanted to have a better life for the family, to make a better life for the family. And my mom had a sister who lived here already who was willing to be a sponsor. She was pretty well set up here. Here in the States. So she had a lawyer friend who could help here, and that's how we got over here. She was our sponsor."

According to Anna, my grandfather Gilberto Navarro Valdez was born in El Rey, Arizona, in 1916. What she called "El Rey" was the Mexican immigrant name for Ray, Arizona (also sometimes called el Ray, Sonora), a mining-boom ghost town north of Tucson. Ray was demolished in 1958 when the Kennecott Mining Company began an open-pit mine on that spot and relocated the community to the corporate-planned town of Kearny. Ray itself was a town constructed by the previous mine company, the Ray Copper Company. My grandfather, however, was not a US citizen.

The specifics of this curious information had been family lore for many years, especially when more of my mother's history of her undocumented status as a child emerged. Gilberto had lived most of his youth in Mexico. Raised on Ranchito Llano near Guasave, Sinaloa, Mexico, he moved to Cananea, Sonora, Mexico, as a teenager—just before the stock market crashed in 1929. He married Rosaura Rioseco in 1936.

In order to probe further into her educational experience and possible mentors, I asked Anna who helped her with her English when she first started school in Bisbee. "When you first arrived," I asked her, "how much English did you understand?"

"I didn't speak no English. I didn't have nobody to talk to, or practice with. Well I was little, so it didn't matter much to me. But I had a really nice teacher; her name was Mrs. Bonham, and she was bilingual but not Mexican. I never had a Mexican teacher, and only that one bilingual teacher. She helped me a lot. I guess she kind of liked me or something. She was my first teacher in Bisbee, in first grade."

An interesting further contrast between the first English exposures of Anna and Robert emerged as she continued her memory of Mrs. Bonham, her first mentor. I began to see that this teacher brokered Anna's sponsorship of English and the dominant language. I also had a suspicion that gender may also have been an issue, and that Anglo teachers may have treated Mexican girls differently than they did boys. Gender relations in Bisbee during this time were subject to heavily policed surveillance of the town's Mexican male populace from the youngest of ages, for supposed Communist and anti-American activities (Benton-Cohen) because of labor organizing in the copper mines.

Anna explained how her teacher tutored her after school using her Spanish skills already partially developed in her one year of school in Mexico. "I remember she first started giving me papers in Spanish. And she would see—I think—I could do it in Spanish, and then slowly she started introducing me to the language. And if I didn't understand it, she would write down what I said. And it was just a way like, you know? It took her own time . . . I was very fortunate because she helped me a lot." Mrs. Bonham's bilingualism directly affected how she taught Anna. She assessed Anna's literacy skills in Spanish and translated these into English education scaffolds for building on strengths.

It would seem that Mrs. Bonham did not think of her language-minoritized students' languages as deficits, and with elements of biliteracy transition into English the method of recognizing and utilizing bilingual strengths in social communication, it seems, was in practice—but in the context of an English-only school during after-school hours. Again, it is also important to consider what sorts of "safe spaces" were available for immigrant parents to gather with others in a common educational endeavor on the Arizona borderlands during this era. Even then, as now, schools would have benefited by reaching out bilingually to communities who share common interests.

Mrs. Bonham communicated directly with Gilberto and Rosaura about Anna's progress. "She spoke good Spanish too. And she would talk to my mom and dad about how I was doing." Mrs. Bonham also followed Anna's progress for a few years after finishing her first year with her. According to Anna, she also stepped in to help with her older siblings as well. "Sometimes she would help my sister and brother too, but not all the time. But they were picking it up too, with their friends and stuff."

To reiterate, nothing had changed in school policy when Anna began attending elementary school four years after my father started. She did not remember any Spanish-speaking students disciplined in the way Robert narrated. There was still no bilingual program at the school, but Anna recalled how Mrs. Bonham organized her class in order to address the specific needs of her emergent bilingual students.

"How did she help the Spanish-speaking students?" I asked Anna.

"She would get all us kids who spoke Spanish in a group. There were a few of us. I remember there was this boy, Emilio. He had a hard time. Poor kid. He couldn't grasp it, it was hard for him. It was hard for him to grasp the English. For me it was easier, but with him it was hard. And she would get frustrated with him with that. And he acted like he didn't want to learn it. And she [Mrs. Bonham] knew that this other little girl and me wanted to learn it, so she helped us more. Poor chamaquito (little guy). Pues (well), and she would help us more. And with that little boy, I didn't know what happened. The teacher wanted him to learn English, but he didn't want to." Anna pointed to a gender issue in the classroom, that either girls were more linguistically adept than boys, or Bisbee teachers favored girls. Girls may also have been more compliant to authority than boys. The hint that Mrs. Bonham grew frustrated with Emilio seemed to imply that the "sink or swim" mentality, that of individualizing success or failure, was not uncommon, and that perhaps this was the case for Robert. What this individualist mentality overlooks, however, are the structural conditions by which schools permitted or even expected some students to slip through the cracks. That even Anna subscribed to this mentality, assuming that Emilio "didn't want to" learn English, demonstrates the power of English-only subtractive ideologies to colonize one's internalization of social norms as individual failures and successes.

DECOLONIZING SUBTRACTIVE SCHOOLING

Subtractive schooling has had marked effects on the educational experiences both of my parents and of my generation in my family. This critical autoethnography is my attempt to decolonize the complications that subtractive schooling has made in my education, while also decolonizing the notion that researchers bring objectivity to their studies. By understanding these networked intersections in my example from family oral histories, I demonstrate how critical autoethnography can reflexively turn to lived experiences as subjects for critical analysis, for storytelling, and potentially for a decolonial option that disrupts subtractive modes of schooling and literacy research. Holding negative views of Spanish in its many local dialects leads to subtractive English-only discrimination. Robert experienced subtractive schooling, based primarily on the racial hierarchy of the Arizona borderlands over fifty years ago. Subtractive schooling practices neglect to recognize that children come to schools with complex sets of histories, as members of diverse families and communities. Understanding the stories of subtractive schooling that come from critical autoethnography can uncover emergent bilingual counters to dominant narratives that tend to individualize failure on students and their communities without examining the structural inequalities that permeate education.

As a researcher, conducting this critical autoethnography enlightened me about the intersections of race, gender, class, and lived experience in my parents' stories. This opened my eyes to the research trajectory I have established for myself where I have challenged these structural inequalities in English-only policies and literacy research for immigrant families. Valuing linguistic diversity in the classroom means collaboration with the families of students to build on already present literacies, while also being cognizant of structural inequalities that influence student opportunities. For emergent bilingual students, learning about the stories of students who have learned English, the pains of becoming bilingual in schools that insist that students "sink or swim," can become powerful tools for understanding what impact subtractive schooling may have had on their own lived experiences, thus opening spaces for decolonizing such ideologies. Learning how these policies shaped schooling that "subtracted" Spanish from my experience meant I would never point the finger of blame at my parents. Blaming the parents is always too easy, and that goes for my family, and all families in marginalized communities.

As I described earlier in this chapter, racial discrimination in Bisbee, Arizona, during the 1950s was so terrible that Mexicans generally earned lower wages reserved for "nonwhites." Yet some rare spaces were reserved in the "white" category for Mexicans who assimilated well—Mexicans who conformed to the dominant culture, which emphasized monolingual English spoken with an American accent, that is, English spoken without a Spanish accent. My parents, acting out of the need for survival, internalized this model of domination, and as a result of their labors to be integrated and accepted as American, they fully acculturated their children, and at the same time internalized both resentment and guilt about Spanish-accented English.

Though my grandparents made the sacrifice of migration for their children's benefit, their children—my parents, Robert and Anna—did not. Anna migrated as a child, but recalled her father out of work for months at times because of meager opportunities available for Mexican immigrants. My parents' stories taught me that I had an easier life than they did, particularly on those days when Robert and I went to work as custodians for the bank my parents cleaned for eighteen years. I heard similar narratives from Anna when working with her, also as a custodian, though at a medical clinic. I went to work with both my parents landscaping and cleaning offices, movie theaters, banks, and parking lots during college vacations. When considering my aspirations to leave Safford, Arizona, for New York City, and also my parents' aspirations for me, I had to rely on the clichés such work experience provided me: an internalized orientation from my habitus, or a laborer's work ethic.

When I tell colleagues that my parents cleaned offices for a living, and that I know what it feels like to work, real physical work, I remind myself that I am nostalgic for a class positionality I no longer inhabit. Yes, I used to accompany my parents when they cleaned offices in the evening, sometimes doing my homework while I waited, and other times helping out with what I could—usually vacuuming and picking up trash from bins. My efforts there brought no special notice from them, but when I won awards from school my parents were always proud, and Robert told me from a long time back that I was doing things that never really appealed to him because he did not have what he termed my "ambition." Schools subtracted his educational ambitions when he was young. I was ambitious in ways he was not, Robert said, and he credited this to social class for shaping my entitlements to dream the way I could.

Robert and Anna felt political pressures and racism in the language they internalized on the US borderlands, and in the US mainstream. Their five children grew up speaking English, "like Americans," or like "normal people," according to Robert. This meant English as our home language. Though Anna had insisted on using Spanish, she ultimately followed suit with her husband, who demanded that his children be monolingual English speakers. Though some Spanish did remain with the children—mostly words for food or relatives—English far and away dominated the third generation's linguistic repertoire. Research on generational language shift argues that Spanish seldom lasts beyond the second or third generation, and that economic, historical, social, and political factors determine these subtractive patterns (Ovando, Combs, and Collier; Rumbaut, Massey, and Bean; Portes and Rumbaut). Like Robert and Anna, I did not have any bilingual courses during my schooling, though by the time I was growing up such classes were available in the state of Arizona. During the 1950s, however, such classes were not. If they had been, my parents would both likely have been enrolled in them. In my case, like Robert and Anna, I attended only public schools.

Both my parents spoke about accents at length. Despite our family's English dominance, we still spoke a marked variety of English. Chicanx English is the racially marked form of English which is my home language. Chicanx English may constitute the linguistic interference from Spanish that native speakers experience when learning English, but one cannot assume that this holds true in every case. While Chicanx English's phonology, morphology, syntax, and lexicon differentiate it from standardized English, its features also characterize a language independent of Spanish (Duchnowski). The transition into Spanglish (Zentella) is only one marker of collisions and adaptations of languages and cultures. When voiced in English, the Chicanx English accent remains, and this often goes unnoticed by its native speakers. Chicanx English remains distinct from standard English or "Anglo" English by illustrating its speakers' ethnic identities and declaring their cultural ties with Mexico.

Robert did pick up English, and perhaps overcompensated by making an active push to forget Spanish and to assimilate to English only. I could not help wondering whether my father's English-accented Chicanx Spanish wasn't some form of overcompensation to further distinguish himself from what he perceived as linguistically Mexican, to affect the "normal" US accent. Even his English had a pronounced drawl to it. His variety of Chicanx English was localized to the regional Mexican American accents of Texas and New Mexico. His English had a Texan twang to it, but also the cadences of standard English and nonstandard Chicanx English. In rural Arizona, though, his self-regard for his accent was "normal." After all, speaking "normal" English was one way to prevent being sent behind the classroom door. This same accent pervaded my Spanish, but in a much more English-pronounced way. As Otto Santa Ana writes, contrary to the hegemonic assumption that Latinxs choose *not* to speak English, "to prove their loyalty to the hegemony of Anglo-American culture, Latinos cannot retain two public languages. They must appear to be monolingual English speakers" (289). This appearance of "normal" or American English was the public face for participation as a citizen. Richard Rodriguez's *Hunger of Memory* displaces bilingual curricula on these grounds, reflecting a dominant public identity grounded in speaking and writing "American" and not like an "immigrant."

My place along the Arizona-Sonora border affected my perceptions of subtractive schooling and language loss. My father mentioned how some individuals in his family wished they had the "normal American" English, or what he deemed nonaccented English, so they could live better lives. Upward mobility for ethnic minorities and recent immigrants conflates social class and national identity transformations. One "loses" both class-based roots and ethnic roots to get ahead. I write this about my biography, to offer a contrast to my parents, but also, I hope, to complement the richness of their words, their oral histories. This family oral history exercise offers rich potential for storying about ourselves, and, for writing students, storying about their lived experiences, and the lived experiences of those for whom they express care. And because of that, I must always honor my family's stories, and learn from their wisdom. Their story is my story, and my story is the continuation of theirs. This is a storying that makes connections to decolonizing notions of subtractive schooling.

CONCLUSION

This chapter engaged critical autoethnography to explore my family's language loss over a generation through migration and assimilation into the US mainstream. My parents both recounted their relations to their families and their home languages, and offered a window into why my literacy research was a personal endeavor. This exercise into critical autoethnography located the contexts for a decolonial counter to the subtractive schooling ideologies in my family's experience by analyzing how dominant and minoritized languages in my parents' generation stifled the bilingual potential of the coming generations. Context and history of course affected how I shaped this autoethnographic research, and I argue that context influences my observations and perceptions of language, literacy, learning, and identity. This, in turn, has been a family and personal matter for me, as well as a central concern for my research, to break systems of subtractive schooling for emergent bilingual learners.

The autoethnography of my own family experience and my position as literacy researcher also must be acknowledged. My trajectory entailed educational frustrations, cultural disconnects, and ultimate monolingual literacy in the dominant language, and consequently a limited form of social mobility. Motivated to position myself in this research, to "show" my linguistic and cultural journey as a second-generation Mexican American and how it intersected with my research, this critical autoethnography discloses the positionality every researcher brings to projects, though not all research includes the self-reflection of what I learned about myself when composing my inquiry. My English literacy and bilingual family background are fundamentally related to the orientation my research program has undertaken. As an ethnographic researcher, then, my experience with language loss and immigration became a biographical foundation for conducting the study, an experience of "being there," an attitude "sufficient to experience the mundane and sacred, brash and nuanced aspects of socio-cultural life and, through observations, encounters and conversations, to come to an understanding of it" (Lewis and Russell 400). My history and life trajectory brought me to "be there" in different communities to study literacy as practiced, and to learn more about myself in the process.

This brings me back to a central question that has affected my research since graduate school: why did I desire to earn my PhD in the first place? I knew I wanted to study for the rest of my life, for one. There were also the stark differences between direct experience and book-learning that made me rethink an academic life as a means to examine my history. Yet I had second thoughts about pursuing my PhD in English, which I thought would entrap me in an ivory tower where research would leave me alienated from community involvement and service.

My search for the truths in direct experiences versus the truths represented symbolically in texts first led me to venture away from southern Arizona. I remember my father telling me a similar story about when he left Bisbee after enlisting in the Army at seventeen. He was never a great student, he said, so he decided to drop out of high school, lie about his age, and sign up for the service. Despite being a self-described "bad" student, Robert was a voracious reader, and—as I still recall clearly—when I asked him why he joined the Army, he said, "to see the world." He had only read about it, and he wanted to see it. My father's narrative and my own were examples of rural working-class, ethnic minority American youth enclosed in a local area. The difference was that Robert internalized subtractive schooling that taught him he was a bad student for being different, whereas I internalized a sense of monolingual English entitlement for educational success. No doubt, being a cisgendered male with phenotype certainly helped.

During my interview with my mother, I asked Anna if she had ever had any experiences like Robert's behind-the-door punishment.

She shook her head. "He went through a lot of stuff when he was younger, when he started school. I imagine he probably suffered, you know. Humiliating, too. And I don't think he wanted any of the kids to be like that too . . . I didn't have the bad experience like he did. I had a good experience. I think if he had had a good teacher like I had, it could have been different. Look, I can see where it's coming from—I can see it. And he was just a little kid, too, you know."

Yes, I know. Now I know.

The challenge I faced researching my parents and their educational histories dealt with connecting to my Mexican identity, what I knew of myself, who I'd become, and, of course, where it was I would go, and helped me with some identity work and decolonizing certain deeply implanted ideologies. Like Spanish, being Mexican American in the academy had been another challenge, but in ways different from the challenge that many Mexican Americans faced, and by this I mean various forms of discrimination. Some social privileges came with being an assimilated American of Mexican descent: recasting the challenges of my diminished Mexican identity and my emergent Spanish as gifts was one such privilege. My privileged positionalities have guided me in my scholarship, but always as challenges for me to better understand myself in a larger picture, to dialogically frame my immediate experience: a Mexican American struggling to maintain and negotiate my Latinx and American cultural identities under constant cultural and linguistic insecurities. These stories of my family history, however, have made me stronger, and they are the stories that guide my research as an ethnographer who appreciates the nuances of narratives, language, and lived experiences as forms of community wealth.

WORKS CITED

Alba, Richard, and Victor Nee. *Remaking the American Mainstream: Assimilation and Contemporary Immigration.* Harvard UP, 2003.

Alvarez, Anna. Personal interview. 25 May 2011.

———. Personal interview. 2 June 2011.

———. Personal interview. 9 June 2011.

Alvarez, Robert. Personal interview. 29 May 2011.

———.Personal interview. 6 June 2011.

———. Personal interview. 11 June 2011.

Alvarez, Steven. *Brokering Tareas: Mexican Immigrant Families Translanguaging Homework Literacies.* State U of New York P, 2017.

———. *Community Literacies* en Confianza: *Learning from Bilingual After-School Communities.* National Council of Teachers of English, 2017.

Benton-Cohen, Katherine. *Borderline Americans: Racial Division and Labor War in the Arizona Borderlands.* Harvard UP, 2011.

Bourdieu, Pierre. *Sketch for a Self-Analysis.* Translated by Richard Nice, Polity Press, 2007.

Boylorn, Robin M., and Mark P. Orbe, editors. *Critical Autoethnography: Intersecting Cultural Identities in Everyday Life.* Left Coast Press, 2014.

Brodkey, Linda. "Writing on the Bias." *College English*, vol. 56, no. 5, 1994, pp. 527–47.

Chang, Heewon. *Autoethnography as Method.* Routledge, 2008.

Denzin, Norman K. *Interpretive Ethnography: Ethnographic Practices for the 21st Century.* SAGE, 1997.

Duchnowski, Dawn. "Chicano English: Language Issues and Their Relationship to Culture." *Virtual International Classroom: The English Language: American English(es) and World English(es).* Western Connecticut State University, Apr. 1999, http://courses.wcsu.edu/valkommen/dawn.htm#note2. Accessed 3 Aug. 2017.

Durand, Jorge, Douglas S. Massey, and Chiara Capoferro. "The New Geography of Mexican Immigration." *New Destinations: Mexican Immigration in the United States*, edited by Víctor Zúñiga and Rubén Hernández-León, Russell Sage Foundation, 2006, pp. 1–20.

Farr, Marcia. *Rancheros in Chicagoacán: Language and Identity in a Transnational Community.* U of Texas P, 2006.

Farr, Marcia, and Elías Domínguez Barajas. "*Mexicanos* in Chicago: Language Ideology and Identity." *Building on Strength: Language and Literacy in Latino Families and Communities*, edited by Ana Celia Zentella, Teachers College Press, 2005, pp. 46–59.

Glaser, Barney G., and Anselm L. Strauss. *The Discovery of Grounded Theory: Strategies for Qualitative Research.* Routledge, 2017.

Heath, Shirley Brice. *Ways with Words: Language, Life, and Work in Communities and Classrooms*, Cambridge UP, 1999.

Hoggart, Richard. *The Uses of Literacy: Aspects of Working-Class Life*. Penguin, 2009.

Holdman Jones, Stacy, Tony E. Adams, and Carolyn Ellis, editors. *Handbook of Autoethnography*. Left Coast Press, 2013.

Horne, Gerald. *Black and Brown: African Americans and the Mexican Revolution, 1910–1920*. New York UP, 2005.

Lanza, Elizabeth, and Bente Ailin Svendsen. "Tell Me Who Your Friends Are and I Might Be Able to Tell You What Language(s) You Speak: Social Network Analysis, Multilingualism, and Identity." *International Journal of Bilingualism*, vol. 11, no. 3, 2007, pp. 275–300.

Lewis, Susan J., and Andrew J. Russell. "Being Embedded: A Way Forward for Ethnographic Research." *Ethnography*, vol. 12, no. 3, 2011, pp. 398–416.

Massey, Douglas S., Jorge Durand, and Nolan J. Malone. *Beyond Smoke and Mirrors: Mexican Immigration in an Era of Economic Integration*. Russell Sage Foundation, 2003.

Mignolo, Walter D. *The Darker Side of the Renaissance: Literacy, Territoriality, and Colonization*. 2nd ed., U of Michigan P, 2003.

Onwuegbuzie, Anthony, and Nancy Leech. "Validity and Qualitative Research: An Oxymoron?" *Quality & Quantity: International Journal of Methodology*, vol. 41, no. 2, 2007, pp. 233–49.

Ovando, Carlos J., Mary Carol Combs, and Virginia P. Collier. *Bilingual and ESL Classrooms: Teaching in Multicultural Contexts*. 4th ed., McGraw-Hill, 2006.

Portes, Alejandro, and Rubén G. Rumbaut. *Legacies: The Story of the Immigrant Second Generation*. U of California P, 2001.

Pratt, Mary Louise. "Arts of the Contact Zone." *Profession*, 1991, pp. 33–40.

Reed-Danahay, Deborah E., editor. Introduction. *Auto/ethnography: Rewriting the Self and the Social*. Berg, 1997, pp. 1–17.

Rodriguez, Richard. *Hunger of Memory: The Education of Richard Rodriguez*. Bantam, 1982.

Rose, Mike. *Lives on the Boundary: A Moving Account of the Struggles and Achievements of America's Educationally Underprepared*. Penguin, 2005.

Rumbaut, Rubén G., Douglas S. Massey, and Frank D. Bean. "Linguistic Life Expectancies: Immigrant Language Retention in Southern California." *Population and Development Review*, vol. 32, no. 3, 2006, pp. 447–60.

Santa Ana, Otto. *Brown Tide Rising: Metaphors of Latinos in Contemporary American Public Discourse*. U of Texas P, 2002.

Valenzuela, Angela. *Subtractive Schooling: U.S.-Mexican Youth and the Politics of Caring*. State U of New York P, 1999.

Zentella, Ana Celia. *Growing Up Bilingual: Puerto Rican Children in New York*. Blackwell, 1997.

4

Arabizing Vernacular Discourse: A Rhetorical Analysis of Tunisian Revolutionary Graffiti

Fatima Zahrae Chrifi Alaoui
San Francisco State University

THE "ARAB SPRING"

SINCE DECEMBER 17, 2010, THE TERM *Arab Spring*[1] has been adopted to describe a set of demonstrations inaugurated by the self-immolation of a fruit vendor named Mohamed Bouazizi (Adib-Moghhaddam; Al-Ali; Kraidy; Matar). Within weeks, what originated as Bouazizi's dissent against police brutality emerged as a turmoil that astounded the Arab region and rest of the world. Hence, the general concept of the "Arab Spring" is that of a movement that started in Tunisia and swept across North Africa and into the Middle East. This movement then led to the ousting of the Tunisian, Egyptian, and Libyan governments and saw significant unrest in other countries (Adib-Moghhaddam; Al-Ali; Kraidy; Matar).

However, soon after the emergence of the "Arab Spring," academics and media experts ran to provide diverse interpretations in regard to the origins and the motives of the demonstrations and the revolutions as a whole, as well as what and who should be "blamed" for the movement. For instance, the US media coverage of the "Arab Spring" was based mainly on Orientalist storylines that categorized the "Arab Spring" as either a sweep of extremism and zealotry or a sweep of democratic reform (Adib-Moghhaddam; Al-Ali; Matar). However, such dichotomous framing ignores the stories and the bodies of the many Arab men and women within these revolutions. Additionally, those framings reinforce the inevitable narratives of the clash between the West and the East; a logic that demonizes the revolutions and flattens the complex realities of the "Arab Spring" and its subjectivities. Therefore, I call for an analysis of one of the productions of the "Arab Spring," Tunisian revolutionary graffiti, through the lens of decolonial vernacular discourse to challenge the Euro-Americano-centric legacies of Orientalism in Western academia as well as popular culture, and to offer "new" readings of the representations of Arab[2] and Muslim[3] bodies and subjectivities.

To pursue this analysis, I consider the "Arab Spring" as an event in the Deleuzian sense (as cited in Puar). In *Terrorist Assemblages,* Jasbir Puar calls for looking at events within a Deleuzian framework that reflects "an assemblage of spatial and temporal intensities, coming together, dispersing, reconverging" (xviii). In other words, considering the "Arab Spring" as an event refuses binaries between past and present, between a "history-making moment" and a "history-vanishing moment," between "politicality" and "stability" (Puar xvii–xx). The "eventness" of the "Arab Spring" collapses past, present, and future and looks at the "Arab Spring" as a movement between the before and the after. Situating the "Arab Spring" as an event helps me look at the cultural productions of the uprisings as an assemblage of theoretical interests, meaning there is not one stand, but rather as ideas that converge, diverge, and merge, a movement that did not "just" emerge, rather a movement that is "always-becoming" (Puar xxiv). Foregrounding the political urgency of surveying the productions of the "Arab Spring" as a vernacular discourse is imperative in forging new ways of understanding communication in postcolonial/neocolonial settings.

Contemporary postcolonial scholars have analyzed images and misrepresentations of Arab and Muslims within different cultural artifacts (see Adib-Moghhaddam; Haddad; McAlister; Said, *Covering Islam* and *Orientalism*). However, there is little work done on how Arabs and Muslims are negotiating their identities vis-à-vis these representations and what strategies they are using for empowerment and resistance. For those reasons, I argue for the use of a vernacular discourse to look at the Other side of representations and knowledge production. Hence, through a review of vernacular discourse, I illuminate how the vernacular functions not only in opposition to but also as a threat to hegemonic control as it is the means for expressing the multiple realities of people who use it. Therefore, I argue for the critique of vernacular discourse as a critical decolonial methodology to illustrate the hidden power dynamics and discursive strategies used to empower marginalized identities and further mobilize social change. Building on these concepts, I contend that, by considering and analyzing the dynamic construction of discourses by those interpellated by them, we can better understand how marginalized communities construct an ontological status as a collective self through the comprehension of how they create varied subject positions. I argue how the uprisings of Arabs and Muslims that took hold across the Arab world and the struggles that continue today do not just undermine authoritarian regimes, they also unsettle mainstream representations of seemingly war-torn, sectarian, oppressed, and repressed "Eastern" societies. Hence, through a decolonial critical vernacular discourse analysis of the graffiti, I want to engage in a different kind of conversation in regard to the Middle East and North Africa.

Thus this essay first explores the foundations of critical vernacular discourse and its links to ontology and epistemology, and argues for the importance of examining different artifacts produced by marginalized groups. Second, the essay contextualizes and analyzes the vernacular discourses of the Tunisian revolutionary graffiti to explore other forms of knowledge production. This analysis unveils the complexity underlying the discussion around issues of identity, agency, and knowledge production in the Middle East and North Africa, demonstrating the need for critical studies in the region beyond the binary approach that has been practiced and applied by academics and media analysts. Finally, the essay articulates a framework for analyzing the construction and positioning of marginalized identities. It locates a way of studying and theorizing the dialectic between agency and the subject by looking at how the larger dominant structures are reproduced and contested through these discourses as well as how marginalized groups construct their own subjectivities through the use of vernacular discourse. In the context of my study of Tunisian graffiti, this approach to analyzing the vernaculars produced by Tunisian activists offers significant potential for locating new potentialities with regard to discursive contestation. It highlights discourses by members of marginalized communities that have largely been foreclosed to serve the interest of corrupted leaders and officials.

CRITICAL VERNACULAR DISCOURSE

I want to begin by arguing for the importance of studying and examining discourses developed by marginalized groups. Here I am echoing the work of rhetorical critics Kent A. Ono and John M. Sloop, who argue that rhetoricians should focus on the rhetorics of the oppressed. Through privileging the vernaculars of the oppressed, Ono and Sloop suggest, the split between everyday acts of activism and the academic pursuit of criticism could finally collapse. They write that critical rhetoricians

> [c]annot take the tools they have now and blithely apply them to the study of cultures. Rather, new methods, approaches, orientations, even attitudes, toward cultures need to be created. . . . critical rhetoric must be reconceived in light of the vernacular discourse that challenges approaches founded within Western notions of domination, freedom, and power. (40)

In other words, the traditional theory and praxis of rhetoric focus on dominant systems, structures, and classes, while neglecting the discursive forces of power that dismiss as well as erase the discourses and bodies of those in the margins. Furthermore, Ono and Sloop contend that vernacular discourse has two primary elements that could be examined: cultural syncretism and pastiche (21–25). These two characteristics are key to the construction and deconstruction of rhetorics. Their critical approach attempts to destabilize the subject position of the community of vernacular users while also de-essentializing vernacular discourses on "freedom," for instance, as the main artifact of marginalized bodies and voices (26). In doing so, Ono and Sloop demonstrate how vernacular discourse is a fluid process that is changeable and adaptable to the everyday lives of the people it is used by. That is, vernacular discourse could either operate in a way where it affirms the identities of the marginalized communities or essentializes the discourse of the people while supporting hegemonic structures. Therefore, the usage and the fluidity of vernacular discourse allow for a rhetorical praxis that is adaptive to the rhetorical situation or context to which it is applied.

Ono and Sloop, then, advance the idea that vernacular discourse could be used as a counterhegemonic and resistive practice against dominant systems that affirms oppressed voices (23). They term this discursive function *cultural syncretism,* a characteristic of vernacular discourse that not only contradicts dominant ideology but also expresses vernacular beliefs of that culture. They argue that vernacular discourse "[a]ffirms various cultural expressions while at the same time protest[ing] against the dominant cultural ideology" (20). Vernacular discourse, that is, demonstrates how its discursive aspects are always in negotiation and development. In other words, the dynamics of vernacular discourse reveal how the focus of analysis is shifted toward the cultural productions of marginalized identities, as well as how those productions embrace dominant ideologies and resist them.

Pastiche is the second function of vernacular discourse highlighted by Ono and Sloop. Pastiche has the tendency to use fragments and artifacts from popular culture to produce as well as create new effects and meanings: "Pastiche implies that vernacular discourse may borrow from, without mimicking, popular culture" (23). In other words, pastiche enables vernacular communities to establish their own identities and cultures outside hegemonic ideologies and systems. Pastiche has the tendency to use fragments and artifacts from popular culture to create new effects and meanings (23). It is a "[u]nique discursive form [constructed] out of cultural fragments" and "motivated by a concern for local conditions and social problems" (23). In other words, pastiche is a dynamic and inventive process that takes elements from popular culture, which enables vernacular communities to establish their own identities and cultures outside hegemonic ideologies and systems. However, because of the nature of borrowing, Ono and Sloop argue, aspects of dominant discourses and cultures could be found in the vernacular discourses of the oppressed. (Paradoxically, Ono and Sloop minimize the role of popular culture in vernacular discourse by failing to acknowledge how popular culture employs the vernacular for its revitalizing drive.)

Bernadette Calafell expands Ono and Sloop's critique by locating the counterhegemonic, affirmative, and community-centered characteristics of vernacular discourse within other forms of knowledge production that are not merely textual, but embodied/performative. In her book *Latina/o Communication Studies: Theorizing Performance*, Calafell writes how such discourses expose other forms of knowledge:

> This vernacular discourse does not divorce language or words from their embodied nature . . . . My desire in using this method is to highlight certain meaning and rhythms in language and the choice of words while privileging the importance of orality in historically marginalized cultures. (20–21)

Hence, Calafell's rhetorical-performative perspective advances the argument that critics should pay attention to rhetorical discourses that are not merely textual but also visual, verbal, and performative in order to understand how history, power, and social location have shaped the form of discourses produced by and manifested within marginalized communities, specifically, in her case, Latin@ communities. Furthering this point, Calafell and Dawn Marie D. McIntosh invite scholars to examine "how the bodies of people of color are always and already 'counter' to dominant ideologies that govern the public sphere" (217). By articulating the body "as/is rhetoric/al" (204), they bring to our attention the importance of studying the ignored and "everyday acts of survival, resistance, and empowerment" (202), which are important in understanding how people of color use these strategies—in both the public and private spheres—to resist oppression and produce empowering spaces.

Hence, by analyzing vernacular discourse within a revolutionary moment, it is possible to theorize how marginalized communities constructed their own (counter)subjectivities to the challenged power structure. Therefore, by evaluating the Arab Spring as a an event that produced a vernacular discourse, I will be able to highlight new ways of understanding communication from a decolonial[4] perspective.

In this essay, I analyze how vernacular discourses in the Tunisian revolutions demonstrated revolutionary potential. Through the use of the synthesized concept of "embodied vernacular discourse," I examine the art of graffiti collected in Tunisia to discuss vernacular discourse from three angles: content, agency, and subjectivity. To highlight the emergence of decolonial vernaculars in these communities, I selected these graffiti for close rhetorical analysis. Employing the synthesized concept of embodied vernacular discourse, my analysis attempts to examine how the selected graffiti and body rhetorically constructed a Tunisian/Tunisian-Arab community by addressing the following questions: How did they challenge dominant ideologies while simultaneously affirming their own rhetoric ("cultural syncretism")? How did they borrow from the language of the mainstream in order to challenge it ("pastiche")? How did different personal and institutional agencies help shape or constrain their discourses? How did they construct their subjectivities?

GRAFFITI AS DECOLONIAL PRACTICE

During my data collection in 2013, I came across one of the most radical visual shifts in Tunisian streets, graffiti. The graffiti scrawled across the walls, advertising billboards, street signs, flower pots, park benches, and any other surface changed the "disciplined"—and what the government called "civil"—outlook of Tunisian streets into an uncensored open book full of Tunisians' political sentiments. This visual shift captured for me the two most important historical developments that we can identify at the end of the third year of the ongoing Arab uprisings and transformations: first, the birth of Arab citizens who feel they have socioeconomic and political rights and are prepared to speak out, mobilize, and take action to achieve those rights; and, second, the birth of a public political sphere in which citizens can express themselves and compete peacefully for the exercise of power. Citizens occupying street walls through the graffiti capture those two developments quite nicely.

The content and language used in the graffiti are equally telling. The formal public space of Tunis (billboards, advertisement panels, newspapers, and magazine covers) was dominated by admonitions to vote "yes" to a referendum to support the interim government that had been installed after Ben Ali's overthrow. The content sprayed on walls and other informal spaces reflected many more varied views, including the very common statement "ash-shab yurid isqat annitham" ("The people want the downfall of the regime"). Other graffiti called the current leader a killer or warned that another revolution was imminent. The actual variety of languages used is equally significant. The graphic and stylistic methods of communicating, used in conjunction with various languages, were important structural and qualitative tools. That is, while English was overwhelmingly used, non-English languages were significant as well, given that this global conflict has political implications around the world. For instance, the graffiti I photographed in Tunisia contained messages *not only* in the Tunisian dialect, but also in Arabic and French, which are considered to be native languages of the North-African region.

This presence of English graffiti was not surprising, especially given that English is seen to be the mainstream international language of expression, as well as a means to seek *international* support and solidarity through such messages. The additional use of vernacular Tunisian languages in graffiti, however, also reinforced a particular sense of *nationality* among the people. Similar to Benedict Anderson's argument that the creation of imagined communities became possible because of "print capitalism" (7), which enabled presses to use the vernacular instead of Latin, the Tunisian readers, speaking various local dialects, became able to understand one another, and a common discursive structure emerged. The hybridity of the graffiti, that is, created an imagined community based on a shared identity that brought together the personal and cultural feeling of belonging to the "nation." Thus, the imagined citizens that the vernacular of the graffiti targeted was mainly the Tunisians—the North Africans who shared a history of French colonialism and Arab influence that consequently influenced the existence of vernacular languages expressed in the graffiti.

However, this same imagined community—developed through the use of the graffiti—could also be understood as a global/borderless community representing a decolonial multitude. The hybrid linguistic and visual usage in the graffiti allowed multiple communities to connect locally in Tunis and across the region. This confirms the approach to the vernacular as a strategy that allows for the formation of affirmative and community-centered coalitions that engaged in border crossing (Calafell; Bhabha). Also, the wide dissemination of the graffiti into other states in the Middle East and North Africa as well as over social media created a collective existence of a community based on demands for social justice, which defied geopolitical borders. This formation of the global/borderless community will be exemplified in the analysis of specific graffiti below.

Here is it important to first note that the appointed government in Tunisia tried in places to paint over the graffiti, but gave up after every wall it painted white was full of graffiti again twenty-four hours later (Ben Mhenni). Hence the new public political sphere—which continues to experience its birth across Tunisia—lurches back and forth between popular sentiments that support and oppose all three principal actors who have dominated the public power structure in the past few years—the old guards of the ex-president Ben Ali (who are also the holders of the French colonial legacies), the police, and the Nahda Party (similar to the Muslim Brotherhood). The new element today that Tunisia still displays, however, is that those who control the power structure do not totally control the public sphere. Inscribing graffiti on the walls of Tunis became a visual and a verbal voice for the people. A Tunisian graffiti artist, Oussama Bouajila, who inscribed several slogans and paintings on the streets of the capital, Tunis, says,

> We created this graffiti movement because no one speaks about us and the problems of unemployment, poverty and marginalization that we face. So, we have decided to speak for ourselves. Why graffiti? Graffiti is more accessible for the Tunisian [citizen] who does not have access to Facebook, for instance. (qtd. in Mtiraoui)

Hence, the graffiti was transformed into a (trans)national news outlet for how these communities are viewing and interpreting the events of the uprisings. This shift in body politics of thought is what Walter Mignolo describes as decoloniality, which is a "programmatic" of de-linking from coloniality that "brings to the foreground other epistemologies, other principles of knowledge and understanding" ("Delinking" 453), where social movements are fighting for "social liberation from all power organized as inequality, discrimination, exploitation, and as domination" (Quijano 178). That is a meaningful milestone on the third year of the Tunisian and other Arab uprisings that cannot be denominated in seasons of the year, but rather only in the attitudes of individual citizens who are determined to express themselves politically and in public.

The graffiti's vernacular discourses can be understood as decolonial in two ways. First, the graffiti artists helped create a new framework for the Tunisian/Arab community in the streets and in mediated images, such as domestic and internationals newspapers, Facebook, and Twitter. As a consequence, they created a "new humanity" (Mignolo, *Darker Side* 52). Second, the graffiti established a hybrid vernacular subjectivity by crossing the borders between national origin, race, religion, class, and other social categories rhetorically. For instance, Tunisian street artists did not only use local revolutionary symbols, but also reused Western and Latin American revolutionary icons. The Tunisian protesters also used rhetorical strategies including identification, satire, assemblages/mixing, and transculturalism as vehicles for content that was potentially critical of mainstream hegemonic discourse. Meanwhile, these rhetorical techniques helped establish their own vernacular rhetoric ("cultural syncretism") and thus helped build a personal, creative, and liminal Tunisian/Arab community in the streets.

This is evident in a piece of graffiti found in the walls of Sousse, central East Tunisia (Figure 4.1). The graffiti is a painting of an angry, desperate man in black and white, with a caption written in Arabic in red and black that reads “We, the employed and the unemployed, are against injustice and exploitation.” The graffiti is signed by the name “Zwewla.” The term *zwewla* in Tunisian dialect means “the poor,” and refers also to a street art community that is famous for its graffiti in support of the poor and marginalized groups in Tunisia (Ben Mhenni). In this graffiti, the group Zwewla used identification—or “one of us”—rhetoric to address issues about the Tunisian/Arab community. Identification refers to the means by which an author may establish a shared sense of values, attitudes, and interests with his or her audience (Burke). The more an author can talk in the audience’s language through “speech, gesture, tonality, order, image, attitude, idea, identifying attitude, idea, identifying [his or her] ways with [the audience’s]” (55), the more effectively s/he can persuade the audience. Using the

Figure 4.1. Graffiti done by Zwewla.

strategy of identification, the group Zwewla constructed their graffiti persona as a struggling working-class Tunisian/Arab with whom their Arab audience could easily identify. Like many other graffiti, the "words" and "paintings" were ordinary and familiar. By setting an artistic demonstration in the walls and writing in both modern and colloquial Arabic, the group Zwewla treated their audience as their friends, and conversed about their ideas, feelings, and stories. The content of the graffiti addressed heavy and complex issues. The group criticized the mainstream regimes' mistreatment of Tunisian and Arab citizens by drawing upon the popular image of what an "Arab" looks like and using the Arabic language.

In their graffiti, Zwewla also sought to resonate with their Tunisian/Arab audience by reminding them of their shared struggles and demands. The graffiti group frequently used the pronouns "we," "our," and "us" in Arabic to break the boundaries between themselves and their audience and construct themselves as members of the community. The delinking between the "people" and the "government" was an important strategy to create this new humanity. By identifying with their audience, they voiced the outrage that the people ought to have—one that should protest against the injustices exerted upon them by the authoritarian/elitist regimes in the region. However, the use of the modern Arabic language mixed with the Tunisian dialect in the written captions of the graffiti, as well as the employment of Arabic calligraphy in the drawings, communicate a hybrid and embodied discursive space. The vernacular discourse of this graffiti speaks directly to the Tunisian and Maghrebi community as the written words *khadam w battal*, "we the employed and unemployed," are written in Tunisian/Maghrebi colloquial, not in modern Arabic. Hence, the message is establishing an exclusive cultural identity of a shared Tunisianness/Maghrebiness through the use of a colloquial language that could only be understood by this specific community, not all Arabs. There is an articulation of a discursive imagining of a community (Anderson) that is not Arab, or Western, but rather Tunisian/Maghrebi. Therefore, this message is decolonial as it is both affirmative of the Tunisian/Maghrebi identity and counterhegemonic of the widely accepted notion of a pan-Arab, or a unified, identity. The fact that the text is written in Arabic letters does not make it accessible to all Arabs, and refutes the hypothesis that all Arabs share "one" Arab "Spring."

The second part of the text in the graffiti is written in modern Arabic, which reads *deda addulm wa istighlal*, "we against injustice and exploitation." Unlike the first part of the caption of the graffiti, the discourse of this text is open to all Arabic-speaking identities; it is not only open to Tunisians/Maghrebis, but also Arabs. Thus, this part of the text constructs a discursive pan-Arab unity that was not present in the first part of the text. It also communicates different meanings and resists the constructed understanding of Arabness. First, the issue of access to employment and social class are articulated as problems that Tunisians/Maghrebis are—specifically—suffering from; however, "injustice and exploitation" are issues that are shared among the Arab communities but under different circumstances and social categories. Second, it is important to note that the diversity of what constructs Arabness and its issues are important rhetorical constructions that Zwewla established in the caption of this graffiti. Through the verbal fragments of the graffiti, the group Zwewla suggests the presence of hybrid, diverse, embodied Arab identities. Zwewla, as rhetors, employ hybridity as a decolonial political strategy to construct their subjectivities. In other words, through the deployment of different languages in their graffiti, Zwewla confirm that their identities are "a product of multiple cultures, having a tolerance for ambiguity" (Calafell and McIntosh 18). I would also add that such work establishes a decolonial thinking that acknowledges subaltern reason (Mignolo, *Local Histories* 88) and subjectivity.

According to Bhabha, hybridity as a political strategy suggests a subjectivity that troubles the boundaries of social classifications and exerts its positive influence by dancing along the borders. The graffiti artists, then, are engaging in border crossing, articulating variegated discourses that are composed of many overlapping forces beyond race and ethnicity. In other words, this nuanced articulation of demands in Arabic, but through the usage of two different layers—Tunisian/Maghrebian dialect and modern Arabic—both affirms and resists simultaneously the notion of pan-Arab unity that is widespread not only in the Middle East and North Africa, but also in the West—a colonial process that always considered the Arab as "one" and as "the other." The caption of this graffiti creates new meaning that is affirmative of a shared Arabness, while at the same time rejecting the non-polyvalent aspects attached to Arabness, and constructs an individual identity of being a Tunisian/Maghrebi. It is a borderless understanding of identity. I unpack this notion of Arabness more in depth in later examples, but this concept asserts what Calafell and Delgado discussed in terms of the powerful abilities of visual arts. They affirm that "[a]rt has the ability to communicate because it can collect images and artifacts of cultural and ideological resonance and reposition them within a given frame to *echo long-held sentiments while articulating new meanings*" (5, emphasis added). Hence, these Tunisian political artists employed rhetorical or discursive strategies of identity construction and invention to articulate "identities-in-the-making" (Calafell and Delgado; Mignolo, *Local Histories*).

Another frequently used technique in the graffiti is the deployment of assemblage or mixing, a type of "pastiche" (Ono and Sloop). The group Zwewla mixed many fragments of the Western mainstream discourse to serve their own argument, particularly in the form of images in their graffiti. For instance, the drawing included in this graffiti is the popular Internet meme character "Trollface," or rage comic. Trollface is an Internet character/troll that was originated in the United States and drawn by the artist Carlos Ramirez; it is a very simple black-and-white drawing, asymmetrical and with an enormous grin showing two enormous rows of teeth (Brad). Due to the unattractiveness of the face, the meme is aptly named. Also, the face is known to appear in rage-filled or sarcastic comics. Hence, the group Zwewla borrowed the American Trollface concept, and mixed it with Tunisian/Arab political affects. The graffiti's drawing portrays an angry, desperate trollface, but the angry affect shown in the troll's face is rearticulated through the text to communicate discontent and disappointment in a Tunisian regime that let down its own citizens. Hence, the trollface is an affirmation of the Tunisian/Arab cultural identities' expressing frustration and resistance. The angry face of the troll in this graffiti could also suggest that this is a counterhegemonic message vis-à-vis the Orientalist trope that considers angriness an Arabic trait. Here, the "anger" is recontextualized in terms of a resistive movement against historically created colonialist injustices and exploitation. This is also what the decolonial scholar Aníbal Quijano encapsulates as social movements seeking, as noted above, "social liberation from all power organized as inequality, discrimination, exploitation, and as domination" (178).

As this analysis suggests, Zwewla strategically used the "we/us" rhetoric, assembling/mixing, and satire to concurrently (dis)/identify with a Tunisian, Arab community (communities) and—at the same time—challenge the mainstream discourse. Constructing a persona as an ordinary Tunisian/Arab citizen and talking in a personal manner, the group of artists turned this graffiti into a conversation in which they shared their personal feelings and demands with a community. This created a unique graffiti-style decolonial vernacular, which is rhetorically different from that of conventional speeches in which rhetors attempt to "educate" or "preach" to their audience. Moreover, the images drawn by these political artists by default served to create a new look for the Tunisian/Arab community. In challenging the preconceptions of the community prevalent in the mainstream media—angry without a cause, passive, supportive of dictatorship, and obedient—these Tunisian graffitists appeared to be expressive, and rebellious in a creative way. Hence, the graffiti is not only counterhegemonic of the stereotypes of an "Arab" persona is the West, but also resistive of the "obedient" character that the ruling regimes of the Middle East and North Africa have established for years in describing their citizens. The embracing of a *politics of disobedience* is also what Mignolo ("Delinking"; *Darker Side*) sees as a strategy for radical politics within decoloniality. Seen in this light, this graffiti forces a decolonial appeal in how it simultaneously creates vernacular discourses while contesting mainstream discourses.

Another graffiti drawn by the group Zwewla that is worth examining is one that was created after the Tunisian revolution (Figure 4.2), when there was a rebirth within the Islamist political structure as they became part of the government following the overthrow of former leader Zine al-Abidine Ben Ali in 2011. This particular graffiti was in the same area as the previously discussed graffiti, in Sousse, central East Tunisia. The graffiti portrays headshots—in black and white—of four personalities with names written in upper-case English under their faces. From left to right, the headshots include the following names: BELAID, CHAVEZ, BRAHMI, and MANDELA. Over the faces of Belaid and Brahmi, you can see red ink spots, signifying blood spots that are also touching the heads of Chavez and Mandela. Finally, the graffiti is signed by the group's name—Zwewla—in Arabic. Mohamed Brahmi and Chokri Belaid were both opposition leaders who were considered to be symbols of the Tunisian revolution that ousted the dictatorial regime in Tunisia, and both were critical of the actions of the new Islamist party. When Belaid and Brahimi were assassinated, this created turmoil in the Tunisian political scene and forced demonstrators to go back to occupy Avenue Habib Bourgiba (Gall). Moreover, the presence of the headshots of Hugo Chavez and Nelson Mandela suggest that

Figure 4.2. Graffiti done by Zwewla.

Zwewla embraced these leaders as political symbols because—like the Tunisian graffitists themselves—they fought against marginalization, oppression, and the suppression of the voice of the people.

Hence, this second graffiti by Zwewla is producing culturally specific rhetoric within the Tunisian population. First, the graffiti represents an affirming vernacular as it speaks to all the Tunisians who are resisting the new political assassinations and supporting the oppositional leaders who were killed. The drawing is thus syncretic as it protests the mainstream discourse of the new oppressive government that is allowing political violence against the opposition, while simultaneously constructing its own community's rhetoric to engage them.

Moreover, the vernacular discourse in this graffiti is also constructed out of fragments of national and international cultures. The images of Latin American and African revolutionaries and leaders as well as other elements from Western culture (for example the use of the English language) had been coopted by those young Tunisian graffitists to express their discontent with the post-revolutionary political scene. The vernacular discourse constituted within this graffiti is a form of pastiche of different elements that have been taken from diverse contexts and placed in the graffiti for the purpose of establishing new meanings and effects (Ono and Sloop 23). First, the graffiti could be accessible only to the Tunisian population. Non-Tunisians who are not familiar with the political leaders of Tunisia could misunderstand the placement of Chavez and Mandela in the graffiti. The graffiti in this instance represents what Ono and Sloop call "a broken language," since in this context there are images that "cannot be understood by the hegemonic culture and therefore [function] syncretically, to affirm and protest, through a pastiche of other languages," or in this example, images (24).

Zwewla is thus bringing together different cultures to create specific cultural expressions for their community. With regard to this fragmented strategy of pastiche used by the graffitists to produce their art, Michael Calvin McGee affirms, "Rhetors make discourses from scraps and pieces of evidence. Critical rhetoric does not begin with a finished text in need of interpretation; rather, texts are understood to be larger than the apparently finished discourse that presents itself as transparent" (279). Hence, the members of Zwewla used fragments of mainstream and diverse revolutionary images to construct their own subjectivities. Their graffiti represents a transnational form of art where those graffitists, instead of rejecting globality (they are embracing it through art and revolutionary symbols) reinterpret it for their specific histories and to match their needs. This process is a recognition of the interconnectedness of coloniality through using both local (Belaid and Brahmi) and global (Chavez and Mandela) figures of resistance as symbols of those who denounced oppression and the promises of modernity and were silenced. This identification of the impact of the oppressive power of global coloniality shows how Zwewla are embodying action and constructions of knowledge through their art.

DECONSTRUCTING ARABNESS

In this way, the Tunisians/Arabs represented through this graffiti inhabit subjectivities articulated by a vernacular discourse that is beyond issues of nationality as well as traditional concepts of "the Arab." For instance, the "Trollface" graffiti exemplifies this hybrid and embodied subjectivity by combining Tunisian dialect and modern Arabic, to highlight the diversity within "Arabness," combating the misconceptions and biases against the notion of the "one" Arab identity, at least implicitly. Also, Zwewla's artistic works demonstrate that they, as Tunisians, are not limited to speaking only a Tunisian-specific vernacular discourse in the graffiti. Instead, they rhetorically worked with other vernacular communities to criticize the hegemonic discourse regarding class, nationality, and social oppression. They also tried to construct decolonial hybrid vernacular subjectivities in their graffiti by challenging racial and social essentialism, rhetorically mobilizing a political mobility and solidarity. This confirms how the "Arab Spring," visually, verbally, and performatively "reinvented" both the Arab subject and the collective (Calafell and Delgado). As noted earlier, the works of postcolonial scholars such as Edward Said's *Orientalism* highlights how the Orient was essentially invented and constructed by Western empires in order to execute imperial ambitions and convey cultural superiority. Correspondingly, Aníbal Quijano and Immanuel Wallerstein confirm that decolonization of occupied territories did not eradicate coloniality, "it merely transformed its outer form" (550). Through analysis of the graffiti, we can see how the group Zwewla are "reinventing" the Orient as well as how the "Arab Spring" is producing knowledge of the Orient. There is agency vis-à-vis the construction of one's identity, discourse, and space.

The Arab uprisings, through the graffiti, brought attention to vernacular discourse as a decolonial medium of dissent. The graffiti artists reaffirmed the centrality of the vernacular, more specifically, in public struggles around cultural, social, and economic ideals that are bound to animate the emerging body politic. Thus, the visibility and appearance of vernacular discourses are indicative of the characteristics of larger dilemmas around national identity and political participation in the Arab states. Scholars have long argued that Orientalist discourses about the voices and the bodies of Arabs and Muslims reinforce processes of domination and "Othering" in a neocolonial context (Abu-Lughod; Ahmed; Puar; Said, *Covering Islam)*. As demonstrated by the graffiti examples above, the Arab vernacular can provide an important site of investigation, beyond both the Orientalist gaze and postcolonial thought, to study the process of political meaning making within national histories that are informed by but irreducible to colonial experience. Hence, unpacking and distinguishing local political discourses disturbs the fixed binaries of East/West and provides more insights into the complex realities of "Arab" subjectivities, providing agency to (re) create the Orient and its knowledge production.

In the process, the vernacular discourses in the "Arab Spring" also address the role of citizen in steering a democracy. As opposed to representations of the "Arab" unable to engage in democracy, the rhetorical strategies exhibited in the graffiti influenced the general climate of public opinion and helped to create an alternative political public sphere. The vernaculars of the Arab Spring, that is, created a solid argument in the region that the *citizen* matters. This argument started to put in place the essential building blocks of democratic systems, from the implementation of pluralistic citizen participation, to creating more mechanisms of accountability. The vernacular graffiti in Tunisia disclosed how members of Tunisian society discovered and clarified their shared interests and engaged in exchanges that shaped their opinions on issues of common interest. Paying close attention to how members of society engage in public dialogue reveals a picture of citizens who are contentious on matters that affect their lives. As such, the graffitists' work can also be seen as contributing to the conceptual framework of decolonial vernacular discourse enabling researchers to understand how the rhetorical character of formal and informal communication is formed and expressed, and how it shapes identities.

More important, the project of examining Arabs' communicative expressions is crucial in highlighting the "voices" of the people and in creating new ways of understanding communication from a decolonial approach. The vernacular discourses of the "Arab Spring" voice specific communicative practices from localized Arab communities and explore these practices' significance for Arab subjectivities in terms of the politics of national and cultural belonging. The graffiti sought to explore the plurality of Arab discourse and cultural expression and the resonances that make a pan-Arab identity, as well as the hybridity that comes from multiple voices and bodies. The goal of this project is forwarding a theoretical and methodological grounding for the study of Arab communication, or decolonial vernacular discourse. In other words, through the employment of a "metatheory" (Holling and Calafell) and decoloniality (Mignolo, "Delinking" and *Darker Side;* Quijano), this research systematizes a model for studying Arab voices and symbolic practices sensitive to a nuanced understanding of embodiment, identity, resistance, and power.

In other words, vernacular discourses of the "Arab Spring" created complex articulations of identity construction and performances in "new/complex" political spaces that—simultaneously—embrace and challenge dominant ideologies and cultural practices. The complex conceptualization of decolonial vernacular discourses of the revolutionary body in this project opens up issues of agency, identity, and representation that have been discussed in merely dichotomous ways and voices a revisionist model of reading Arab communicative practices to move beyond reductionism and embrace multiplicity. The graffiti askes to be "heard in a variety of ways, and in different positionalities" (Holling and Calafell xviii).

CONCLUSION

In many ways the "Arab Spring" can largely be understood as the movement of voices, bodies, and ideas connected to political and social objectives across political borders through the medium of visual, textual, and embodied vernaculars. This analysis has demonstrated how the "Arab Spring" that started with Bouazizi's self-immolation in December 2010, which initiated a regional revolt strengthened by a set of solid principles and demands, developed not in the pages of a scholarly article or the work of a recognizable analyst but through the bodies of normal citizens and the improvised protest-graffiti that circulated in the congested squares of Arab neighborhoods from Tunisia to Syria. The vernacular discourses of the "Arab Spring" destroyed the censorships and the fears that kept the voices and the bodies of the Arab citizens "hidden" for years in their respective countries. The cultural (re)production of the decolonial vernacular from such blazing revolutionary language as "karama" (dignity), "assulta lisha'b" (power to the people), and "thawra" (revolution) gave new meanings to the voices and to the identities of the people. It reconstructed a powerful active vernacular and gave rise to new citizenry and to active political spheres. The "Arab Spring" has proven that even with the high level of security control that citizens endured for years, the dynamic, counternarrative discourses that were articulated by countless individuals overtook the regime's rhetoric, and indeed its control over the people and the state. The spontaneity of people's vernaculars also helped make the uprisings inevitable and unstoppable in the face of control.

This vernacular language provides critical socio- and politico-vernacular sites that contribute to a fuller understanding of the overall regional situation and the localized iterations of the Arab revolutionary moment. In Tunisia, the critical discourse analyses of the graffiti (and language used) help to demonstrate and interpret mass-scale popular reactions in and outside of a politico-decolonial-vernacular context. Relying largely on the framing works of Ono and Sloop, Calafell, Holling and Calafell, Mignolo, and Quijano, my findings support the theory that decolonial vernacular discourse acts as a carrier and conveyor of revolutionary sentiments, as well as a visible validator of the voices and bodies of the marginalized who created an identification space allowing the people to embody the "thawra" (revolution).

As for the brave individuals who continue to struggle against violent oppression and express themselves fearlessly with a new-found strength and collective consciousness that gave birth to the "Arab Spring" as well as its many vernaculars and sociopolitical identities, it is critical that academia respect the absolutely irreducible complexities of what these demonstrators, artists, and everyday citizens are doing. The graffiti artists formulate the discourse of identity formation, analyzed by Michelle Holling and Bernadette Calafell, as well as Lila Abu-Lughod, within a vernacular of overlapping tensions that is vital to consider in analyzing the interrelations of vernaculars, resistance, and national identity in the "Arab Spring." Identity formation, according to Abu-Lughod, takes place "[b]etween practices and their justifications, between ideals and behavior, between simple prescriptions and multiple interpretations, between a sense of the universal and the complexity of local and individual experience" (Introduction 25). Indeed, the identities of the revolutionaries protesting in Tunisia and across the Arab region are being formed and re-formed in the between spaces of politics, society, culture, religion, economics, and, importantly, the vernacular. Hence, the revolutionaries created "[s]paces for connection across difference based on shared feelings of Otherness, [and/]or collectively [that] should not be downplayed where there are possibilities for coalition building, particularly in contemporary political climates" (Holling and Calafell 22).

My findings also offer examples that resonate with the theory and the praxis of a decolonial vernacular discourse. In the case of the "Arab Spring," the discourse acted as a carrier and conveyor of revolutionary sentiments (see Ono and Sloop; Calafell; Holling and Calafell; Mignolo, "Delinking" and *Darker Side;* and Quijano). Employing the strategies of vernacular discourse, cultural syncretism, and pastiche, the graffiti artists Zwewla challenged hegemonic views about Tunisians/Arabs while simultaneously establishing their own vernacular rhetoric and thus (re)building a new community through the graffiti. They also constructed hybrid subjectivities by traveling along the borders of different vernacular communities, and deconstructing the differences among Tunisians/Maghrebis and Arabs. Their graffiti represents a transnational form of art where those graffitists, instead of rejecting the West, are embracing it through art and revolutionary symbols, but reinterpreting it to their specific histories and to match their needs.

Moreover, the revolutionary language used in the uprisings is an important finding to note. The language is affirmative of the hybrid Tunisian subjectivity that crosses the borders between French and Arabic. It is a language of a multicultural identity. Hence the usage of the graffiti, and of revolutionary and hybrid language, serve as an event-catalyst by providing communicative expressions that can readily and quickly travel across borders. These communicative expressions are tools and weapons in the hands of the graffiti artists and the mouths of the demonstrators as they offer a resource and technique with which to strengthen a resistance on the individual and collective levels against what they articulate as domination, corruption, and injustice, or simply the stagnation of the status quo. These voices, images, words, rhythms, and bodies form a vernacular of opposition that can, as this research project argues, be considered the language of the "Arab Spring," and it is a vernacular used transnationally in the Arab region that in and of itself is a critical form of revolutionary activism. That said, it can also be, and is, used to push physical actions toward social change to further a regional, yet highly localized, political reform agenda.

The decolonial vernacular discourse of the "Arab Spring" initially aimed at initiating the downfalls of long-time dictators and succeeded with incredible rapidity at ousting the regime of Ben Ali, in the case of Tunisia. The vernacular discourse of the "Arab Spring" communicates a set of attitudes and ideologies that are, arguably, born out of a spirit of anger and frustration, and of the desire to improve one's standing and to change society and the nation-state, for the better. This revolutionary spirit is perhaps summarized best in the transnational political phrase that swept across Tunisia and the rest of the Arab region, and built the collective political consciousness: "Dégage" (leave). The Arab Spring started an incredible movement of dynamism, self-expression, activism, revolutions, uprisings, and all different kinds of activities that continue to shape the Arab world. The Arab uprising is consistently changing and it has a wide variety of different manifestations and different conditions in different countries. There is no single "Arab Spring," there is no single Arab revolution or movement; there is a wide variety of citizen dynamism and activism, expressing grievances and complaints, and aspiring to a better world.

Citizens of the Arab world are striving for a better world that they want to create with their own hands, responding to their rights as citizens and human beings to be treated fairly by their own societies. However, the changes that are going on in the Arab region are very complex, varied, and rapid, which makes it difficult to encompass all the details of the current situation or to predict accurately the future of the Arab revolution. Rather, it is important to reflect on what has happened in the last few years and think about what can be identified as new, significant, and lasting, and what is just fleeting and temporary. Also, it is important to think about what has been achieved by the revolution and what has not, as well as what should be anticipated to happen in the future. However, the dilemma I faced in executing this research is that all the events that are happening are at the same time *sequential, simultaneous,* and *cyclical.* By "sequential," I refer to the fact that the sequence of events that are happening is never-ending. For instance, every week, every month, there is something new (either positive or negative) that happens; a whole process of major historical development that keeps occurring in every country. By "simultaneous," I refer to how the Arab countries are trying to do something new that no other country in the world has ever tried to do. Every single state of the twenty-two Arab countries is experiencing some level of activism, citizen expression, and demand, from demonstrating in the streets to tweeting online. However, they are simultaneously trying to achieve what in Western countries, like the United States, was achieved over a period of two hundred years, from wars to revolutions to bringing forward new constitutions and granting equal rights to citizens. The implementation of a democratic system of governance in Western countries was indeed a long process that did not address all the issues of its societies at the same time. The difference in the Arab world is that Arab citizens are trying to solve all the issues they are facing at one time. It is very complex to simultaneously define the constitution, shape the nature of the political system, address the issue of minority rights, tackle the issue of religious pluralism, address the issue of national identity and national values, address the issue of civilian/military/police balance, address the issue of the role of women in society, and address the issue of the relationship between the central government and the regional provinces; yet all these issues are being treated at the same time. The problem is that it is beyond human capacity to achieve satisfactory outcomes in all those areas at once. For instance, I found out from the Tunisian people I talked to that if the government achieves some agreement on the role of Islam in the constitution, for example, there will be a disagreement on the role of women in the constitution, or freedom of the press, or foreign aid . . . . In other words, there is no linear breakthrough of the process that could be achieved. If we look at the case of Tunisia, for example, first we have citizens' revolts, then the overthrow of the president, then the election of a new government, and then the drafting of the first democratic constitution, all within a short period.

Finally, by "cyclical" I refer to how the progress of the revolution or postrevolution is taking a step forward toward a democratic transition, and then a step backward toward the old authoritarian regime. In the case of Egypt, we can see how the people ended the authoritarian rule of the military, and then—democratically—elected the Muslim Brotherhood into the government, and then ousted the democratically elected president and returned to military rule. Hence, the transition is indeed a cycle of achievements and failures. The sequential, simultaneous, and cyclical nature of these issues of nation building, state building, political definitions, national values, societal relationships, and identity redefinitions will take time to achieve a clear outcome for these populations.

This research project on the vernacular discourse of the "Arab Spring" brought attention to the significance of analyzing how normal citizens use hybridity as a decolonial political strategy to construct their subjectivities. The deployment of hybridity as a decolonial political strategy refers to a subjectivity that troubles the boundaries of social classifications and exerts its positive influence by dancing along the borders (Bhabha; Mignolo, *Darker Side*). In other words, the hybridization of subjectivity disrupts its traditional formation, and establishes a queer and ambiguous subjectivity, which offers a new space where the discursive (re/de)constructedness is witnessed. That is to say, for a critical discourse analysis, it is important to engage in border crossing, articulating variable discourses that are composed of many overlapping forces beyond focusing on one single identity. For instance, the deployment of different languages in the Tunisian graffiti challenges the essentialized categorizations that reinforce a Euro-Americano-centric perspective of an authentic "Arabness," and employs a hybridity strategy that articulates discourses by traveling along the borders of several intersecting groups involved in subjectivity construction (e.g., Arabs/Tunisians/Maghrebians/French; an assemblages of multiple cultures and historicity).

To summarize, the synthesizing of a hybrid articulation of a decolonial vernacular discourse urges scholars to consider the vernacular discourse of the "Arab Spring" as hybrid in terms of subjectivity, content, and agency and to explore the processes of its hybridization. The project also calls for employing hybridity as a decolonial political strategy to examine how everyday citizens use this method to (re/de)construct their subjectivities.

NOTES

1. In this research project, I chose to use the phrase "Arab Spring" between quotation marks to denote the controversy around the naming of the uprisings, and to communicate a political stance in alliance with other Arab scholars and citizens (see Rami Khoury; Ibrahim N. Abusharif; Maytha Alhassen) who do not describe the movement as a "blooming" awakening from a "winter slumber," but rather as a movement that has been years in the making (mostly naming it "Karama"/Dignity). The phrase "Arab Spring" is also widely used mainly in the West, not necessarily in the Middle East and North Africa.

2. In this research, by Arab people, I refer to those who identify linguistically, culturally and diasporically as Arabs (not only genealogically).

3. By Muslim, I refer to a larger understanding of Muslimness that is not merely faith-based but cultural and diasporic as well. It is not necessarily a series of dogmatic doctrines; the definition is fluid and dynamic. In some instances, it could also refer to bodies that are mistakenly identified as Muslim just because of their skin color.

4. In this research, I am borrowing Walter Mignolo's (*Darker Side;* "Delinking") theorization of decoloniality to denote how social movements in North Africa are embracing a decolonial thinking to eliminate colonial and postcolonial Western thoughts in their countries, as well as "delinking" from the colonial legacies in their respective governments. This decolonial process empowers radical politics and epistemological shifts that push for the emergence of a new body politics of knowledge, similar to that of the Zapatista movement (Mignolo, "Delinking"). Hence, instead of following postcolonial thought that focuses on the transformation within the academy (Mignolo, "Delinking" 452), I am focusing on a decolonial approach that celebrates the citizen, the activist, and the movement.

WORKS CITED

Abu-Lughod, Lila. "Do Muslim Women Really Need Saving? Anthropological Reflections on Cultural Relativism and Its Others." *American Anthropologist*, vol. 104, no. 3, 2002, pp. 783–90.

Abusharif, Ibrahim N. "Seasons of a Phrase." *The Chronicle of Higher Education*, 2013, *ProQuest*, https://search-proquest-com.jpllnet.sfsu.edu/docview/1327255405?accountid=13802.

Adib-Moghhaddam, Arshin. "The Arab Revolts, Islam and Postmodernity." *Middle East Journal of Culture and Communication*, vol. 5, no. 1, 2012, pp. 15–25.

Ahmed, Leila. "Western Ethnocentrism and Perceptions of the Harem." *Feminist Studies*, vol. 8, no. 3, 1982, pp. 521–34.

Al-Ali, Nadje. "Gendering the Arab Spring." *Middle East Journal of Culture and Communication*, vol. 5, no. 1, 2012, pp. 26–31.

Alhassen, Maytha. "Please Reconsider the Term 'Arab Spring.'" *HuffPost,* 10 Feb. 2012, https://www.huffingtonpost.com/maytha-alhassen/please-reconsider-arab-sp_b_1268971.html.

Anderson, Benedict. *Imagined Communities: Reflections on the Origin and Spread of Nationalism.* Verso, 1983.

Ben Mhenni, Lina. "Graffiti in Tunisia: Art or Crime?" *Your Middle East.* 1 Dec. 2012. Accessed 15 Mar. 2014.

Bhabha, Homi K. *The Location of Culture.* Routledge, 1994.

Brad. "Trollface/Coolface/Problem?" *Know Your Meme.* (n.d.). Accessed 28 Mar. 2014.

Burke, Kenneth. *A Rhetoric of Motives.* U of California P, 1950.

Calafell, Bernadette Marie. *Latina/o Communication Studies: Theorizing Performance.* Peter Lang, 2007.

Calafell, Bernadette Marie, and Fernando P. Delgado. "Reading Latina/o Images: Interrogating *Americanos.*" *Critical Studies in Media Communication*, vol. 21, no. 1, 2004, pp. 1–24.

Calafell, Bernadette Marie, and Dawn Marie D. McIntosh. "Latina/o Vernacular Discourse: Theorizing Performative Dimensions of an Other Counterpublic." *What Democracy Looks Like: The Rhetoric of Social Movements and Counterpublics,* edited by Christina R. Foust, Amy Pason, and Kate Zittlow Rogness. U of Alabama P, 2017, pp. 201–24.

Gall, Carlotta. "Second Opposition Leader Assassinated in Tunisia." *The New York Times,* 25 July 2013. Accessed 15 Feb. 2014.

Haddad, Yvonne Yazbeck. "The Post-9/11 *Hijab* as Icon." *Sociology of Religion*, vol. 68, no. 3, 2007, pp. 253–67.

Holling, Michelle A., and Bernadette M. Calafell. "Tracing the Emergence of Latin@ Vernaculars in Studies of Latin@ Communication." *Latina/o Discourse in Vernacular Spaces: Somos de Una Voz?,* edited by Holling and Calafell, Lexington Books, 2011, pp. 17–30.

Khouri, Rami. "Arab Spring or Revolution?" *The Globe and Mail*, 18 Aug. 2011, *ProQuest*, https://search-proquest-com.jpllnet.sfsu.edu/docview/884113104?accountid=13802.

Kraidy, Marwan M. "The Revolutionary Body Politic: Preliminary Thoughts on a Neglected Medium in the Arab Uprisings." *Middle East Journal of Culture and Communication*, vol. 5, no. 1, 2012, pp. 66–74.

Matar, Dina. "Contextualising the Media and the Uprisings: A Return to History." *Middle East Journal of Culture and Communication*, vol. 5, no. 1, 2012, pp. 75–79.

McAlister, Melani. *Epic Encounters: Culture, Media, and U.S. Interests in the Middle East, 1945–2000.* U of California P, 2001.

McGee, Michael Calvin. "Text, Context, and the Fragmentation of Contemporary Culture." *Western Journal of Communication*, vol. 54, no. 3, 1990, pp. 274–89.

Mignolo, Walter D. *The Darker Side of Western Modernity: Global Futures, Decolonial Options.* Duke UP, 2011.

———. "Delinking." *Cultural Studies*, vol. 21, no. 2-3, 2007, pp. 449–514.

———. *Local Histories/Global Designs: Coloniality, Subaltern Knowledges, and Border Thinking.* Princeton UP, 2000.

Mtiraoui, Emine. "Two Tunisian Graffiti Artists Face Trial." *Nawaat*, Nov. 13. Accessed 13 Mar. 2014.

Ono, Kent A., and John M. Sloop. "The Critique of Vernacular Discourse." *Communication Monographs*, vol. 62, no. 1, 1995, pp. 19–46.

Puar, Jasbir K. *Terrorist Assemblages: Homonationalism in Queer Times.* Duke UP, 2007.

Quijano, Aníbal. "Coloniality and Modernity/Rationality." *Cultural Studies*, vol. 21, no. 2-3, 2007, pp. 168–78.

Quijano, Aníbal, and Immanuel Wallerstein. "Americanity as a Concept, or the Americas in the Modern World-System." *International Social Science Journal*, vol. 44, no. 134, 1992, pp. 549–57.

Said, Edward W. *Covering Islam: How the Media and the Experts Determine How We See the Rest of the World.* Pantheon Books, 1981.

———. *Orientalism.* Pantheon Books, 1978.

5

La Cultura Nos Cura: Reclaiming Decolonial Epistemologies through Medicinal History and Quilting as Method

Iris D. Ruiz
University of California, Merced

Sonia C. Arellano
University of Central Florida

A MINI-COUNTERSTORY . . .

> Local setting: A writing program faculty meeting on promoting diversity in the classroom held at a Hispanic Serving Institution in California.
> Global setting: The United States of America, where Latinxs are the largest minority.
> Discursive exchange:
> Science Writing Professor: "I don't teach content, so I don't have to worry about diversity in my classroom."
> Latina Composition Professor: "Wait, you don't teach content? If you don't teach content, what do you teach?"
> Science Writing Professor: "I teach students how to write strong, stylistically sound science writing."
> Latina Composition Professor: "Well, where did those concepts come from? Who defines them?"
> Everyone in the room: Awkward silence . . .

We aim to cognitively and culturally depart from an arguably hegemonic and colonial perspective in the field of composition and rhetoric (comp/rhet), and thus we interrogate how comp/rhet scholars have traditionally favored historical, historiographic, and material research methods and scholarship that are based upon colonial—read Eurocentric—forms of knowledge creation, dissemination, and preservation, engaging in exclusionary and provincialized (Sánchez) epistemological practices indicative of imperial scholarship (Delgado). Raúl Sánchez calls out this epistemic provincialism in "Writing," where he claims that definitions of writing are predicated upon a provincialism "that treats Western/European perspectives on knowledge, culture, and language as universal" (78). This provincial perspective favors alphabetic writing systems, which, while dominant, are only one type of semiotic system of communication. Overlooking other sign-systems in favor of hegemonic definitions of writing delegitimizes other definitions of writing while concealing their own provincialism.

Writing is not the only keyword featured in *Decolonizing Rhetoric and Composition Studies: New Latinx Keywords for Theory and Pedagogy* (Ruiz and Sánchez). The book chapters make several attempts to perform the decolonial option to epistemically delink from provincial, colonially defined terms. In this chapter, we perform a similar rhetorical move that questions provincial, colonial research methods that overlook ties to Western-based epistemological traditions. Continuing to rely only on Western ways of knowing and creating knowledge, furthermore, works to maintain an epistemically imperial position, which makes it difficult for comp/rhet decolonial scholars, like us, to challenge its claimed objectivity and hegemonic eminence.

The counterstory offered above demonstrates this difficulty in an exchange between a Latinx and a white colleague. The unquestioned definition of "stylistically sound writing" in the above scenario is reminiscent of how comp/rhet practitioners use conventional and disciplinary methods to adhere to disciplinary research standards without questioning the Eurocentric and Germanic epistemic traditions that underlie such methods (Ruiz, *Reclaiming*). Further, the above discursive exchange is reminiscent of using writing textbooks which claim objectivity but which are actually exercises in colonial and hegemonic literacy and linguistic training. For example, the textbook *They Say/I Say: The Moves That Matter in Academic Writing* is described on Amazon.com as a textbook that "identifies the key rhetorical moves in academic writing," "shows students how to frame their arguments as a response to what others have said[,] and provides templates to help them start making the moves." This description sounds finite: "key rhetorical moves" and "academic writings," for example, provide no space for critique. These nouns are things that exist unproblematically and one is presumed to be able to access them easily through reading this particular textbook. With such claimed objective and unquestioned attributes, one rarely stops to think how these types of decontextualized writing instructional tools are the most desired by students and the most recommended by practitioners without any hesitation as to the aims of such books to teach imitation of colonial discursive practices. However, claims of objective knowledge have recently come under strict scrutiny as being provincial and hegemonic with an increasing presence of compositionists of color joining the profession, who are beginning to contribute to and create their own epistemologies through alternative research methods, such as the decolonial historical and material methodology offered here.

Before going on to describe the ways that both of these methods speak back to the traditional—read colonial—research methods, it is worth noting the entrance of decolonial theory, thought, and possibilities for creating spaces for alternative knowledge-making practices in the history of comp/rhet. There is no doubt that scholars of American Indian rhetoric Ellen Cushman, Victor Villanueva, Mary Louise Pratt, and Damián Baca have provided a path for the entrance of decolonial critiques and epistemological contributions into the field with a focus upon indigenous knowledge and experiences that are seen as marginal, and sometimes invisible, to the field's current focus upon other "critical" forms of knowledge-making such as feminist historiography, feminist research methods, critical revisionist historical methods, and critical material research methods. While there are certainly other American Indian rhetorical studies scholars who study indigenous rhetorics and ways of making knowledge in comp/rhet, all the scholars listed above, with the exception of Baca and Ruiz, neglect the ways that Chicanx/Latinx scholars also contribute to indigenous rhetorical traditions and epistemological contributions to the field as American Indians in a time when more Latinxs are attempting to reclaim an indigenous past that was lost due to colonial conquest (Acuña) and identifying on the US Census as "American Indian" (Decker). This is an oversight of the field that is partly accounted for in this chapter. So not only are we claiming that colonial research methods continue to maintain an unquestioned standing and continue to relegate decolonial research methods to colonized spaces of alterity—we are also claiming a space within an area that has yet to acknowledge Latinxs as contributors to a decolonial tradition that has only recently accommodated a space for Mexica[1] rhetorical studies. Here we add to that space by proposing decolonial historiography as medicinal and reclamatory and decolonial material studies as integral to the corporeal bodies of American Indians on the other side of the Mexican border.

We understand the challenge of gaining epistemological legitimacy due to limited access into colonized epistemological spaces such as comp/rhet and its textual storehouses of knowledge, which are produced in tightly woven and maintained networks of scholarship. Through these limited spaces and epistemological constraints, however, as two Chicanx female scholars, we engage the concept of *epistemic disobedience*, drawn from Walter Mignolo's theory of decolonial options, in order to problematize the colonial epistemologies that legitimize traditional research methods in comp/rhet. Epistemic disobedience operates by unveiling "epistemic silences of Western epistemology and affirming the epistemic rights of the racially devalued, and considering decolonial options to allow the silences to build arguments to confront those who take 'originality' as the ultimate criterion for the final judgment" (162). We engage in this task to assert a decolonial option and to consider ways our field currently does research. We specifically critique a claimed objectivity of established, dominant, and legitimized comp/rhet historical and material methods and scholarship. In other words, current historical and material methods still value objectivity and Eurocentric notions of methods and research.

In this chapter, we begin by examining some legitimized mainstream comp/rhet methods and methodologies. Through a decolonial lens, we see comp/rhet traditions as deeply steeped in empirical historical and materialist methods and methodologies that are mired in colonialism—read: the blood, genocide, and destruction in the histories of compositionists of color—because of these traditions' blatant overlooking of the colonial histories that legitimized certain forms of knowledge and knowledge making while simultaneously delegitimizing alternative and indigenous ways of knowing and being in the world. Additionally, scholars in positions of power in comp/rhet have been guilty of perpetuating a deafening silence of minoritized voices and experiences that do not align with traditional Western values in its imperialist scholarship (Ruiz, "*Reclaiming*"; Delgado). Although the field has grown and expanded to be more inclusive of minoritized voices, approaches, and research areas, there is much work to be done in aligning what we say we value and what we demonstrate we do value through positions of power, policy, engagement with community, and even views expressed in prominent textual and physical spaces of the field.[2]

DECOLONIZING HISTORICAL AND MATERIAL COMP/RHET METHODS: BUILDING FROM DECOLONIAL EPISTEMOLOGIES

The methods we present here are decolonial responses to colonial methods in comp/rhet, and as such, both our methods engage in both healing and a reclamation of marginalized people's ways of making knowledge and of being in the world. While Iris Ruiz presents decolonial historiography as an alternative way to engage in reclamation critically, Sonia C. Arellano presents a decolonial way of material composing as an approach to center and reclaim human stories. Ruiz argues for the necessity of a decolonial historiographic method, *medicinal history*—also known as historical recovery or historical *curanderisma* (Levins Morales). Arellano suggests comp/rhet scholars engage in a decolonial feminist material method—such as *quilting as method*—which involves composing through textiles. We offer these as decolonial options that engage what Mignolo refers to as "epistemic disobedience" by departing from traditionally valued knowledges and knowledge making in comp/rhet. We present such methods because they contribute to a growing body of sustainable decolonial methods and methodologies for scholars interested in decolonizing methods and for the colonized scholars in the field.

Our discussion of decolonial methods here draws from Mignolo's concepts of decolonial epistemologies and decolonial options. In "Epistemic Disobedience, Independent Thought and Decolonial Freedom," he claims that Western epistemology has hidden self-serving interests and that the work of decolonial thinking is to reveal such epistemic silences in order to affirm "the epistemic rights of the racially devalued" (162). In other words, Western ways of creating knowledge have been established as the norm by those whom they serve. Decolonial thinking advocates for marginalized groups not only to make visible this self-serving norm, but also to challenge it so as to value other ways of knowing.

Mignolo claims there are two paths to knowledge, de-Westernization and a decolonial option, and the main point of departure is that the former does not question what is eliminated for the sake of modernization, while the latter "starts from the principle that the *regeneration* of life shall prevail over primacy of the *production and reproduction* of goods at the cost of life" (161). In the historical and material methods put forth here, we center alternative ways of knowing and thinking about critical historical and material methods to demonstrate that indigenous, decolonial epistemologies and  ontologies are not just differences in approaches, but are essential parts of human life that have had to undergo severe levels of trauma in order for colonial forms of knowledge making and education to prevail while, at the same time seeing their own communities deteriorate and compete for resources, as seen with #NODAPL and the current immigration crisis where infants are being separated from their parents.

As we build from decolonial options in this chapter, it is important to point out the nuance of decoloniality not being in opposition to colonialism, but in consideration of colonial wounds. Mignolo claims that those engaging in the decolonial option have one commonality: colonial wounds, which are the effects on groups of people historically "classified as underdeveloped economically and mentally" (161). If we start from a point of colonial wounds, then the decolonial option is based upon a reaction to a colonial legacy. Mignolo also claims that "[d]e-colonial thinking presupposes delinking (epistemically and politically) from the web of imperial knowledge (theo- and ego-politically grounded) from disciplinary management" (20). Colonial wounds are, therefore, the remnant effects of a colonial legacy and provide a commonality for those engaging in a decolonial option. As a decolonial option assumes a delinking from imperial knowledge, we can see that the work of decolonial options and delinking is in reaction to colonial legacies. Delinking and decolonial options, therefore, are not to remove the colonial legacy completely but, instead, acknowledge and challenge its effects.

Decolonial epistemologies, then, ask those who suffer from colonial wounds to challenge the normalized Eurocentric ways of knowing and value other ways of knowing. Within comp/rhet, claims to knowledge have been directly connected to histories of colonialism and continue to colonize alternative perspectives by relegating them to the margins of illegitimacy (Ruiz, *Reclaiming;* Prendergast; Royster; Royster and Williams; Ramirez; Baca, *Mestiz@ Scripts*; Connal). As Mignolo suggests, it is not enough to change the conversation; the terms of the conversation must also be changed, and in order to do that, we must call into question the control of knowledge (162). To do that, Mignolo claims we must shift the focus on the knower and therefore the "assumptions that sustain locus enunciations" (162). By presenting historical and material methods here, we intend to do just that within comp/rhet: question who controls knowledge in the field (locus of enunciation) and suggest other ways of producing knowledge (decolonial option).

CONTRIBUTING CRITICAL DECOLONIAL METHODS TO COMP/RHET

While we acknowledge the rich, necessary, and vast tradition of both quantitative and qualitative research methods which create the epistemologies of the field of comp/rhet (Kirsch and Sullivan; Glenn and Ratcliffe; Moss; Heath; Sternglass; Banks), initially we want to look specifically at historical methods common in the field, particularly those that are traditional (Brereton; Connors; Kitzhaber) and those that are "critical" (Glenn and Ratcliffe; Faigley; Crowley). In comp/rhet, scholars have discussed the history of the field for a long time and continue to revise this history so as to be more inclusive. The field addresses some historical and material methods and has worked to critically reclaim stories of those who have been erased by dominant histories and narratives. However, it still has distance and epistemological space to traverse before it can claim to understand the colonial worldviews it purports to dismantle but nonetheless maintains. In order to understand the significance of the contribution of our decolonial historical and material methods to the field, we briefly discuss room for inclusion in the existing scholarship.

Western historiographic practices continue to be consubstantial to comp/rhet studies. Such practices are underwritten by the presupposition that knowledge production began in a specific part of the planet and a proposition that knowledge spread thereafter from East to West and/or from the archons of Athens to modern America. This created a kind of normative historical thinking in the field that continues to have rhetorical and ideological consequences. Such consequences include the denial of rhetorical histories and practices elsewhere and otherwise. The fact that Western historiographic practices attempt to manage and control what counts as knowledge demands an ethical project of both recovery and restoration work.

The same can be said for histories of composition studies (such as those of John Brereton, Albert Kitzhaber, and Robert Connors). We know there are absences and have worked to recover them. However, the existing work has not yet acted on behalf of methodologies that work to reclaim lost/erased knowledges and rhetorical traditions associated with the Chicanx/Latinx rhetorical traditions as part of American Indian rhetorical studies. For example, Villanueva acknowledges the Puerto Rican history of the indigenous Taino in "Memoria Is a Friend of Ours: On the Discourse of Color."[3]

Furthermore, while some histories have been critical in noting absences with regard to location, gender, and class (see for example the works of Lynn Bloom, Lester Faigley, Wallace Douglass, Richard Ohmann, and Susan Miller), few address the absence of race in these histories (García de Müeller and Ruiz; Ruiz, "Race"). Still, these critical histories are regarded as providing "critical" and unofficial perspectives to the "Harvard History" because they have worked to recover silences—yet they still do not question the very delivery of the types of knowledge production they are compliant with. Ultimately, current histories of rhetoric are limited in scope and adherent to the Western tradition, and are so at the expense of ceding that rhetoric existed "elsewhere and otherwise" (Baca; Sánchez). The same can be said about histories of composition studies, which have yet to establish a history located in the Southwest with many colonized people (Ruiz, *Reclaiming*).

Moving on to material methodology, we see that, currently, scholarship in comp/rhet takes up "material" studies in a variety of ways. Some feminist scholars study specific material objects such as textiles (see for example Goggin and Sohan), and academic journals craft special issues to examine the rhetorical value of material projects such as the AIDS Memorial Quilt (Morris). Other scholars briefly mention textiles (quilts) to support their own theories concerning cultural "mnemonic devices" (Banks) and as a metaphor to build their own theories concerning nonlinear readings (Deleuze and Guattari). Some scholarship takes up new materialist rhetoric and object-oriented rhetorics, which vary based on approach but tend to focus on human and nonhuman actors that contribute to a nonstatic rhetorical context that affects human hierarchies (see Gries; Rickert; Riedner and Mahoney). Another common area of study in comp/rhet involves the subversive potential of maker culture and DIY (do it yourself) (e.g., Shivers-McNair).[4]

All of these areas—scholars studying material objects, new materialist/object-oriented rhetorics, and maker culture/DIY—continue to make important contributions to comp/rhet. However, they also continue to value a Western rhetorical tradition either in whom they study, how they approach their research, or what their data includes. Moreover, none of these areas are new, but are simply attending to knowledges and populations previously ignored. For example, indigenous populations have a rich history of making material things, considering their relationships to nonhuman actors, and valuing the knowledge generating potential of tactile processes. Now that scholars who align with a Western intellectual tradition are doing these same things, they have a seemingly new intellectual and rhetorical value.

Additionally, this scholarship is not challenging the colonial legacy of comp/rhet. In their introduction to *Text + Field: Innovations in Rhetorical Method*, Sara McKinnon et al. provide an example of scholars working within traditions that are not actually traversing the epistemological distance they claim to be. In discussing the topoi of judgment in rhetorical scholarship, McKinnon and her coauthors claim that "feminist scholars who disrupt traditional understandings of what counts as a text worthy of criticism and who intervene in the implied subjectivity of the rhetorical critic (as individual, white, male, and professional) also maintain the primacy of the rhetorical critic's judgment" (15). In other words, these scholars are being progressive by expanding notions of texts worthy of study while maintaining a colonial legacy in assuming that their individual judgment is superior to or more important than that of others. However, the material and tactile rhetoric we discuss attempts to address some critiques such as the one from McKinnon et al. First, we depart from the abovementioned scholarship because we use material to mean literal and tactile forms of discourse, which again is not new, but is also not widely valued in our field. In other words, alphabetic, verbal, and visual rhetoric are not the only ways that people can be moved. Material things can convey and create meaning through touch, which is underdeveloped in comp/rhet.[5] Moreover, scholarship that has discussed textiles discusses their visual rhetoric as a static text and not the action of making textiles as research (Goggin; Sohan).

Looking outside our field, approaches such as arts-based research move past the critique of McKinnon and her coauthors that research facilitates a critic's judgment as the final assessment of research. In their book *Arts Based Research,* Tom Barone and Elliot Eisner state that "arts based research is a heuristic through which we deepen and make more complex our understanding of some aspect of the world" (3). They claim that arts based research has modest aspirations to facilitate another angle or a deeper understanding of what we are investigating as researchers, not a concrete conclusive declaration of a Truth. In the material method forwarded here, the researcher is engaging in the practice of making a quilt as research with a modest goal of deepening the understanding of a particular phenomenon.

MEDICINAL HISTORY AND QUILTING AS METHOD

The previously mentioned Western tradition of knowledge making can be ideologically ruptured if one engages in the decolonial option to shift the geopolitical center of "epistemological" discoveries and practices away from the West. However, we caution against an identity politics approach to epistemological recentering. In other words, we are not suggesting a method that makes broad generalizations about groups of people based on superficial, prescriptive identity categories, nor are we suggesting replacing one way of knowing with another because it is superior. We instead suggest that decentering the currently valued way of knowing in our field and in academia and recentering other ways of knowing will glean nuanced understandings of the world that may facilitate knowledge production in positive ways for marginalized people. Here we suggest medicinal history and quilting as method as approaches that recenter and reclaim minoritized ways of knowing to provide nuanced ways of being in the world and conducting research.

Medicinal history is a decolonial method that allows for the practice of historical reclamation and healing by recentering the knowledge production of the indigenous Nahua, the Mexica

(Levins Morales). For example, medicinal history as an act of decolonial delinking and of reclaiming history allows for a comparison between Western and non-Western understandings of the human relationship to the universe and particularly to human existence here on earth. Many indigenous peoples of the Americas conceived of the human relationship to the Earth quite differently than did Europeans. This comparison is classified as "medicinal" because it also heals that which was severed through colonial relations and colonial renditions of the human relationship to the Earth. When Christians imposed their belief systems on the Americas to facilitate colonial projects, Nahua belief systems were undermined and demonized—the Nahua were said to have worshipped many gods and practiced the most heinous and inhuman crimes (León-Portilla 13).

Medicinal history allows these biased, ill-informed renditions of Mexica religious practices to lose legitimacy when their colonial motives are exposed, and further allows one to heal and regain the symbiotic philosophy of Mexica conceptions of the human relationship to the land and the heavens. Duality was a much privileged and natural concept for the Nahua goddess Coatlicue (later named Tonantsi) and other female goddesses; however, through colonization, binary opposites such as good and evil were the only concepts available. René Descartes, famous for his contributions to rational thought and to the Enlightenment as well as the claim, "I think, therefore I am," inaugurates what is known as the Cartesian split. There is no equivalent for this type of split in Mexica thought and philosophy. The smoking mirror, for example, which is associated with Tezcatlipoca, signifies introspection and reflection, but it does so holistically, as it is one of the four aspects of Nahua Ollin, which means "harmony" in Nahuatl, the Mexica indigenous language.

The Mexica spirit died through colonization, and the human being became inhumane and an object to be enslaved and delegitimized through the Europeans' wanting land and riches. The decolonial delinking of history allows for this knowledge to come to the fore because we purposely delink and place our center from which to gaze as a historical method located at the center-point of

Mexica consciousness and belief systems. This is the medicine in the decolonial practices of performing an act of decolonial, epistemic disobedience and of engaging in the method of decolonial historiography.

While medicinal history is a decolonial method that facilitates reclamation and healing, quilting as method is a decolonial feminist practice that facilitates reclamation and knowledge production. To understand the ways we approach research and in order to situate that research within the discipline of comp/rhet, we first explain how we are influenced by Gloria Anzaldúa's refusal of dichotomies in some areas and the promotion of both/and approaches to the world. She claims that "[i]n trying to become 'objective,' Western culture made 'objects' of things and people when it distanced itself from them, thereby losing 'touch' with them. This dichotomy is the root of all violence" (59). Moreover, she claims that the creative and the intellectual should not be split and refers to the need to study art as nonstatic actions that are part of everyday life (88–89). This desire for objectivity, the objectification of things, and the splitting of the creative and intellectual can be seen in the field of comp/rhet, in personal interactions—like being told our work is not rigorous enough, theoretical enough, or quantitative enough—as well as in institutionalized policies—such as tenure and promotion guidelines that value written publications over creative efforts.[6] Anzaldúa's work influences our desire to offer quilting as a method for reclaiming stories of migrant lives that will never have a chance to provide written contributions to comp/rhet. Quilting as a method can also facilitate knowledge production through creative methods.

Quilting as method is an approach to research that advocates for the expression of data through textile compositions. Instead of solely relying on an alphabetic text to demonstrate research and knowledge production, we consider how a textile can convey the same knowledge. In developing quilting as method, we seek to center ourselves and our experiences as a starting point for our research and to study and develop creative methods such as quilting to provide explanations of the nuances of tactile rhetoric. Additionally, a focus on migrant lives reinforces a decolonial option of delinking that places human lives above disciplinary transformation and epistemically centers on the corporeal rather than privileging the abstract site of knowledge production (20).

Developing the concept of quilting as a feminist decolonial material method, we assert that composing a quilt provides researchers an approach that conveys their research through colors, textures, materials, and visual as well as alphabetic texts. Tactile rhetoric refers to the ways that rhetoric is and can often be tactile and, as a result, can be emotionally and physically felt. In other words, through creating and touching a textile object, one can feel the affect emotionally, and one can also feel the effect physically. The tactile lends itself not to thinking of things as objects, but to considering how knowledge is produced through human interaction with textiles. In providing a tactile rhetorical approach, this material method functions to expand notions of what counts as rhetorical, what count as texts worth studying, and what counts as knowledge production within comp/rhet (such as is seen also in Baca's work with codices in *Mestiz@ Scripts* and Licona's work with zines). When we expand our notions of what counts as rhetorical work, the intellectual, creative work of women, artists, and activists becomes an imperative area to engage rhetorically in our field.

The value of a material method of rhetorical analysis lies in the possibilities of learning varied information through this particular nonalphabetic approach. Just as the information gleaned from a close reading of an alphabetic text, from conducting an ethnography, and from conducting archival research will all be different, quilting as a method of research provides the opportunity to engage in a tactile rhetorical approach through making a quilt with one's hands. Insofar as the field of comp/rhet is concerned with both composition *and* rhetoric, creating a quilt is thus situated so as to be a useful research method within our field. The quilter carefully considers the composition of the quilt as it is being created, and making a quilt to represent data creates many possibilities for research. In other words, the quilter-researcher is a rhetorician considering the rhetorical.[7] Moreover, quilter-researchers are engaging in a composing process as they make the quilt. For a comp/rhet scholar, creating a quilt is another possibility of data representation that delinks from traditional notions of research—alphabetic, empirical, and single-authored—as quilting employs a material method of research—tactile, experiential, and collaboratively constructed.

THE RECLAIMING WORK OF HISTORICAL AND MATERIAL METHODS

Acknowledging that decolonial historical methods are more expansive, and useful beyond the Chicanx[8] community, we use Chicanxs as an example because we are a colonized population, direct descendants of the colonized indigenous of the Americas to various extents. We can, therefore, identify as American Indians on the US Census, but we cannot claim rights due to our indigenous past as other American Indians can within the United States; however, that doesn't mean that Chicanxs are not indigenous to this land. In his powerful piece, "Xicana/o Indigenous Epistemologies: Toward a Decolonizing and Liberatory Education for Xicana/o Youth," Martín Sean Arce explores the importance of "the recognition and embracing of the Xicano/Xicana connection to the land of this continent, that which reifies their existence and humanity as Indigenous" (25). So, for Chicanxs, it can be detrimental to our conception of our humanity if we are not allowed to reclaim our connection to this land both spiritually and physically. If this sounds essentialist, it is imperative that the reader understand that one does not adopt the politically and historically conscious term *Chicanx* unless one is also aware of their colonized status and their indigenous past in an effort to reclaim lost and stolen parts of that past. As a matter of fact, reclaiming indigenous notions of the spirit can be essential for Chicanxs who have lost their way in an educational system that Arce claims is based on the dehumanization of those with colonial histories, namely Chicanxs.

To quote Margarita Berta-Ávila: "The experiences of oppression in the United States can be described as a mental-spiritual and social-material domination that is fueled by manipulation and alienation" (117). The erasure of these traditions has been detrimental for Chicanxs seeking to decolonize and reclaim our identities, especially within educational institutions that do not recognize us as Native Americans native to this land. It is disempowering when one group's worldview is discounted and outright ignored, when their "methodologies" for understanding their humanity are shunned, and when the world around them and their place within it are delegitimized. Berta-Ávila expands this notion:

> Xicanas/Xicanos are indigenous to the land on which they live. The land is the connection to their identity and their understanding of life. This connection is a threat to the growth of capitalism in the United States, thus making it necessary to impose on Xicanas/Xicanos a dehumanizing cultural hegemony. When Xicanas/Xicanos enter the schooling system, they come with a sense of displacement. Xicanas/Xicanos are not sure how to view themselves. . . . (qtd. in Arce 25)

Chicanxs' relationship to the Earth and the way we view our relationship to the Earth are not the same as the Cartesian split, as mentioned above. However, Chicanxs have been forcibly removed from their intimate ties to the land as capitalism views the land as a resource from which to extract resources for profit. This forced removal, both physical and spiritual, has caused a double displacement for Chicanxs, who are intimately tied to the history and lands of the Americas. The reclaiming of history through indigenous methods is, therefore, as much a spiritual practice as it is an intellectual practice because it draws upon indigenous ways of knowing and of making knowledge, also known as methods and methodologies. It is akin to the practice of curanderismo because it invites the practice of healing and serves as a type of "medicinal" practice that cures and revives while it reclaims the practices already in existence before colonization.

Also, the reclaiming work of quilting as method asserts that recentering tactile rhetorics support a methodology that values other ways of knowing including a nonalphabetic representation of research, creative labor, and the narratives of colonized people. These decolonial values reflected in material methods identify epistemic silences and colonial wounds to question disciplinary norms. Quilting as method addresses the epistemic silence surrounding quilt making as knowledge making and the colonial wounds that cause migration in order to tell the narrative of migration through tactile knowledges. The example used here is derived from the personal experience of creating a quilt for the Migrant Quilt Project, a group of volunteers that creates quilts from clothing left behind by migrants crossing the southern Arizona desert. Each quilt they create documents the names (or uses the term *unknown* for unidentified migrants) of migrants who have died in the Tucson Sector each year.[9] The quilt Arellano created documents 205 migrant deaths from 2002 to 2003 and maps each death onto an image of the state of Arizona to demonstrate visually the grave consequences of the US Border Patrol's Prevention through Deterrence program.[10] Although we discuss this quilt project and quilting as method here, we ask scholars to consider the value of other research projects and other tactile methods as well.

Quilting as method engages the tactile rhetoric of textile projects, like the Migrant Quilt Project, and allows scholars of rhetoric to contemplate the boundaries of what counts as rhetoric. Often scholars study traditional notions of rhetoric (alphabetic writing and speech) and visual rhetoric as separate areas of study. Although some scholarship complicates these demarcations, we believe we could benefit from considering a project such as quilts that facilitates the composing of alphabetic, visual, and tactile rhetorics all in the same text. With a textile project such as the Migrant Quilt Project, the quilter not only incorporates the names of dead migrants, but also creates beautiful and sometimes somber visual compositions. Additionally, the quilter incorporates tactile elements to feel the experience of migrants crossing the desert physically (for example, a self-mended pair of jeans) and emotionally (for example, the words copied from a love letter found in a pair of jeans). This method, then, rejects the confines of traditional alphabetic rhetoric, rooted in Western epistemologies, and reclaims the possibility of nonalphabetic composition research.

On the left: the words from a love letter found sewn into the waistband of a pair of jeans. This was included in the 2001–2002 quilt made by Cornelia Bayley. On the right: A self-pair of jeans mended at the hem because they were likely too long. This was included in the 2002–2003 quilt made by Sonia C. Arellano.

In order to heal the creative/intellectual split, quilting as method delinks from valuing only intellectual labor and values the creative labor of quilting as method—and rejects the idea that intellectual and creative labor are dichotomous. Frantz Fanon's claim that mastery brings one closer to being *"a real human being"* (qtd. in Mignolo 7) is reified in comp/rhet as we continue to undoubtedly value theory and quantitative work and still struggle to value creative labor as well. Quilting as method suggests that our field must move past valuing only alphabetic representations and empirical research and recognize that creative labor (along with the physical and emotional aspects of such labor) is a legitimate form of knowledge production. For example, in completing this quilt, Arellano felt physical pain from pressing an incredible number of seams and from drawing blood by pricking her fingers. She cried deconstructing a pair of child's jeans with the brand tag "Refuge" on the waistband and while writing the name of a girl who was the same age as she was in 2003, when she died crossing the desert and Arellano was on her way to college. These examples demonstrate how quilting as method is necessarily a kind of creative and intellectual labor that function together for the quilter to make meaning. In other words, reclaiming both sides of the creative/intellectual divide facilitates nuanced and expanded epistemologies.

Attempting to explain a phenomenon through storytelling, quilting as method values the work and narratives of colonized people. Therefore, quilting as method reclaims the stories and lives of dead migrants that the US government attempts to erase. The Migrant Quilt Project documents a (re)constructed narrative of migrants who, as the result from legacies of colonization, are forced to migrate. Most quilters intend to tell a story of migration that helps others understand the hardship migrants all too often face. As the quilter composes the quilt from various articles of clothing likely belonging to various people, a narrative is created by putting stories of the colonized side by side. Providing qualitative data representation as colonized people's stories asks the viewer to consider their narratives as a human story and less cold and distant than statistics.[11] Moreover, because the Migrant Quilt Project is grounded in recovering and reclaiming materials connected to the histories and violences of the geographical area, quilting as method facilitates the telling of these narratives in a tactile way. The decolonial nature of this is reclaiming the stories of dead migrants who otherwise would not be recognized. Perhaps this quilting project is the most powerful reclamation work of quilting as method, as implemented in the Migrant Quilt Project: Telling the stories of those who are actively being killed and erased by the US government.

Ultimately, quilting as method is not only beneficial for a researcher but also to a teacher. Arellano says, "My pedagogy is affected, regardless of the course I'm teaching, by the reclamation work of quilting as method. I ask my students to push the boundaries of rhetoric and composition to consider what can fall under these terms so we can value more than written texts and Western rhetors. I facilitate multimodal projects so students can consider composing more broadly and employ various rhetorical strategies to successfully consider their intellectual and creative labor as one." Lastly, Arellano asks her students to be critical in the projects they take on, particularly when considering marginalized populations. She asks them to write a document called "situating the researcher" to ar-

Wilson Graham Photography

ticulate their methods and methodologies, but, more important, to connect their human selves to their areas of study. This helps them to be critical of themselves and others regardless of the populations they are writing about or writing with. As with most methodologies, the reclaiming work of quilting as method affects research and teaching in seamless ways.

To end this section, we would like to offer some practical methods for performing a decolonial historical method that practices a type of healing through medicinal history. Here are some starting points to consider when engaging this highly sensitive practice. It involves shedding self-destructive notions of being an imposter and of being marginal, "not-good-enough," "uncivilized," and "emotional." The actions suggested in this toolkit will be difficult, contradictory, emancipatory, and healing to the heart, mind, and spirit of the colonized. The actions may upset others around you but may ultimately lead you to help create a more sustainable existence on earth. It also involves having the courage needed to see through on the following decolonial historical and material methods toolkit, which calls on one to:

- acknowledge that canonical notions of Western epistemology are in service to those whose work aligns with Eurocentric notions of rhetoric, typically the white male majority of academia;
- realize that shifting the center of understanding from the West to locations elsewhere involves an unwavering commitment to cultural and epistemological research and reclamation;
- be continually willing to shatter and delink from old notions of self with a profound commitment to constant renewal and spiritual recovery;
- be willing to constantly return the gaze from the colonized to the colonizer;
- create a social text such as a quilt to insert yourself as a researcher;
- draw from familial and tactile knowledges as an essential part of your research process;
- consider what can be gleaned from a material representation of your research; and
- consider and recognize whose colonial stories are being told or examined and by whom.
- Additionally, critical reflection is a key part of the toolkit. We suggest contemplating your place (how you are impacted and

implicated) within the social issue at hand and considering what is gained from considering the tactile rhetoric of your work.

LOOKING FORWARD IN COMP/RHET

Conquest, colonization, and racialization stem from a privileging of the West. In such a world, Eurocentrism is the default from which to measure everything that counts as knowledge and has produced what many scholars and researchers refer to as claims to objectivity and empirical observation of reality. The methods suggested here intend to challenge discursive effects of our colonial legacy by offering methods that delink from the colonial matrix of power. As we have demonstrated here, a decolonial method of historiography intends to see the value in cosmological understandings of the universe and the role that all humans play in the symbiotic, cyclic flow of life such as indigenous philosophies and epistemologies. Additionally, a feminist decolonial material method suggests scholars consider what the tactile has to offer in knowledge creation. Aligning with other contributions in this collection, we offer these methods as decolonial options in order to delink from the colonial matrix of power and demonstrate decolonial knowledge-making practices.

NOTES

1. Mexicas were a Nahuatl-speaking indigenous people of the Valley of Mexico who are known today as the rulers of the Aztec Empire.

2. What we refer to here is the professed need for more minoritized people as editors of prominent journals, as chairs of departments, and as heads of professional organizations; policies such as tenure and promotion that value community work and nontraditional and collaborative research; resources that allow academics to engage communities to benefit the communities, not just provide research for academia or feed atrocious discussions on listservs and in executive committees that present a complete disregard for minoritized people's ways of creating knowledge.

3. It should be noted that this article was in a special issue of *College English*.

4. Although the study of maker culture is not new in academia, its current popularity in our field is apparent with projects such as a *Digital*

Rhetoric Collaborative blog carnival in 2016 on the topic, as well as a half-day workshop at the 2017 Conference on College Composition and Communication titled "Handcrafted Rhetorics: DIY and the Public Power of Made Things."

5. For more on this argument see *Rhetorical Touch: Disability, Identification, Haptics,* by Shannon Walters.

6. For example, at my institution, within the category titled "Research and Creative Activities," the only mention of creative endeavors still discusses a creative work published in a journal, assuming the creative work is alphabetic writing.

7. Here I define *rhetoric* as the ways an object can intentionally move people to accomplish a particular goal as the rhetor is composing her text—a quilt.

8. Drawing upon Rubén Salazar's definition of *Chicano/a,* the term *Chicanx* brings an added element to the word *Chicano.* According to Salazar's "Who Is a Chicano? And What Do Chicanos Want?" "a Chicano/a is a Mexican-American with a non-Anglo view of him/herself" (B7). Today, when in the word *Chicanx* the "x" replaces the "o/a," it is intended to remove the gender binary and recognizes the European imposition of gender codes brought upon the indigenous by Spanish colonizers.

9. The Tucson Sector is determined by the US Border Patrol and encompasses almost the entire state of Arizona. The US Border Patrol and the Pima County Office of the Medical Examiner document migrant deaths per fiscal year, October 1 to September 30.

10. Prevention through Deterrence is a tactic implemented by the US Border Patrol to heavily patrol the more urban areas where migrants cross, intentionally pushing migrants to cross at more remote and dangerous areas in order to deter crossing. See DeLeón for more on how this tactic functions to blame nature and migrants for migrant deaths while absolving the US government of any blame.

11. Although there is plenty of work accepted about nonalphabetic rhetorics, the topic and author of that work affect its reception. As textiles are mostly written about by women, and also mainly made by women, this area is particularly underaddressed in the field.

WORKS CITED

Acuña, Rodolfo. *Occupied America: A History of Chicanos.* 2nd ed., Harper & Row, 1981.

Anzaldúa, Gloria. *Borderlands/La Frontera: The New Mestiza*. Aunt Lute, 1987.

Arce, Martín Sean. "Xicana/o Indigenous Epistemologies: Toward a Decolonizing and Liberatory Education for Xicana/o Youth." *"White" Washing American Education: The New Culture Wars in Ethnic Studies*, edited by Denise Sandoval, Anthony Ratcliff, Tracy Lachica Buenavista, and James R. Marín, Praeger, 2016, pp. 11–42.

Baca, Damián. *Mestiz@ Scripts, Digital Migrations, and the Territories of Writing*. Palgrave Macmillan, 2008.

———. "Rethinking Composition, Five Hundred Years Later." *JAC*, vol. 29, no. 1/2, 2009, pp. 229–42.

Ball, Helen K. "Quilts." *Handbook of the Arts in Qualitative Research: Perspectives, Methodologies, Examples, and Issues*, edited by J. Gary Knowles and Ardra L. Cole, SAGE, 2008, pp. 364–69.

Banks, Adam J. *Race, Rhetoric, and Technology: Searching for Higher Ground*. Lawrence Erlbaum and National Council of Teachers of English, 2006.

Barone, Tom, and Elliot W. Eisner. *Arts Based Research*. SAGE, 2012.

Berta-Avila, Margarita. "The Process of Conscientization: Xicanas/Xicanos Experiences in Claiming Authentic Voice." *Journal of Hispanic Higher Education*, vol. 2, no. 2, 2003, pp. 117–28.

Bizzell, Patricia, and Bruce Herzberg. *The Rhetorical Tradition: From Classical Times to the Present.* 2nd ed., Bedford/St. Martin's, 2000.

Bloom, Lynn Z. "Freshman Composition as a Middle-Class Enterprise." *College English*, vol. 58, no. 6, 1996, pp. 654–75.

Brereton, John C. *The Origins of Composition Studies in the American College, 1875–1925*. U of Pittsburgh P, 1996.

Connal, Louise Rodríguez. "Hybridity: A Lens for Understanding Mestizo/a Writers." *Crossing Borderlands: Composition and Postcolonial Studies,* edited by Andrea A. Lunsford and Lahoucine Ouzgane, U of Pittsburgh P, 2004, pp. 199–217.

Connors, Robert. *Composition-Rhetoric: Backgrounds, Theory, and Pedagogy.* U of Pittsburgh P, 1997.

Crowley, Sharon. *Composition in the University: Historical and Polemical Essays.* U of Pittsburgh P, 1998.

Decker, Geoffrey. "Hispanics Identifying Themselves as Indians." *New York Times,* 3 July 2011. https://www.nytimes.com/2011/07/04/nyregion/more-hispanics-in-us-calling-themselves-indian.html.

De León, Jason. *The Land of Open Graves: Living and Dying on the Migrant Trail.* U of California P, 2015.

Deleuze, Gilles, and Félix Guattari. *A Thousand Plateaus: Capitalism and Schizophrenia.* Continuum, 2008.

Delgado, Richard. "The Imperial Scholar: Reflections on a Review of Civil Rights Literature." *University of Pennsylvania Law Review,* vol. 132, no. 3, 1984, pp. 561–78.

Douglass, Wallace. "Rhetoric for the Meritocracy." *English in America: A Radical View of the Profession,* edited by Richard Ohmann, Oxford UP, 1976, pp. 97–132.

Faigley, Lester. *Fragments of Rationality: Postmodernity and the Subject of Composition.* U of Pittsburgh P, 1992.

García de Müeller, Genevieve, and Iris Ruiz. "Race, Silence, and Writing Program Administration: A Qualitative Study of U.S. College Writing Programs." *WPA: Writing Program Administration,* vol. 40, no. 2, 2017, pp. 19–39.

Glenn, Cheryl, and Krista Ratcliffe, editors. *Silence and Listening as Rhetorical Arts.* Southern Illinois UP, 2011.

Goggin, Maureen Daly. "Visual Rhetoric in Pens of Steel and Inks of Silk: Challenging the Great Visual/Verbal Divide." *Defining Visual Rhetorics,* edited by Charles A. Hill and Marguerite Helmers, Lawrence Erlbaum, 2004, pp. 87–110.

Graff, Gerald, and Cathy Birkenstein. *"They Say/I Say": The Moves That Matter in Academic Writing,* 4th ed., W. W. Norton, 2017.

Gries, Laurie E. *Still Life with Rhetoric: A New Materialist Approach for Visual Rhetorics.* Utah State UP, 2015.

Heath, Shirley Brice. *Ways with Words: Language Life and Work in Communities and Classrooms.* Cambridge UP, 1983.

Herrick, James A. *The History and Theory of Rhetoric: An Introduction.* 5th ed., Pearson, 2012.

Kirsch, Gesa, and Patricia A. Sullivan. *Methods and Methodology in Composition Research.* Southern Illinois UP, 1992.

Kitzhaber, Albert R. *Rhetoric in American Colleges, 1850–1900.* Southern Methodist UP, 1990.

León-Portilla, Miguel. *The Broken Spears: The Aztec Account of the Conquest of Mexico.* Translated from Nahuatl into Spanish by Ángel María Garibay K., English translation by Lysander Kemp, Beacon Press, 1962.

Levins Morales, Aurora. *The Historian as Curandera.* The Julian Samora Research Institute, Working Paper #40, Michigan State University, 1998.

Licona, Adela C. *Zines in Third Space: Radical Cooperation and Borderlands Rhetoric.* State U of New York P, 2012.

Martinez, Aja Y. "A Plea for Critical Race Theory Counterstory: Stock Story versus Counterstory Dialogues Concerning Alejandra's 'Fit' in the Academy." *Composition Studies*, vol. 42, no. 2, 2014, pp. 33–55.

McKinnon, Sara L., et al. "Introduction: Articulating Text and Field in the Nodes of Rhetorical Scholarship." *Text + Field: Innovations in Rhetorical Method*, edited by McKinnon et al., Penn State UP, 2016, pp. 1–21.

Mignolo, Walter. "Epistemic Disobedience, Independent Thought and Decolonial Freedom." *Theory, Culture and Society*, vol. 26, no. 7–8, 2009, pp. 159–81.

Miller, Susan. *Textual Carnivals: The Politics of Composition.* Southern Illinois UP, 1991.

Mohanty, Chandra Talpade. *Feminism without Borders: Decolonizing Theory, Practicing Solidarity*. Duke UP, 2003.

Morris, Charles E., III, ed. *The AIDS Memorial Quilt at 20: Commemoration and Critique of the Epidemic Text.* Spec. issue of *Rhetoric & Public Affairs*, vol. 10, no. 4, 2007, pp. 557–754.

Moss, Beverly J. "Ethnography and Composition: Studying Language at Home." *Methods and Methodology in Composition Research*, edited by Gesa Kirsch and Patricia A. Sullivan, Southern Illinois UP, 1992, pp. 153–71.

Ohmann, Richard M. *English in America: A Radical View of the Profession*. Oxford UP, 1976.

———. *Politics of Letters*. Wesleyan UP, 1987.

Pratt, Mary Louise. *Imperial Eyes: Travel Writing and Transculturation*. 2nd ed., Routledge, 2007.

Prendergast, Catherine. *Literacy and Racial Justice: The Politics of Learning after Brown v. Board of Education*. Southern Illinois UP, 2003.

Ramírez, Cristina Devereaux. *Occupying Our Space: The Mestiza Rhetorics of Mexican Women Journalists and Activists, 1875–1942*. U of Arizona P, 2015.

Rickert, Thomas. *Ambient Rhetoric: The Attunements of Rhetorical Being*. U of Pittsburgh P, 2013.

Riedner, Rachel, and Kevin Mahoney. *Democracies to Come: Rhetorical Action, Neoliberalism, and Communities of Resistance*. Lexington Books, 2008.

Royster, Jacqueline Jones. *Traces of a Stream: Literacy and Social Change among African American Women*. U of Pittsburgh P, 2000.

Royster, Jacqueline Jones, and Jean C. Williams. "History in the Spaces Left: African American Presence and Narratives of Composition Studies." *College Composition and Communication*, vol. 50, no. 4, 1999, pp. 563–84.

Ruiz, Iris D. "Race." *Decolonizing Rhetoric and Composition Studies: New Latinx Keywords for Theory and Pedagogy*, edited by Iris D. Ruiz and Raúl Sánchez, Palgrave Macmillan, 2016, pp. 3–16.

———. *Reclaiming Composition for Chicano/as and Other Ethnic Minorities: A Critical History and Pedagogy*. Palgrave Macmillan, 2016.

Ruiz, Iris D., and Raúl Sánchez, eds. *Decolonizing Rhetoric and Composition Studies: New Latinx Keywords for Theory and Pedagogy*. Palgrave-Macmillan, 2016.

Sánchez, Raúl. "Writing." *Decolonizing Rhetoric and Composition Studies: New Latinx Keywords for Theory and Pedagogy*, edited by Iris D. Ruiz and Raúl Sánchez, Palgrave Macmillan, 2016, pp. 77–89.

Shivers-McNair, Ann. *Making, Marking, Mattering: What We Can Learn about Writing, Rhetoric, and Technology from a Makerspace.* 2017. U of Washington, PhD dissertation.

Sohan, Vanessa Kraemer. "'But a quilt is more': Recontextualizing the Discourse(s) of Gee's Bend Quilts." *College English*, vol. 77, no. 4, 2015, pp. 294–316.

Sternglass, Marilyn S. *Time to Know Them: A Longitudinal Study of Writing and Learning at the College Level.* Lawrence Erlbaum, 1997.

Villanueva, Victor, Jr.. *Bootstraps: From an American Academic of Color*. National Council of Teachers of English, 1993.

———. "Memoria Is a Friend of Ours: On the Discourse of Color." *College English*, vol. 67, no. 1, 2004, pp. 9–19.

———. "The Rhetorics of the New Racism and the Four Master Tropes." *FYHC: First-Year Honors Composition*, vol. 1, 2006.

Walters, Shannon. *Rhetorical Touch: Disability, Identification, Haptics*. U of South Carolina P, 2014.

Yacatsol. "La Cultura Nos Cura." *YouTube,* https://www.youtube.com/watch?v=LvRu9DXRmf8.

6

Beyond Colonial Hegemonies: Writing Scholarship and Pedagogy with Nyāyasutra

Shyam Sharma
State University of New York, Stony Brook

> तन्त्राधकिरणाभ्युपगमसंस्थतिि: "सद्धिान्त:" . . . . सर्वतन्त्रा वरिुद्धस्तन्त्रेऽधकि्रृतोऽर्थ: "सर्वतन्त्रसद्धिान्त:" ।।१।१।२६-२८।।
>
> —*The Nyāya Sūtras of Gotama* first century CE
>
> Translation: An established tenet is a [principle] resting on the authority of a certain school, hypothesis, or implication. . . . A [principle] of all schools is [or becomes] a tenet which is not opposed by any school. . . .
>
> —Satis Chandra Vidyâbhusana

> By pointing out that academic traditions of Western universities are built on several centuries of economic and cultural imperialism, [postcolonial] theory demands that scholars and teachers of literature and literacies ask rhetorical questions the answers to which had been for many years assumed: who speaks? on behalf of whom? who is listening? and how?
>
> —Susan Jarratt

> I invite us to read all of [the comments] through, once again, and listen to ourselves. . . . [observing] a disturbing consistency that may reflect the culture, I fear: invective; intentions to disparage, humiliate, defeat; exclusivity; sarcasm; cynicism. . . . How about urbane, democratic, cultivating, respectful, tolerant, edifying, mentoring, compassionate, friendly. . . ?
>
> —Chris Paris

Chris Paris's invitation above is his appeal to prior commenters to be less antagonistic to Joseph Kugelmass, a then doctoral student in English at a California university who had written an article they didn't like. The comments had criticized Kugelmass and/or his writing as ill-informed, disingenuous, baffling, disappointing, flabbergasting, distressing, sloppy, an embarrassment for the venue and to his graduate school as well as himself, likely to scare away search committees on the job market, playing a zero-sum game, and squabbling over crumbs that fall from academy's table. In his response, Paris urges the scholars to take a different approach that "edif[ies] each other . . . through the process of rhetoric that shares invention, agreement, disagreement, diversity, disparity . . . ," asking them to consider "mentoring" the writer by simply recommending appropriate readings instead of "contradict[ing] invitation with denigrating hegemonic word choice and tone." Indeed, viewed differently, the writer seems to be using common academic skills taught in graduate school: making an "intervention" in the scholarship by using strong "arguments" and "contention" to create a "niche" and to "occupy" it. In the accusations in the comments section that the student writer was essentially claiming first-year writing as a territory of English using that same agonistic approach, it is hard to miss echoes of territorial struggle. The aggressive defenses of composition studies remind us that disciplines, like nation-states and other social institutions, are built upon power dynamics, colonial legacies, and imperial forces, as well as ideologically constructed histories. The history of rhetoric and composition is a construct that is claimed to parallel the establishment of the United States as a colony, then back to the British, then Roman, then Greek empires (Jarratt; Baca)—while it largely continues to ignore other cultural and intellectual inputs as well as the destruction and suppression of other rhetorical traditions and histories along the way. What is striking, and pertinent to my argument, is how  confrontation/countering and domination/defense get normalized as an essential aspect of mainstream agonistic rhetoric, which has for the most part made other types and elements of rhetoric all but invisible in the West and increasingly beyond, as well as in how scholarly discourse and disciplines function more broadly.

The second quotation in the epigraph is from one of the scholars of rhetoric or composition who have called for or used postcolonial or decolonial theories which, I will argue in this chapter, can help us productively explore histories and dynamics of power, including how disciplines normalize conflict, develop intellectual complacency about marginalization, and perpetuate hegemony,[1] as well as how academic discourses describe argument as confrontation, persuasion as conversion, scholarship as product, quality as rigor, and so on. Besides Susan Jarratt, who draws on postcolonial theory, I will draw on Damián Baca as another rhetoric and composition scholar whose work draws on decolonial theory and therefore provides relevant perspectives for theorizing power and ethos in this chapter. To borrow the words of Sabelo Ndlovu-Gatsheni, the decolonizing of knowledge production, as distinct from postcolonial critique of its hegemony in the global era, involves the "teasing out [of] epistemological issues [and] politics of knowledge generation, as well as questions of who generates which knowledge, and for what purpose" (11). While building on postcolonial critique of the hegemony of Greco-Roman-Anglo-American agonistic rhetoric, I offer decolonial strategies for countering that hegemony in scholarship and pedagogy.[2]

The Sanskrit words and their translation in the first quotation above describe consensus-building rules for productive argumentation established by the Nyāyasutra tradition[3] of ancient South Asia. In Nyāya rhetoric, a rhetor must work from a position of fairness and truth, by positively "ascertaining" facts and propositions, determining questions "through the removal of doubt," and engaging and hearing out both or all sides. Hence, the more accepted the tenets behind a rhetorical process the more reliable the outcomes of argumentation.

The three excerpts in the epigraph above are *not* meant to juxtapose the different rhetorical practices or cultures with one another, or to generalize about them. Instead, I intend to foreground the element of "justice," which I posit is present in any rhetorical tradition or practice but is suppressed when other elements are dominant—as we see in the call for a different approach by the commenter on the *Inside Higher Ed* article. My objective in this chapter is to illustrate how perspectives from outside rhetoric and composition, namely postcolonial and decolonial theory as well as Nyāya rhetoric, can help us appreciate the sense of justice as a critical element of ethos and therefore of sound arguments and productive rhetoric. I argue that such a foregrounding of justice can help the study and practice of rhetoric to radically rethink dominant views about argumentation. It would help us explain, for instance, how the seemingly naïve suggestion of mentoring an "adversary" would be feasible, even necessary, in order to alleviate the "threat" of ignorance, ego, or aggression, thereby creating room for professionally and socially beneficial discourse out of difference and conflict. I argue that we must find ways of framing rhetoric as a means for seeking truth and understanding, especially toward effecting social justice. In order to do so, we must shift our discipline's focus from debate and confrontation toward more engagement, from persuasion and conversion toward more conversation, from rejection and exclusion toward more inclusion, from hierarchy and hegemony toward more harmony—at least where such shifts are intellectually productive or socially feasible. Thus, this chapter builds on Jarratt's questions for and Baca's critique of our discipline for examining what discourses dominate in the discipline and who speaks them, as well as applying Keith Lloyd's ("Culture"; "Multivalent"; "Rethinking") explanations of argumentation toward a three-dimensional theory of ethos that relies primarily on justice (Nyāya or similar rhetorics) and offsets the effect of power/domination (agonistic rhetoric) and identity politics (postcolonial discourse). My interest is in advancing a conversation about what rhetorical traditions and approaches from beyond the Western mainstream could be drawn upon and adapted for pursuing greater equity and fairness through scholarship and pedagogy of writing and rhetoric as we also seek the advancement of our discipline.

To set the context with a brief preview of Nyāya tradition before I explore its value for scholarship and discuss its potential uses in pedagogy, the process of a typical Nyāya argument involves "a proposition, a reason, an explanatory example, an application of the example, and statement of the conclusion" (Sinha 171) whereby rhetors participate in (rather than just presenting or trying to impose) their argument *(tarka)*. Perception-enhancing conversation *(vada)* with the audience is foregrounded against the rhetor's own position and her or his need for persuading the audience. The sutras (rules or procedures) recommend confutation as a means for establishing validity of a statement *only* if the opposite seems absurd or contradictory—not because the rhetor wants to confute it based on desire, ego, or benefit for self. In fact, to counter a position for the sake of victory would be "wrangling" *(jalpa)* rather than engaging in fair argumentation *(vada)*: "Wrangling aims at gaining victory by means of quibbles and analogues" (Sinha 171) and is therefore prohibited, in all its manifestations like cavil (merely attacking opposing views), fallacy (erratic reasons), quibble (opposition using alternative meanings), and analogue (opposition based on unsupported similarity or dissimilarity). As pointed out by Lloyd ("Culture"), a scholar who has made the greatest contribution toward familiarizing Western audience with the Nyāyasutra tradition, one way to understand Nyāya argumentation is to view it as a unique combination of Aristotle's enthymeme and example: "Rather than reasoning through a chain of inter-related statements, Nyāya develops the idea that reasoning must be based in a dominant analogy" (77). This chapter draws upon Lloyd's theorization of Nyāyasutra, as well as building on a source text by Vidyâbhusana (including my own translation of Sanskrit text in the case of a few terms).

SCHOLARSHIP: FROM HEGEMONY TO HARMONY

> Composition specialists often perceive their vocation from a colonial vantage point. As seen from within a Eurocentric narrative, Composition's rhetorical history is rationalized across the globe from East to West, from Ancient Greece to Modern America. (Baca 229)

Scholars of rhetoric have sought to create intellectual and curricular space for studying and teaching different rhetorical traditions, especially by pointing out limitations and insufficiency, contradictions and difficulties posed by mainstream Western rhetorical theory. As Roberta Binkley and Marissa Smith state, "While Aristotelian theory provides powerful conceptual tools and vocabulary, scholars such as Enos, Glenn, Jarratt, Neel, Swearingen, and others have well documented its limitations, frequently offering the sophistic tradition as an alternative"; broadly put, as the authors further note, citing Thomas Miller, the one canonical rhetorical "tradition" is largely a fiction that has outlasted its usefulness. And as Baca illustrates in the article quoted above, the teaching and study of writing have historically played, and continue to play, a sociopolitical (broadly, colonizing) role in US society and on a global scale today. Yet even though composition scholars are aware of the colonial legacy of their discipline and even though they theoretically subscribe to the notion of "diversity," they continue to buy into the "Eurocentric myth [that links] the Western Roman alphabet to rationality, critical agency, and social equality" (Baca 230–31), thereby helping perpetuate colonial legacies and their hegemonic forces within the discipline and in society.

The hegemony of agonistic rhetoric is so prevalent that academic mentors advise students to avoid being seen as challenging the canon, as happened in my own case when I first started writing this work about a decade ago. Growing up in Nepal and India, I had read about Nyāya rhetoric and I understood the terminology (some of which was used in daily life[4]); later, when I started teaching writing as a graduate student instructor in the United States, I was so inspired by how productive concepts from this tradition were for teaching writing that I wanted to share my teaching experience through a journal article. Unfortunately, even though I found some writing on the subject (e.g., Lloyd, "Rethinking"; Stroud) in rhetoric journals, I kept developing and discarding drafts for several years because I couldn't muster the courage to make an "intervention" as I understood scholarship to be by definition at the time. My anxiety stemmed from reading harsh responses to unconventional perspectives in the scholarship,[5] as with online discussions like the above; indeed, I learned to define intellectual progress in terms of barriers not engagement, scarcity not opportunity, victory not fairness. The manner in which power and hegemony shape scholarship is reflected, as I now see, at the end of ten bullet points that stayed at the top of my latest discarded draft from about seven years ago: "Be careful not to criticize the history of rhetoric, or 'brand' yourself as the person who wrote about an 'exotic' topic." As a graduate student on the job market, I took that piece of advice, given by a senior scholar in the department, so seriously that I gave up on the topic, once again. Since then, I instead kept learning about, and developing courses that focused on or integrated, different rhetorical traditions, strategically avoiding or diluting the "exotic" element in the process. I gave up because I didn't realize how misleading the metaphor of "space" could be when it comes to disciplines as intellectual and cultural domains rather than physical (physically limited) and political (limiting due to power dynamics) ones. As I return to the topic and reread the advice about not writing oneself into an exotic corner, I am struck by how its pragmatism is shaped by hegemony and how disciplinary socialization uses "disciplining" rather than creating increasingly inclusive communities within and across political/cultural borders.

Scholarship and pedagogy of rhetoric and composition have certainly, and tremendously, helped to advance literacy education, enlightening millions of students in North America and beyond, especially empowering increasingly diverse learners whom institutions send to writing classrooms and programs for learning basic to advanced communicative skills. Many writing scholars also teach about society and culture, with justice and dignity for all as the content and often the objective of the rhetorical education. Knowledge and pride in this fact, however, should not prompt members of the discipline to ignore the fact that rhetoric and composition have also been put to less dignified use and still have the potential to perpetuate injustice and unfairness for some students (see esp. Baca). As Native American and African American scholars, and increasingly Asian American and other minority scholars, have shown through their work, claims and contradictions of Greco-Roman-Anglo-American rhetoric are not just abstract and innocuous intellectual issues; historically, some of the them have been distant and not-so-distant kin to ethnonationalism and racial supremacy, colonization and cultural destruction. A case that Scott Richard Lyons relays from the story of Luther Standing Bear illustrates how literacy education has been used to enforce ethnonationalist and racist policies. When children arrived at a school, they saw a number of "white men's names" on the board. Those "arbitrary, meaningless names were selected by students . . . [which were] then written on cloth and sewed on the back of each student's shirt" (448). Lyons interprets this incident as symbolic of the imposition of the dominant literacy and epistemology upon the native peoples. So, for instance, when I face a Native American student in a writing classroom, I cannot just be proud about it as an encounter of one "global citizen" with another, ready to start "working on" global or local issues. As a sensitive educator, I must also see it as an occasion for understanding and helping to counter the legacy of marginalization and injustice that the student may still be affected by. As scholars and educators, we must learn and grow from every occasion we can.

More than thirty years ago, Carolyn Matalene called for greater attention to cultural differences in writing styles, pointing out the American history of rhetoric as ultimately ethnocentric, which she argued was a "less and less appropriate response" in a globalizing world (790). J. Vernon Jensen drew similar contrasts and urged scholars of rhetoric and writing not to ignore other rhetorical traditions:

> Our profession since its origin has dutifully analyzed the rhetoric of Greece, Rome, Britain, and the United States, but has ignored over half of the globe. We have exhausted ourselves probing the Western rhetorical heritage. . . . [but] have overlooked the rhetorical heritage of the East, which honors nonexpression, silence, . . . and the avoidance of clash of opinion in order to preserve harmony. (135)

In the 1990s, even as more scholarship on non-Western rhetoric was produced in the field of rhetoric, mainstream scholarship on composition pedagogy did not show much enthusiasm for drawing on the broadening base of rhetoric. Instead, scholars and teachers of writing seemed interested in advancing (or making relevant) North American writing studies elsewhere in the world, an interest that continues to be expressed in a variety of ways, ranging from disrespectful to informed about other societies and cultures.

The desire to learn from and use rhetorics from other cultures remains less common than an interest in "globalizing" the discipline, as in expanding its reach. For instance, Mary Muchiri and her coauthors lamented that in spite of "huge growth" in the profession, "composition remain[ed] largely restricted to the United States and Canada" (175); the authors' objective was to examine "what happens to the published literature on [North American] composition in [the academic] contexts" (176) of other countries. While writing pedagogies from other countries are increasingly shared in the scholarship, most authors do not ask whether the flow of knowledge is occurring in the other direction, from the rest of the world to North America (see Donahue). In fact, by separating academic exchange from the colonizing influence of multinational corporations and development agencies, scholars ignore the hegemony that exchange of knowledge can perpetuate if they do not address the unequal political and economic conditions of that exchange. Good intentions do not help to counter the global hegemony of Western knowledge.

More generally, the selection and exclusion of geopolitical spaces, assumptions about political regimes and cultural values, and the mode of production of disciplinary knowledge and practices of dominant societies is part of the "theoretical narrative" within which composition works in the North American university (Binkley and Smith) and seeks to grow into a globally relevant academic discipline. As Arabella Lyon and Banu Özel have argued more recently, the knowledge of discursive traditions of other societies and cultures is still lacking in composition studies, even more so than in theoretical scholarship in rhetoric. In spite of the recognition of the "global turn" in both rhetoric and writing studies (Hesford), significant conversations about how to engage with the "imagined global geography" are yet to emerge in mainstream scholarship.

In the past few years, a more diverse set of scholars have started to respond to the calls for the diversification of rhetoric, also creating more resources for writing pedagogy. Responding to Wendy Hesford's call for reflection about that possibility, especially by examining "ways in which scholars imperil or safeguard disciplinary identities and methods that take for granted the nation-state and citizen-subject as units of analysis and ignore the global forces shaping individual lives and literate practices" (789), Morris Young points out examples of work by scholars[6] who have started foregrounding that "global geography" that not only straddles national boundaries but is also obscured right within the history of nations like the United States. Then he argues that there is much more to be done to understand how "global forces shap[e] individual lives and literate practices," asking:

> How does challenging the nation-state and citizen-subjects as the object of analysis reveal larger networks of activity? . . . How do we think across space both in terms of movement across actual borders between nations or locations and movement across discursive spaces that regulate the status and activity of people? (131)

The questions that Young asks do not just describe theoretical and hypothetical possibilities of shifting focus from nation-state and citizen-subject as units of analysis, and the global turn is not just about facing political forces with intellectual arguments today: it is also about making visible and audible people and communities who were obscured by disciplinary histories shaped by colonialist and imperialist national histories and hegemonies.

One of the reasons that new voices and perspectives have been very slow to appear and are still very limited in mainstream scholarship seems to be a consistent resistance and defensive response to calls for change. Scholars of feminist rhetoric have been the most prominent group who have critiqued tradition and offered new perspectives for a long time; but their work seems to be met with resistance or uninterest decade after decade. For instance, when C. H. Knoblauch and Lil Brannon critiqued the teaching of rhetoric and writing in North America and called for seriously broadening the scope of rhetoric, instead of responding to the call critics faulted the book for assuming that the "Western" tradition was a monolithic one. In a conference paper, Lloyd ("Multivalent") systematically illustrated how scholars who do not like new proposals made by feminist scholars—for instance, toward adopting more invitational rhetoric—have used the same old agonistic rhetoric to reject the proposals. In making such a proposal, Sonja Foss and Cindy Griffin, for instance, had acknowledged the need for different kinds of rhetoric in different contexts, but their critics rejected the suggestions by arguing that invitational rhetoric "presupposes" the "rare" condition of "equality among interlocutors"—such as at country clubs and in boardrooms. Such framing new approaches within either/or arguments—which cast new ideas as radical, useless, uninformed, or simply similar to what already exists in the dominant tradition—is very common.

The same agonistic view of discourse shapes academic disciplines and professions, defining, for instance, the "quality" of scholarship by "rigor" in the sense of the most informed and authoritative ideas in the mainstream. While such focus on rigor has rapidly advanced knowledge and greatly improved both the methods and the quality of scholarship, the assumption that competition is always productive has also turned exclusion into an ideal and often into an actual measurement of quality (such as the percentages of rejections by journals). This dominant regime also justifies the obsessive demand for a polished surface as essential to quality, even though it is more of a byproduct of exclusionary mechanisms. It also prevents quality from being defined in more than one way—such as theoretical and practitioner-based, rigorous and experimental, procedural and product-focused, experiential and objective, communal and translocal, competitive and conversational—even as such possibilities are becoming more practicable with modern technology and already implemented in some scholarship venues.

Postcolonial critique of hegemonic organizations and processes helps us explain problems with quality based on exclusion; unfortunately, its demand for inclusion and resistance can often lead to the creation of specialized margins (such as "special interest groups" at conferences, "special issues" in journals, and separate collections like this book) that the majority can conveniently continue to ignore. So to the extent to which this dynamic of who gets to speak and what subjects and perspectives are included in the conversation goes into the domain of power and hegemony, theories of power and resistance need to be supplemented with theories of justice and fairness, viewing "space" not as literal and necessarily limited but as a misleading metaphor that may need to be rejected. New theories of ethos and authority must be adopted for also rethinking such issues as the "prestige" of scholarship in terms of numbers and diversity of contributors (postcolonial view) and further by asking what causes were pursued by the contributors beyond their own self-interest (view of justice).

Enhancing theories of power and of identity with rhetorics of justice, such as that of Nyāya, could also help alleviate anxieties among scholars who often worry that they may coopt or abuse marginalized or new traditions for their own benefit, misrepresent those traditions, or fail to "do justice" to their uniqueness or complexity. LuMing Mao states that "Chinese American rhetoric became viable and transformative not by securing a logical, unified, or unique order, but by participating in a process of becoming. . . ." ("Rhetorical" 426). When we shift attention from tradition, resistance, and representation, we can prevent the perfect from being the enemy of the good. Similarly, for scholars who typically avoid difficult topics because they are not "experts," Nyāya offers the powerful idea of an ethos of social and intellectual purpose, instead of prior knowledge and expertise. Cause-based rhetoric can also avoid the weaknesses of postcolonial perspectives that often discourage novices, outsiders, and insiders alike—especially in relation to specialized or politically sensitive topics—from entering the "fray" because it locates ethos in identity and subject position. It also doesn't easily let scholars and scholarship in the mainstream "off the hook." In light of such inhibitions and entry barriers, Nyāya is capable of inviting and engaging different groups and interests because it finds ethos in the purpose of justice and the pursuit of truth, discouraging divisions and agonistic dynamics and encouraging collaboration and mutual understanding. While social and intellectual purposes do not in themselves compel anyone to pursue them, a focus on truth and justice can alleviate the challenges of uninterest among powerful or majority groups, as well as mitigating anxiety among powerless or minority communities.

Thus on the one hand, by drawing on postcolonial theory as a political theory of power and representation, we can explain how foundational narratives and concepts shape and maintain disciplinary identity and boundaries, especially by foregrounding exclusionary mechanisms and effects of seemingly apolitical processes like "peer review" and "quality," "experts" and "specialization." On the other hand, because ethos based on the intellectual authority of individuals and the identities of groups is an incomplete vehicle for advancing knowledge and the social work that we want rhetoric to do, we further need versatile theories of ethos, such as theories and strategies for decolonizing knowledge production, that incorporate identity and collaboration, inclusion and equity, justice and fairness in order for our discipline to be productive and progressive.

PEDAGOGY: JUSTICE AS CATALYST FOR CHANGE

> . . . everyone would agree that we are in the midst of reexamining how we study the histories of rhetoric. Unfortunately, no one has said much about how we teach them. (Miller, "Teaching the Histories of Rhetoric as a Social Praxis," 70)

Both of Miller's statements above seem largely true today, even after a quarter-century; while a number of scholars have written about the colonial legacy and cultural hegemony of rhetoric, their contribution seems to have only formed specialized spaces in the margins of rhetoric, making even less impact in mainstream composition pedagogy. In fact, similar observations can be found in scholarship produced in each decade starting with the 1970s,[7] such as when

Scott Stroud states: "Although research has been done concerning the one-sided nature of much of communication theory . . . more work needs to be undertaken to explicitly analyze, justify, and consider alternative ontological orientations in a complete conception of the practice of rhetoric" (147). In this section, I discuss how teaching provides distinct opportunities to effect change, allowing the use of different rhetorical traditions and resources to function as a catalyst. Teaching or drawing upon rhetorical traditions from beyond the hegemonic mainstream can help decolonize knowledge making as well as advancing causes of social justice through writing education.

Nyāya rhetoric can be used for foregrounding the element of justice and fairness, starting with classroom conversation where students are invited to explore issues at hand, contributing to collective understanding rather than trying to change others' minds. It can help prepare students for social and professional lives where understanding is more often necessary and beneficial than persuasion. This argument from and for justice can also help develop future teachers' powerful pedagogical methods, thereby promoting rhetorical education as a means for effecting an informed, civic, and responsible citizenry. The argument in favor of Nyāya, therefore, lies not just in its "practicality" but also in its educational potential and its potential as a catalyst for change.

One pedagogically promising aspect of Nyāya rhetoric is *avayava,* often called "Indian syllogism" but originally a broader method of presenting and exploring arguments. As described by Satis Chandra Vidyâbhusana, avayava is a process described within a rhetorical theory that instructs rhetors to adopt positive elements and uses of rhetoric (1–10 in the following list) while avoiding negative ones (11–16): 1. *pramana:* means of valid knowledge; 2. *prameya:* objects of valid knowledge; 3. *samshaya:* doubt; 4. *prayojana:* purpose; 5. *dristanta:* example/analogy; 6. *siddhanta:* conclusion; 7. *avayava:* the constituents of argument; 8. *tarka:* argumentation; 9. *nirnaya:* ascertainment; 10. *vada:* debate; 11. *jalpa:* disputation; 12. *vitanda:* destructive criticism; 13. *hetvabhasa:* fallacy; 14. *chala:* quibble; 15. *jāti:* refutations; and 16. *nigrahasthana:* points of the opponent's defeat. The most cited avayeva (7) include five stages, including a *pratigya*, or hypothesis/proposition that needs exploration for validity and truthfulness; a *hetu,* or specific reason/statement of reason based on the larger purpose/prayojana or use of the argument for advancing the argument; a *drishtanta,* or example/analogy, which is critical to understanding because it uses a familiar or agreed-upon case for discussing a new or controversial one; an *upanayana*, or reaffirmation (not repetition) that inductively expresses the finding from analogy; and a *nigamana,* or conclusion (or drawing of conclusion) that applies the finding from particularities of the exploration toward a general argument.

Nyāya guidelines like the above can seem overwhelming because they involve a plethora of terms and concepts. However, it is neither necessary nor productive to introduce too many details in writing courses (except when this tradition is a major or sole curricular focus). Instead, writing teachers can explore key features of argumentation, identify useful affordances provided by these new concepts, and highlight distinctions by avoiding simplistic comparisons with mainstream rhetoric. For instance, they could focus on how, instead of an argument starting with a statement and then using "analogy" as part of illustration, the avayeva treats the analogy as an exploratory device where a claim is pending analogical and ethical investigation; they could also show how the argumentation uses "reaffirmation," a distinct step linking analogy to "conclusion" that was at first a potential argument. Analogies, understood as "illustrations" (dristanta, literally meaning "end of sight," which implies caution against blind spots), are a key component of the avayeva and ideally draw on experiences or knowledge that are shared between rhetor and audience. Similarly, the approach encourages using pramana, or means/proof of valid knowledge, that can be tested with perception or direct experience of objects/processes, developed with inferences made from new ideas tested against established knowledge, analogy or knowledge from perception of similarity and difference, and the verbal testimony of knowledgeable people. Likewise, a focus on samsaya, or doubt as to whether a proposition can be validated, emphasizes the need for a debate among those who share a genuine purpose: "Its categories outline the rhetorical context—the method removes doubt by combining perceived and inferred relationships with an acceptable example—while the 'members' provide 'limbs' from which to hang one's arguments" (Lloyd, "Rethinking" 369). What looks like the general premise of Aristotelian syllogism is actually more of a hypothesis rather than a statement of truth, and it is meant to allow rhetor and audience to test its truth value with shared knowledge and experience as needed; the concrete example (rather than an abstract principle or accepted truth) embodies the argument in the making.

While Nyāya does recognize the value of conflict/tension, it recommends purposeful and ethically driven use of "opposing viewpoints" as rhetorical devices rather than "positions" describing and limiting participants. This is certainly not to suggest that other rhetorical traditions don't allow rhetors to shift their position; but Nyāya turns the possibility into a critical aspect of the process of argumentation, also asking rhetors to deliberately remove impediments against changing their own minds. Some modern rhetoricians have argued that "All of Aristotelian dialectic falls within this class of wrangling" (Simonson 205) even while acknowledging that Aristotle did believe that "the end of victory could be approached via the means of fair and unprejudiced argument." But even if we do not cast Nyāya argument in such stark contrast with other approaches, it is significant that in Nyāya the goal is "not" victory and hence the means of argument are "less likely" to be spurious (to use a qualification Simonson notes).

In any writing class and at any level, a Nyāyasutra approach to argumentation can help enhance reading and research, discussion and development of ideas. For example, in an assignment I call a "discussion argument," my students deliberately withhold starting, including, and (if feasible) ending with their "stance" when reading about and discussing complex social issues. By pausing to write about the issue from the perspectives of different audiences (or stakeholders), they also explore and discuss new meanings with one another. In group settings, students swap positions for identifying new perspectives, then compiling, complicating, and enriching them—as well as noting strengths and weaknesses in their understanding as a group, rather than refuting one another's arguments. They finally compare the new strategies with traditional ones, discussing what they found useful and worth adding to their rhetorical repertoire. In first-year writing courses, a Nyāya approach enhances discussion by describing it as an "act of knowing" or a "knowledge episode" (Perrett); at the upper-division and graduate levels, my students have used postcolonial framing in combination with a Nyāya approach to, for instance, discuss how education systems can destroy learners' multilingual/multicultural skills and selves in the name of teaching them how to "write," without questioning the conflation of writing with writing in English, for example.

As a teaching tool, Nyāyasutra can be quite useful because it allows instructors to minimize generalization and abstraction while inviting students to explore and present causes, cases, and situations from their experiences—enhancing the Socratic approach to teaching and the use of Rogerian rhetoric for discussion and writing. Whereas questions are used for engagement in the Socratic method, Nyāya method engages students without the element of "pretending" by instead explicitly asking students to collectively identify, understand, and solve a problem at hand. As Lloyd ("Rethinking") observes, while Aristotelian and Burkean rhetorics consider rhetorical/ argumentative "victory" as the goal and then assess the means as fair or unfair afterward, the Nyāyasutra model begins by identifying a cause or problem and considers fairness a prerequisite to conducting the argument. If one of the functions of a rhetorical education is to promote an informed, civic, and responsible citizenry, then teachers can enhance and supplement traditional rhetoric with methods for "just" argument like Nyāya.

Another issue that scholars and teachers often worry about is what to do with student resistance—assuming that students aren't interested in new or foreign cultures and ideas. For instance, discussing the difficulty of teaching critical pedagogy to students who are not used to a political framing of education, Byron Hawk observes that "students cannot simply make the dialectical turn that maps them onto the global space" (214), adding that critical pedagogy "breeds guilt, and guilt often breeds cynicism and passivity, rather than agency" so students end up responding with "whatever" (215). In fact, it is not just students who do not want to encounter painful realities such as racism, ethnocentricity and racial/national supremacy, and colonial legacies; while some teachers avoid difficult topics altogether, others situate the problems in more acceptable contexts or perspectives such as "diversity" or "opportunity." A focus on power can help us to start with the "power" that we wield as teachers, make choices that we can make, and at least educate the next generation of scholars. A further focus on justice can additionally help interrogate potential projection of resistance and anxieties on students, helping us find ways to address resistance on students' part. In *Reclaiming the Local,* A. Suresh Canagarajah cites large-scale global studies that project quite negative consequences of monolingualism and monoculturalism for the politically dominant societies themselves in the next fifty years. Without scholars and educators across borders paying attention and taking up the cause of preserving and promoting the rich diversity of knowledge and cultures of "others" in the world, the diversity of knowledge for all will continue to dwindle at the same startling rate that it already is today.

Teachers, likewise, worry that "alternative" rhetorical traditions and resources are resented by colleagues and students alike because they tend to be perceived as "superior" to their local counterparts—even when not presented as such. This challenge can be overcome by designing discussion of readings, research, and writing assignments for what LuMing Mao calls "reflective encounters," helping students approach new traditions so as to reflect on what they already know, looking in the mirror, so to speak, and not only contrasting the familiar and "exotic" to confirm them as such. Students are usually *not* insensitive or unwilling to learn; it just takes some pedagogical effort to help them come to terms with difficult issues. Describing how he teaches Native American history and issues in writing courses, Daniel Cole states: "A likely reason for [student resistance] may lie in the venerated roles that discovery, colonization, and westward expansion play in the US national mythos, while the consequent dispossession of indigenous peoples is ignored or diminished" (123). While the author "did not expect to fully dislodge the rhetoric of Manifest Destiny in the minds of [his] students," he taught them how colonial forces work, helping them "engage critically with that ideology and examine the ideas with which a great many of them had been taught to identify" (123). When students see how new perspectives and nontraditional rhetorics can help them diversify their knowledge, analytical and research methods, and (for future teachers) pedagogical repertoires, they want to learn how to help stop perpetuating colonial and hegemonic discourses in academe and society. When they know, they care.

Nyāya's focus on context and consensus can prepare students for professions with complex challenges, especially in times that are contentious. For example, a medical team quickly and collectively tries to come to a diagnostic conclusion by examining a patient's condition; members of the team may disagree in the process, but the disagreement is motivated by the common purpose of best understanding the problem and treating the patient. Because the group makes the best decision possible, everyone "wins" the argument. When we are unable to find generally agreeable theses to apply to particular cases (deduction) and also unable to make generalizations from particular cases (induction), we could turn to particular problems and explore them with the simpler goal of understanding the problem on its own terms as much as we can. While experience as the basis of finding common ground may still be debated as shaped by different worldviews, it can be easier to focus on experience than to agree about theory, whether it is before or after a discussion. Especially for societies where people are divided by principle but recognize common problems, Nyāya offers useful methods: it shows how to make debates "honest" *(vaya)* by focusing on "where both sides seek the truth" rather than "hindering" or "tricky" *(jalpa),* "where the goal is to win by fair means or foul," not to mention "destructive" *(vitanda),* where the goal is to "demolish" the opponent by any means (Matilal 2). Replies, similarly, need to deliberately avoid being unfair *(chala),* as when a person picks the weakest part of someone's argument or interprets key terms in their own ways to respond "effectively" while ignoring the principle of honesty and fairness. As Robert Oliver observed, Nyāya and other rhetorical practices of ancient India were part of a larger "common search by speaker and hearer for enlightenment, through penetration of unified truth which encompasses them both and all else besides" (50). While that end was quite often a desire to give up the worldly in favor of being united with the divine, the fact that this same approach was used in civic and political debates and discourses means that it had established secular uses as well. The approach could be tremendously useful during contentious times in any society today.

CONCLUSION

> "Do not be afraid," the voice called to him. "Hang on to the wind and trust!" . . . . Jumping Mouse opened his eyes . . . and the higher he went the clearer [his sight] became. ("Story of the Jumping Mouse," a popular myth from an unnamed Native American tribe, qtd. in Johnson 116)

Every rhetorical tradition and practice has its own merits and affordances, but established traditions can also gradually absorb hegemonic power dynamics from dominant societies and cultures. Often, the merits overlap with blind spots, causing complacency to effectively silence people and suppress ideas. The dominant rhetorical tradition shaping American academic discourses, for instance, promotes productive dialog and defense of one's ideas; however, having adopted competition and contestation as a dominant mode of scholarship, it also prompts academic professions to be territorial and adversarial by default and being inclusive of different traditions and voices, people and perspectives, as a corrective means. Perhaps due to near-universal acceptance of agonistic terms of engagement as the most advanced and effective, scholars themselves use "conflict" as the analytical basis of socioeconomic philosophies such as capitalism and social organizations including diplomacy and the legal system, as well as academic disciplines like rhetoric and processes like scholarly publication. This worldview is so dominant that it is hard to imagine how else society could write its history, maintain institutions and disciplines, and advance knowledge. Postcolonial theory has been an effective means for not only explaining oppression but also for countering hegemony in dominant societies and empires, exposing the same dynamics in academe and the disciplines; but by adopting the same adversarial approach, this theory can also inadvertently reinforce division, especially by allowing those who embrace dominant traditions to stick to the tradition and ignore or dismiss concerns of the marginalized. To address this challenge, the nonadversarial, invitational, and inclusive affordances of rhetorics like Nyāyasutra could be used. While this rhetorical tradition could in itself be impractical and insufficient for our times, by helping us bring out the element of justice where it is suppressed or missing the tradition can foster more ethical stances in our scholarship, in our teaching, and in our public discourse. To use the analogy of the Jumping Mouse in the Native American myth quoted above, we can acquire new perspectives and clarity in our understanding if we venture beyond the historical and geographical limits of our discipline, trusting the good that the winds of globalization might bring, while we also address the risks.

For anyone interested, there is now fairly substantive scholarship about the destruction of indigenous literacies, imperial and racial legacies of education, and patriarchal constructions of the history of rhetoric. But this awareness carefully inhabits special margins of the discipline, rather than considerably reshaping the theory and practice of writing, not to mention reshaping the discipline's foundations. In fact, terms like *colonial* and *imperial* sound overly radical in writing studies, or, rather are radical-ized due to a prevalent hegemony that makes it much easier to contribute by conforming than by interrogating the historical foundations, established methods and practices, and political forces that have shaped the discipline. So, for instance, even though I studied colonization of the native peoples of America, slavery and racism against African American communities, and feminist rhetoric in formal and graduate-level courses, I find it more challenging to enter conversations about these topics than about South Asian rhetoric, which I have only studied independently. In fact, because I am conscious of being partly an outsider to society and culture in the United States, this consciousness considerably affects how I participate in most conversations in the discipline and the profession. Approaching rhetoric and writing as a means of fairness and justice for all my students and for any society and culture, however, begins to alleviate that anxiety. I can then begin to acknowledge that, on the one hand, I am an extraordinary beneficiary of internationalized higher education even as I discuss the insalubrious effects, on students and on education, of the triumphalist narrative of Western education/civilization and of a colonial/imperial world order; on the other, I am reminded that my extremely privileged presence in an American university belies the vast numbers of people left behind by the same global political-economic order. When I take a justice-based approach, I am also able to caution my colleagues against romanticizing the "internationalization" of education, showing how the process is also largely responsible for pushing the "price" of education beyond the means of most middle-class American families—if we take into account the lifetime of debt for many of them. As a noncitizen within an internationalized but nation-based educational regime, when I write about the education of my students—nearly nine out of ten of whom are local and a majority of whom are from low-income families—I pause to think about my "ethos" for advocating fair access and quality education for my students here. It is in that context that I use the "other" rhetorical traditions and practices for addressing the imperial/colonial "entanglements" (see Tuck and Yang)—historical and current, global and local, political and economic—affecting my students and people like them and me elsewhere. I find that my ethos based on justice and fairness in education powerfully enhances my ethos based on knowledge and expertise and my ethos from identity and subject position—even as I write with an almost disabling awareness about how privilege and marginalization, ambivalence and complicity, invitation and gatekeeping are all entangled in colonial foundations upon which a neoliberal global "market" now increasingly shapes access to education for all students.

Fortunately, we as scholars and teachers of rhetoric and writing are uniquely positioned to translate different visions about this discipline into educational objectives, pedagogically implement them, and effect social change. Rethinking the history of rhetoric and teaching writing by drawing on different rhetorical traditions can help us open up conversations about issues of power and politics, colonization and oppression, inequality and injustice. As geopolitical distributions of power shift, the pragmatism that has been used to justify the hegemony of the Greco-Roman-Anglo-American tradition of rhetoric as "the rhetorical tradition" is no longer convincing; the world will not engage in one set of historical constructs forever. The idea of creating inclusive environments and addressing issues of social justice by drawing on diverse traditions of knowledge goes to the heart of who we are as educators—and we can find numerous intellectual mentors in the scholarship, if we look for them, albeit in the margins of the dominant discourse. Nations will do what they must and will do, but educators can and should try to make them better than they are when driven by self-interest and by the whims of politics and power. "As the field rethinks its role for the twenty-first century, [it is for us to] consider how Composition studies itself might join the much larger conversation of disparate and local composing practices throughout history, across the Americas and beyond" (Baca 12). It is "high time" that we asked critical questions about our intellectual responsibilities and update our mainstream scholarship and pedagogy, and not tinker at the margins. How can we use knowledge and awareness about alternative epistemological worldviews to update our own, to connect with others, and to participate in reshaping a vastly uneven playing field where we may be complicit in the ongoing destruction of epistemological diversity in the world? What can we learn by freeing our minds from the hegemony of traditional paradigms and practices? As put eloquently by the commenter in the online article cited at the beginning of this chapter, how about "urbane, democratic, cultivating, respectful . . . friendly" theories and practices of rhetoric and writing that draw upon many rhetorical traditions from around the world?

NOTES

1. All of which an overly ambitious and emerging scholar of a related discipline tried to challenge.

2. For a substantive overview of postcolonial versus decolonial theoretical traditions, see "Postcolonial and Decolonial Dialogues" by Gurminder K. Bhambra.

3. In its broad sense, the term refers to one of six "astika" schools of the ancient philosophical and rhetorical traditions in South Asia. The conceptual basis of the Nyāya rhetorical method was codified by a scholar named Gautama "perhaps as early as 150 BCE, but more probably between 200 and 450 AD" (Lloyd, "Rethinking" 366), with references to "Nyāya" as a study of logic (of laws), philosophy, and spirituality going a few centuries back.

4. The term *vitanda,* for instance, is used in colloquial Nepali to describe aggressive rhetorical behavior, with connotations of street fighting.

5. I discuss the response to Brannon and Knoblauch's work and Lloyd's review of a similar response below.

6. Chanon Adsanatham (whose dissertation on a Thai rhetorical tradition received the CCCC James Berlin Outstanding Dissertation Award), Patrick Berry, Gail Hawisher, and Cynthia Selfe (whose book documents digital literacy practices across national borders), and A. Suresh Canagarajah, whose work has helped mainstream the discourse about world Englishes and translingual practices within writing studies.

7. E.g., Oliver; Gangal and Hosterman; Kirkwood; Garrett; Mao ("Reflective Encounters"; "Rhetorical Borderlands"); Stroud; Mejía; Takayama, Sriprakash and Connell.

WORKS CITED

Adsanatham, Chanon. *"Civilized" Manners and Bloody Splashing: Recovering Conduct Rhetoric in the Thai Rhetorical Tradition.* 2014. Miami U, PhD dissertation.

Baca, Damián. "Rethinking Composition, Five Hundred Years Later." *JAC,* vol. 29, no. 1–2, 2009, pp. 229–42.

Berry, Patrick W., Gail E. Hawisher, and Cynthia L. Selfe. *Transnational Literate Lives in Digital Times.* Computers and Composition Digital P/Utah State UP, 2012. Web.

Bhambra, Gurminder K. "Postcolonial and Decolonial Dialogues." *Postcolonial Studies*, vol. 17, no. 2, 2014, pp. 115–21.

Binkley, Roberta, and Marissa Smith. "Re-Composing Space: Composition's Rhetorical Geography." *Composition Forum*, vol. 15, 2006.

Canagarajah, A. Suresh. *Reclaiming the Local in Language Policy and Practice.* Routledge, 2008.

Cole, Daniel. "Writing Removal and Resistance: Native American Rhetoric in the Composition Classroom." *College Composition and Communication*, vol. 63, no. 1, 2011, pp. 122–44.

Donahue, Christiane. "'Internationalization' and Composition Studies: Reorienting the Discourse." *College Composition and Communication*, vol. 61, no. 2, 2009, pp. 212–43.

Foss, Sonja K., and Cindy L. Griffin. "Beyond Persuasion: A Proposal for an Invitational Rhetoric." *Communication Monographs*, vol. 62, no. 1, 1995, pp. 2–18.

Gangal, Anjali, and Craig Hosterman. "Toward an Examination of the Rhetoric of Ancient India." *Southern Speech Communication Journal*, vol. 47, no. 3, 1982, pp. 277–91. Published online 1 Apr. 2009.

Garrett, Mary M. "'Pathos' Reconsidered from the Perspective of Classical Chinese Rhetorical Theories." *Quarterly Journal of Speech*, vol. 79, no. 1, 1993, pp. 19–39.

Hawk, Byron. *A Counter-History of Composition: Toward Methodologies of Complexity*. U of Pittsburgh P, 2007.

Hesford, Wendy S. "The Changing Profession: Global Turns and Cautions in Rhetoric and Composition Studies." *Publications of the Modern Language Association of America*, vol. 121, no. 3, 2006, pp. 787–801.

Jarratt, Susan C. "Beside Ourselves: Rhetoric and Representation in Postcolonial Feminist Writing." *JAC: A Journal of Composition Theory*, vol. 18, no. 1, 1998, pp. 57–75.

Jensen, J. Vernon. "Teaching East Asian Rhetoric." *Rhetoric Society Quarterly*, vol. 17, no. 2, 1987, pp. 135–49.

Johnson, Flynn. *Journey to the Sacred Mountains: Awakening Your Soul in Nature*. Findhorn Press, 2010.

Kirkwood, William G. "The Turtle Spoke, the Donkey Brayed: Fables about Speech and Science in the *Panchatantra.*" *Journal of Communication and Religion*, vol. 10, no. 2, 1987, pp. 1–11.

Knoblauch, C. H., and Lil Brannon. *Rhetorical Traditions and the Teaching of Writing*. Boynton-Cook, 1984.

Kugelmass, Joseph. "Stop Using Rhetoric to Teach Writing." *Inside Higher Ed.* 23 Dec. 2008, https://www.insidehighered.com/views/2008/12/23/stop-using-rhetoric-teach-writing.

Lloyd, Keith. "Culture and Rhetorical Patterns: Mining the Rich Relations between Aristotle's Enthymeme and Example and India's Nyāya Method." *Rhetorica: A Journal of the History of Rhetoric,* vol. 29, no. 1, 2011, pp. 76–105.

———. "Multivalent Reasoning as a Way to Responsive and Sensitive Rhetorical Practices: Re-considering how Academics Respond to Each Other." Thomas R. Watson Conference, 17 Oct. 2014, University of Louisville, Louisville, Kentucky.

———. "Rethinking Rhetoric from an Indian Perspective: Implications in the Nyāya Sūtra." *Rhetoric Review*, vol. 26, no. 4, 2007, pp. 365–84.

Lyon, Arabella, and Banu Özel. "On the Politics of Writing Transnational Rhetoric: Possibilities and Pitfalls." *Feminist Rhetorical Resilience,* edited by Elizabeth A. Flynn, Patricia Sotirin, and Ann Brady, Utah State UP, 2012, pp. 54–56.

Lyons, Scott Richard. "Rhetorical Sovereignty: What Do American Indians Want from Writing?" *College Composition and Communication*, vol. 51, no. 3, 2000, pp. 447–68.

Mao, LuMing. "Reflective Encounters: Illustrating Comparative Rhetoric." *Style*, vol. 37, no. 4, 2003, pp. 401–25.

———. "Rhetorical Borderlands: Chinese American Rhetoric in the Making." *College Composition and Communication*, vol. 56, no. 3, 2005, pp. 426–69.

Matalene, Carolyn. "Contrastive Rhetoric: An American Writing Teacher in China." *College English*, vol. 47, no. 8, 1985, pp. 789–808.

Matilal, Bimal Krishna. *The Character of Logic in India*. Edited by Jonardon Ganeri and Heeraman Tiwari, Oxford UP, 1999.

Mejía, Jaime Armin. "Ethnic Rhetorics Reviewed." *College Composition and Communication*, vol. 63, no. 1, 2011, pp. 145–61.

Miller, Thomas P. "Teaching the Histories of Rhetoric as a Social Praxis." *Rhetoric Review*, vol. 12, no. 1, 1993, pp. 70–82.

Muchiri, Mary N., Nshindi G. Mulamba, Greg Myers, and Deoscorous B. Ndoloi. "Importing Composition: Teaching and Researching Academic Writing beyond North America." *College Composition and Communication*, vol. 46, no. 2, 1995, pp. 175–98.

Ndlovu-Gatsheni, Sabelo J. "Why Decoloniality in the 21st century?" *The Thinker for Thought Leaders,* vol. 48, 2013, pp. 10–15.

Oliver, Robert T. *Communication and Culture in Ancient India and China*. Syracuse UP, 1971.

Perrett, Roy W. "History, Time and Knowledge in Ancient India." *History and Theory,* vol. 38, no. 3, 1999, pp. 307–21.

Simonson, Solomon. "The Categories of Proof in Indian Logic." *Philosophy and Phenomenological Research*, vol. 6, no. 3, 1946, pp. 400–409.

Sinha, Sweta. "Indian Schools of Logic: A Critical Assessment." *International Journal of Sanskrit Research*, vol. 2, no. 6, 2016, pp. 170–72.

Stroud, Scott. "Ontological Orientation and the Practice of Rhetoric: A Perspective from the Bhagavad Gita." *Southern Communication Journal*, vol. 70, no. 2, 2005, pp. 146–60.

Takayama, Keita, Arathi Sriprakash, and Raewyn Connell. "Toward a Postcolonial Comparative and International Education." *Comparative Education Review*, vol. 61, no. 1, 2016, pp. 1–24.

Tuck, Eve, and K. Wayne Yang. "Decolonization Is Not a Metaphor." *Decolonization: Indigeneity, Education & Society*, vol. 1, no. 1, 2012, pp. 1–40.

Vidyâbhusana, Satis Chandra, translator. *The Nyāya Sūtras of Gotama*. Motilal Banarsidass, 1913.

Young, Morris. "Across Time and Space: The Transnational Movement of Asian American Rhetoric." *Composition Studies*, vol. 44, no. 1, 2016, pp. 131–33.

7

Moving the Body: Preamble to a Theory of Vernacular Rhetoric, or How a Caribbean Rhetoric[ian] Is Composed

Kevin Adonis Browne
University of the West Indies–St. Augustine

> I decompose, but I composing still.
> —Derek Walcott,
> "The Spoiler's Return"

RHETORIC, AMONG OTHER THINGS, IS THE ART OF self-discovery. It is recovery work. Whether they are ephemeral or preserved for posterity, the impetus for studying vernacular archives is founded in the need for practical continuity, the explicit, self-conscious connections made between past and present, historical and contemporary, and the enactment of a vision. When that study responds to a relative dearth in the field, it does so in keeping with the researcher's recognition that such a study is an attempt to stem the veritable erasure of lives—or, more accurately, the erasure of lived experiences as recorded in various texts. For many ethnic and cultural rhetoricians, recovery work is not merely an academic pursuit, but rather a course of inquiry that involves the stirring up of traumas, both personal and public. Every gesture, every word, every claim either enhances or undermines a legacy that is deep in our bones—deeper still in history, that sighing, epic memory. So it is not overstating the case to say that inquiry is not without injury—note that I do not say "the risk of injury." Injury is certain in this line of work—the difference is whether or not we are equipped to perform triage on our battered spirits when the work is done, or whether it will begin at all. In the search for ourselves, and the social [re]construction—or augmentation—of selves that ensues, we find that we are compelled to speak from absences, to [re]create presences from our hallowed echoes. This includes the interaction with vernacular archives and a reflective consideration of what is at stake for the researcher personally invested in the rhetorical exploration of their contents. These archives serve as a locus for initiating public discourse that is mediated (if not predominantly controlled) by the practitioner. It goes without saying, therefore, that the archive and the archivist become the primary sites upon which the utility of Caribbean rhetoric[1] is built, contested, revised, or undone in relation to the numerous other texts of which they are composed.

(Clockwise) Noel Stephens, Rhonda Newton, Dionne Wright, the author, and Leonel Stephens, 1976.

The pathology of Caribbean existence rests, in part, on the fact that we have been conditioned to fear death/destruction/reprisal in the face of its constant presence. The fear, rather than its inevitability, has long been normalized—coalescing, and then calcifying into a "culture" we recognize. Of course, we are familiar with its inevitability; however, between the histories of violence from which we emerged as "Caribbean" and the more recent increases in violence that have accompanied the region's [un]development, there is relatively scant regard for what this reality can generate. Having moved out of that history, through postcolonialism, neocolonialism, and independence, to assume the role of citizen, we are now positioned to colonize ourselves with new knowledge, knowledge of our own making. Unfortunately, this fact has not led to the reality/ies we desire and hope to articulate, which gives ironic and troubling credibility to the notion that we were not really meant to survive, not meant to outlive our usefulness as commodities or capital.

The Caribbean rhetorician is, thus, behooved to explore the means and methods that enable a generative engagement with an unintended past in a struggle to envision a way of knowing and being. Through the enactment of knowing in the process of being, it is assumed that we will arrive at a point of meaning. For the rhetorician possessing some personal investment in this pursuit, the heresy of self-discovery is framed additionally by the compulsion to engage with dead and ephemeral things—that is, not only encountering the past as an abstract (albeit meaningful) context, but also coming face to face with the inevitability of death and the urgency those scenarios present. This is a practice that appears to contradict the typical impulse toward immortality that defines legacy in general and archiving in particular on personal and institutional levels. But it only appears that way, particularly if we fail to consider the following:

1. Subjectivity in the Caribbean is the undiscovered country—all other spaces have been colonized, occupied, awarded, and developed. We are left with limited space to apply even the

most useful tropes of colonization—*decolonization,* for example, which is preceded by the necessary acknowledgment of the situation in which we find ourselves. The self-conscious construction of the subject is all that remains.

2. If there really is no more land, only our bodies and our ideas, then the texts we create, which make up our archives, are the material repositories of our expressive and intellectual topography in specific relation to time.
3. Rhetoric serves as the frame and the compass, the scaffold and the astrolabe, offering both the means to construct and the method to navigate the expanse of what we have constructed.
4. Theories about this rhetoric and its tradition are hidden in plain sight, in accordance with the modes of rhetorical masking, display, and deliberate misdirection.[2]

These provisional tenets go against the traditional structural hierarchy of Caribbean knowledge, which places marginal significance on ordinary contributions—located in letters, notes, receipts, recordings, and photographs—wherein the bulk of alternative enactments of contemporary Caribbeanness may be found(ed). I argue, though, that their function extends beyond the mere desire to speak, or write, back to traditions that have ensured their marginalization. The continuing effects of Empire demand urgency, but not at the expense of a basic declaration of oneself in the world—to ignore that is an effect of Empire in itself, and one we should be careful never to overlook.

Such ontologies of loss and finding—as well as the urgency and clarity they promise—are counterweighted by the acknowledgment of the limits of specific time frames (i.e., lifespans), within which one is able to locate the epistemological and pedagogical value of a project (in archiving, for example) and the subsequent likelihood of a legacy *post mortem*. This is how I enter, by looking past the yield of graves, by disturbing the ashes, and by reminding myself not to mistake movements of the spirit for fortune or mere serendipity.

READING BACKWARDS

It is my feeling that the vernacular self is a bitterly contested site, both the cause and the effect of deep existential conflict, a "zone of ontological struggle" that unfolds and ultimately unravels in the context of a broader imperial—or, if you like, globalist—ontology. This presents us with a problem of establishing workable presences that operate within (and in resistance to) an economy of systematic unseeing, unhearing, and unnaming. In order to more effectively understand how that self begins to coalesce under these circumstances, we have to think in terms of a critical repositioning that places the onus of establishing and sustaining presence squarely on those who require it.[3] When one has cause to consider Caribbean rhetorical traditions, one is reminded that a great deal has already been forgotten—presences, memories fade. One is, as my mother would say, "behind time." The conspicuous absence of these traditions in the field of rhetoric raises crucial questions that are sometimes painful to answer. However, I am obliged to consider not only what I have forgotten, but also what I have yet to know—and exactly how far back I must go to retrieve it. The question becomes: Where best to begin? How do I begin to construct a potentially persuasive argument that would encourage inquiry by interrupting the "trancelike retrospect," disrupting the "silence" with a questioning deep enough to cause astonishment to resonate with reflection—or, better, to replace wonder with inquiry? I must begin where I am and in the time I have. With loss, with the deliberate *countermemorialization of memory,* and with a composition that occurs as a consequence of exploration and heretical exposition.

In *A Small Place,* Jamaica Kincaid declares that "[t]o the people of a small place, the division of Time into the Past, the Present, and the Future does not exist" (53–54). Kincaid's words sting, but they also suggest the need for a methodology for the study of Caribbean rhetoric and its composition that would ultimately undo their irony. All ironies require an undoing. Kincaid's critique serves as a point of prophetic[4] intervention and practical departure that challenges the reader to engage in the critical [re]constitution of the vernacular self—one that complicates the initial claim of Time[lessness], while explicitly refuting the implication that we have no agency and are simply subject to Time's whims. I believe this is what provides Kincaid with the rationale for the additional observation that "[n]o action in the present is an action planned with a view of its effect on the future. When the future, bearing its own events, arrives, its ancestry is then traced . . . at the end of which . . . , the people in a small place reveal themselves to be like children being shown the secrets of a magic trick" (53–54). But it is also where contemporary rhetoricians can begin to situate a methodology of actual practice. If we conclude from Kincaid's formulation of Time[lessness] not only that "here" is always "now," but also that it is "always already," then we may similarly conclude that the fragmented Caribbean "past" is the first "elsewhere" which we possess any real (though only partial) proof of having visited: that is, in the form and function of subjectivity, agency, memory, and various remains. These all demand recognition—critical visibility. Likewise, we may conclude that the consequences of that exploration—the "undiscovered" nonlinearities of the past—are yet to be seen.

The rhetorical understanding of time functions as a troping mechanism in the appreciation, analysis, and distribution of a series of constitutive texts—*and* it could help practitioners recognize and make the connections that would result in the literal making of new knowledge. Similarly, the rhetorical practitioner's manipulation of Time[lessness] ensures the materialization of a particular vision and discovery: the archive.[5] Thus, as I explore the parameters of vernacular archiving in the context of Caribbean rhetoric, my main concern will veer toward the deliberative application of these aspects and their outcomes. At this nexus of activity, I suggest that we would be able to view Caribbean rhetoric, its composition, its practice, and its practitioners concurrently and in multiple dimensions. At stake is how we perceive ourselves as composers of texts that simultaneously compose us. This critical [re]positioning therefore involves the subtle shifting of positions that can lead to [re]created spaces. Once those spaces are [re]created, the transformations that result can lead to changes that are not that radical at all. Rather, the result is an aspiration to the vernacular that necessitates a move away from/beyond reactive response to Empire, and toward a more definitively progressive consideration of rhetorical invention as an existential practice. Excavation—indeed, an exhumation—is required, from which the abstract may be simultaneously sourced, uprooted, *and* used to situate our understanding of what rhetorical invention can mean. This is where we find ourselves: having to go back in time to break new ground—the new ground that *is* the formerly unquestioning self. Incidentally, it is where we are compelled to formulate a rhetorical stand. The Caribbean is an absurdity, but it is ours, along with all it can yield for those who belong to it. This being the case, I rely on the representative anecdote, knowing that, for people who view the Caribbean as a kind of home, the anecdote has functioned as a major form of *praxis,* especially given the institutional limitations to which we have historically been subject(ed).

Anecdote I

In October 1988, my grandfather, Newallo John Wright, died at his house in San Fernando. We all called him "Daddy." He was surrounded by loved ones. At the end of every decade of the Rosary, we added the *Requiem Æternam,* a special prayer for the dead and the dying as they make their way out of this world to a place of eternal rest in wait for (it is hoped) Heaven—or, at least, to Purgatory:

> Eternal rest grant unto him, O Lord.
> And let perpetual light shine upon him.
> May he rest in peace. Amen.

Prayers for the eternal rest of a man who hadn't yet died. For some days he had been drifting in and out of consciousness, losing coherence with every trip. Each time, a longer time, with less and less to report. "Traveling," we call it, though no one could tell where he went. I myself wasn't praying, but I remember the prayers, the bedside confessions, the weeping, and the clearing of throats to keep from weeping. I remember the silence of his nonmovement, the slowing of his breath, turning shallow, until silence. His wallet, its leather dried up and cracked like an old, exposed folio, was the

Newallo John "NJ" Wright, "Daddy," 1960s.

first memento I ever collected—the first *memento mori,* reminding me, at fourteen—of the inevitability of my own death. It was the first archive I recall.

Anecdote II

In October 1997, my aunt Maureen died in the Bronx, where she had lived since 1966. Marjorie, the eldest of her siblings, was a retired nurse. She had already come up from Trinidad, meeting my

Maureen Wright, Central Park, New York, 1980s.

Marjorie Wright-Smith in uniform, date unknown.

mother, Eva, who had emigrated in 1985 to work as a nanny on the Upper West Side and for other wealthy white families in the tristate area. Umilta (whom everyone calls "Dolly") had come in from Canada. Evelyn was back in Venezuela. Lystra remained in Trinidad.

I sat at my aunt's bedside, touching her head, whispering inaudible kindnesses. She was traveling, so I could only hope she heard me. Before I left to go back home to Brooklyn, I wrote my phone number in red ink on a flimsy white napkin. Later that evening, my mother described it all to me by phone (breath by breath, breathlessly) as I paced back and forth between breaths of my own in my apartment , taking it in as it happened:

"Kevin, she going. She going, son. She going."

I remember that my telephone number was written on the napkin. It was discarded, the number forgotten.

Anecdote III

On Friday, April 3, 1981, Peter Wright drowned. His sister Marjorie, being the eldest, was commissioned by Daddy to deliver the news to Maureen, who had emigrated to the United States in 1966, settling in the Bronx. At Daddy's request, Marjorie wrote. The letter is dated April 13, 1981, ten days after the drowning. A Monday. The letter itself would take another ten days to arrive. Seven years later, Daddy would be dead. Nine years later, Maureen would be dead. And fourteen years after that, in 2011, I would find the letter. Thirty years after it was written. I had gone to New York to help my mother move back to Trinidad. She was finally leaving the apartment she had shared with Maureen since moving from Brooklyn in 1996. Many of Maureen's things remained. Going through them, I found a small lockbox. In it were an expired passport, a naturalization certificate, an old Trinidad identification card and other documents, and some letters.

5 Turton St
Les Efforts East
13/4/81

Dear Maureen,

I did promise to write but not so soon anyway I'm forced to do this first to let you know which you already know of the great loss we suffered on the death of our beloved Prime Minister. This has had the entire nation grieved and is still expressing their great loss of a great man. We are having lots of tributes, memoriams condolences in all forms shown to the children and the nation. It was a very touching experience. Well our home circle journeyed to P.O.S to pay tribute. It was a very solemn and touching experience which I could write and write about. I'm hoping to keep all the newspapers of that time. On our return home a second shock was awaiting us. this was that Peter who went to Vessigny to bathe just stepped into the sea with no difficulty whatever and drowned on Friday 3rd April at about 3:30PM. This you could just imagine sent the entire family in chaos when I reached down to Daddy's he was all worked up. Miss Pearl

Page 1 (of 3) of Marjorie's letter to Maureen, April 13, 1981.

THE UNITED STATES OF AMERICA

No. 9731348

CERTIFICATE OF NATURALIZATION

Petition No. 815158

Alien Registration No. A12 768 478

·ORIGINAL·

Personal description of holder as of date of naturalization: Date of birth March 14th, 1936 sex Female complexion Dark color of eyes DarkBrown color of hair Black height 5 feet 2 inches weight 110 pounds visible distinctive marks None Marital status Married Country of former nationality Trinidad

I certify that the description above given is true, and that the photograph affixed hereto is a likeness of me.

Maureen Colvin
(Complete and true signature of holder)

UNITED STATES OF AMERICA
SOUTHERN DIST. OF NEW YORK } ss:

Be it known, that at a term of the District Court of The United States held pursuant to law at New York City on December 27th, 1972 the Court having found that MAUREEN COLVIN then residing at 1937 Davidson Ave. Bronx, N.Y. intends to reside permanently in the United States (when so required by the Naturalization Laws of the United States), had in all other respects complied with the applicable provisions of such naturalization laws, and was entitled to be admitted to citizenship, thereupon ordered that such person be and (s)he was admitted as a citizen of the United States of America.

In testimony whereof the seal of the court is hereunto affixed this 27th day of December in the year of our Lord nineteen hundred and 72

JOHN LIVINGSTON
Clerk of the U.S. District Court
By Deputy Clerk

Seal

DEPARTMENT OF JUSTICE

Maureen Colvin née Wright, Naturalization Certificate No. 9731348.

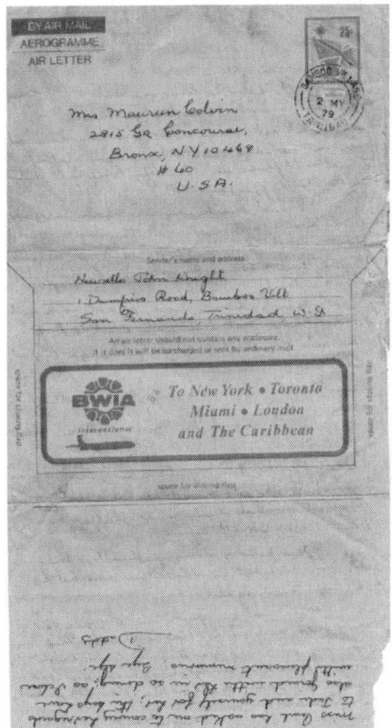

BY AIR MAIL
AEROGRAMME
AIR LETTER

Mrs Maureen Colvin
2815 Gr Concourse,
Bronx, N.Y. 10468
60
U.S.A.

Sender's name and address

1 Dumfries Road, Bamboo Vill
San Fernando, Trinidad, W.I.

To New York • Toronto
Miami • London
and The Caribbean

BWIA

Letter from Daddy to Maureen, May 2, 1979.

Anecdote IV

For three nights in May, 2000, I wore my dead aunt's clothes, my mother's makeup, wig, and pantyhose, and a pair of clunky black Payless pumps to tell the story of my cousin Noel's drowning in 1991. We were the same age when he died: seventeen. He was in Trinidad when it happened. I was in Boot Camp on Parris Island, South Carolina. Although we had been born only a couple of months apart, the gulf between us had now become incalculable. I had a basic agenda, therefore: to make a space where I could justifiably scream, a space to insist myself into a reality that no longer was. A space to help me tell the story. I borrowed heavily from what I could gather of my uncle Peter's drowning in 1981, ten years before Noel. I borrowed from Peter, and from his mother, Pearl, Daddy's second wife, who died in 1986 or 1987. I filled the spaces of a memory I did not have with one of my own—crafting from fragments a story that history and fact alone could never fill. For my portrayal of Noel's mother, Evelyn, I substituted fragments of Miss Pearl's story. It was Miss Pearl, not Evelyn, who had taken out her breast on the shore of Vessigny Beach in Southern Trinidad. Invoking the tenets of her own Pentecostal traditions, it was she who called out to her son, begging him to surface, to come ashore, to come with the tide, if not walk. (All in vain for indifferent waters and their own muddied vanities.) So heavily did I borrow that, holding my belly, doubled over in a heap of dead woman's clothes, it was Peter's name I would scream.

"Why yuh do this to me, son? Oh god, oh God, oh GOOOODDDDD, Peter!"

The scream—the gutted howl—was my mother's. I am my mother's child, as the expression goes, and (being the more emotive of the twins) it was her voice I used, and not that of Evelyn, Noel's own mother. Afterward, I and my audience wept openly before composing ourselves.

Fraternal Twins at First Communion (L to R) Eva and Evelyn, 1957.

Sisters (L to R) Umilta, Evelyn, Eva (my mother), and Lystra, 1962.

COMPOSING OUR SELVES

Absence is an unrefined urgency. And loss—its corollary—demands inquiry, as speculation can sometimes rush in to fill the void. For my part, then, I am thinking of how ancestors, forebears, and the texts they leave behind can complement the pantheon of creatures and imaginings that traverse the in-between (of past and present), the combination of which offers liberatory possibilities for productively synthesizing the consequences of marginalization and resisting various forms of erasure in contemporary settings. Not unlike the lives and deaths of my grandfather, aunt, uncle, and cousin, and the ceremonies that followed—the wake, the funeral, the interment, the repast, the nine nights, the forty days, and so on, into decades—the virtual disappearance of a wallet or a bile-stained napkin had fundamentally influenced the way I would remember them. That is to say two things. The first is obvious: the absence of an object does not necessarily lead to forgetting. Like the fading image of a photograph, the napkin was infinitely ephemeral (and, thus, never really in anyone's possession), providing additional proof of this fact.[6] The second is less obvious: the loss of these objects, accompanied by my regret for not having them, means that I had also abdicated the privilege of taking their respective memories for granted, which the artifacts would likely have enabled. However, in addition to losing that privilege, I had simultaneously been granted an opportunity to devise and enact a way of seeing that relied equally on my uncompromisingly subjective reading of the past in the troubling context of the present and on an infinite number of shifting futures.

What remains, therefore, relies on the deliberate reconstruction of a kind of presence, an imagined presence that functions as a supplement to what was lost among the bones, where many of us have been taught to believe that nothing but whispers exist in the ashes of our ordinary past. The text I had composed—called "Auntie Ada," after my great great-aunt Adrey—is a composite exploration of vernacular rhetorical practice as meaning making—that is, the result of reading, writing, and rewriting with ink and light, and with body and voice, a series of preexisting texts, taken at various

"Auntie Ada," the Author as Archive, May, 2000.

points between inception, perception, and reception. It is, in short, an archival endeavor intended to illustrate that I am, at all times, fully implicated in the practice of being and becoming. More generally speaking, the performance, with its deliberately unvarnished composition of historical revisionism and speculative projection—as a form of rhetorical countermemorialization—is a key example of how our displays unfold in practice.

Culminating with this composite performance in 2000, the anecdotes above illustrate the degrees of increasing latitude one ought to take in crafting a delivery that is assertive on its own merits, comprehensive in its scope, and potentially persuasive when reflected upon and subsequently displayed in public.[7] Turning more directly to the letter, then (included here in its entirety, with notes), we may observe that it not only plays an important role in the process of reflective composition, but it is also the frame—the rhetorical situation—with which to model other encounters and negotiations with our archives and the narratives they help to [re]construct.

5 Turton St
Les Efforts East[8]
13/4/81

Dear Maureen,[9]

I did promise to write but not so soon[. A]nyway I'm forced to do this first to let you know which you already know of the great loss we suffered on the death of our beloved Prime Minister [Dr. Eric Williams]. This has had the entire nation grieved and is still expressing their great loss of a great man. We are having lots of tributes, memoriams, condolences in all forms shown to the children and the nation[.] It was a very touching experience[.] Well our home circle journeyed to P.O.S. [Port of Spain] to pay tribute, it was a very solemn and touching experience which I could write and write about.[10] I'm hoping to keep all the newspapers of that time.[11] On our return home, a second shock was awaiting us.[12] This was that Peter[13] who went to Vessi[g]ny[14] to bathe just stepped into the sea with no difficulty whatever and drowned on Friday 3rd April at about 3:30 PM.[15]

This you could just imagine sent the entire family in chaos[. W]hen I reached down to Daddy's[16] he was all worked up. Miss Pearl had gone to locate the body but to[o] late he could not be found. The search was put on the next morning and as soon as they approached the beach there his blue trunks could be seen floating[.] Some young men went into the sea and brought him out. He was slightly swollen and had slight bruises about[17] his lip and forehead. He was not bitten by fish thank God. Arrangements were made for burial and he was buried on 7th April because of the no burial on weekends. Daddy did take it hard on Friday but after talking to him he cheered up on the weekend accepting condolences for the family. He again broke down slightly on Tuesday this being the first time seeing him after the incident.

With all the nice things said about Peter he did cheer up quickly[.] He thought from all his actions and talks that he was not meant to be here. Miss Pearl broke down complete[ly] after finding the body on Saturday morning[.] She refused meals, avoided interacting with her well wishers and took to bed. Well I had to give her a good shake up on the Wednesday and she did thank me for the talk. She has been somewhat back to normalcy[. T]hat is not with him forgotten[.][18]

I was going to ring you but Daddy suggested that I write[,] not even cable because he knew its [*sic*] not a matter of coming down but he wanted the news delivered gently.[19] We have and we hope you all would console yourselves as God knows best. It could have been any one of us. Daddy had no financial problems as what he had he got from family wise came out to be enough. He received amounts in $300, $200, $100, $400 (friend), some from you which he saved[20] and some from Miss Pearl's brothers. This part went fine and was highly appreciated.

It took me quite a bit of courage to write this letter.[21] Hope I don't have to write a letter of this type again or in a hurry.[22] Cheer up and give Judy our regards. I visited Daddy and they on Sunday and they [ ] except Curtis who is missing him quite a lot as they were pals and he too though[t] that if he didn't go to bathe Peter would be home today. He has gone out to work today Monday. This I think would help him a lot.[23]

Love from all,
Marj.

In a basic sense, my performance in 2000 was of a partial archive that I had composed more than a decade before the letter would be discovered in 2011. Since its rediscovery, it has been endowed with the potential to serve as a codex for my reading of the Caribbean subject, a text with and within which one can make practical sense of what Caribbean rhetoric can mean. Substantiated now by the content of the letter, rather than its mere discovery, the performance in 2000 can be reconstituted as an embodiment of the rhetorical sentiments I had gleaned in my reception and subsequent interpretation of loss and forgetting over the course of decades, both of which the letter was obviously intended to forestall (judging from the general forensic content and Marjorie's deliberative awareness and explicit mention of preservation). But it is more than that: it is a reminder that much of the work of vernacular archiving occurs at the intersection of the texts we discover and the ones we compose, or vice versa. In other words, the letter not only appears to fulfill its role as a forensic record of a family tragedy; it also effectively complements the mythos of Peter's drowning with contextualization and historicization of the key detail. The relative objectivity of Marjorie's reportage in the letter combine with the subjective interpretation of my own storytelling to enrich the overall archive. And the inverse is also true: my performance was a deliberative objectification that, through impersonation, adds nuance to Marjorie's understated subjectivity in her role as author and the bearer of tragic news. Neither can—or should—be separated from the other. What this suggests is that though the periods of drafting differ greatly, following the initial experience in 1981, the publication of Marjorie's letter almost two weeks after Peter's death and my own performance almost two decades later are complementary both in a material sense and a rhetorical one. This is further emphasized in their combined effectivity more than thirty-seven years after the letter was written, more than eighteen years after the performance was staged, and more than seven years after the letter was found. They demonstrate further not only that we suffer the effects of Timelessness, as Kincaid has suggested, but that we can also benefit from our manipulations of time, revising aspects of events for our collective visibility.

The study of this and other texts in the archive[24] is precursory in nature, intended to serve as a discursive and material model—a methodological testing ground—for the study of vernacular knowledge, preservation, and distribution. This reflection marks my attempt to situate these texts' relevance in the current moment—and in the other moments that have led to and follow from this one. In my view, therefore, establishing and understanding a connection—even a preliminary one—is key to understanding discourse in the Caribbean specifically. And, in a more general way, it allows us to examine the role of composition in the author's and audience's participation in public life and their respective contextualization of geopolitical discourse (all of which is multimodally constituted even before being digitized and rereleased). If we mean to understand the function of Caribbean subjectivity as more than a symbolic performance, or a pretense, then there has to be an articulation of and an appreciation for the subjectivities that attend a viable conception of the vernacular self. To do otherwise would essentially relegate the subject to a continuance of phenomenological invisibility. We know, of course, that invisibility, absence, displacement, anonymity, physicality have long been the constitutive acts through which black existence is incorrectly constructed. A relatively revised construction reveals the various complicated expressions of an extant subjectivity that is constantly resisting erasure, silencing, or marginalization.

Furthermore, if the study of such practices is driven, as I argue, by an imperative that advocates for the subjectivity of the practitioners, their communities, and their articulations of place within and beyond those communities, then it is not only counterintuitive to subscribe to an objective approach, it is also quite impossible to do so. There is no meaningful self in the absence of the other; explorations of the self can therefore yield the kind of productive self-interest that we associate with the vernacular, wherein the individual stands a better chance of productively negotiating with the collective in accordance with their shared interests.

Knowledge making is an act of self-determination—an exercise of discursive awareness and, to a lesser degree, subversive power. Self-determination, and not disruption, is the main objective here, but if disruption occurs as a consequence of subjects' collective exercise of self-determination, it should be considered a bonus. The making of knowledge—new or otherwise—involves the conscious manipulation of materials at our disposal, from which emerge opportunities for collaborative articulation. Such articulation forces us to abandon the typical linear reading that we reserve for traditional texts and lean, instead, toward the nonlinear. The existence of such knowledge ought not only to be taken as self-evident, but taken also as an occasion to emphasize the organic nature of vernacular intellectual activity and the subsequent incorporation of the intellectual into the text. Such an act would result in the infusion (rather than the simple imposition) of my motives with regard to the text(s) in question. The aim is not so much to "know," per se, but rather to understand the multidimensionality of what is being displayed, how to meaningfully engage it, and how to ensure that the resulting display reflects our shared understanding.

If we turn to the relevance such a study may hold for the practitioners of the rhetoric embodied in these archives, the need for continuity is significantly amplified. No marginalized group has the luxury of doing anything simply for its own sake.[25] As we have observed from the letter and the performance which both preceded and followed it, these archives are simultaneously evidence of the authors' giving accounts of themselves, how they locate themselves in given situations and as part of a series of social events that make up everyday life. Each object is a declarative statement: that the author-practitioner did, indeed, exist. As such, the inquiry into vernacular archives—and the decision to display them—is not just a question of methodology, but one that describes and expresses the very nature of modern Caribbean existence and the ongoing contestation—in thought, word, and deed—for the significance of the underclassed individual in the constitution of the whole. It is an ethical consideration that occurs in response to an ideology of de facto oppression and resists the internalization of an ideology of self-denial, one that reinscribes a neocolonial-industrialist ethos and places undue value on the productivity of bodies solely in the service of metropolitan imperial power. Inquiry of this kind is also important for Caribbean people because although we continue to be plagued by the idea that a failure to heed the past all but ensures we repeat it, the opposite may be true of texts we fail to preserve: we risk losing a history we alone are equipped to tell, as well as the continuity (problematic or otherwise) that such a telling could provide.[26]

To reiterate, Caribbean rhetoric is an understanding of the vernacular spirit. In the encounter with ancestral knowledge, this means that one is sure to encounter the ancestors themselves. So a major mandate of the Caribbean rhetorician is to understand and give voice to the vernacular spirit. This is the true utility of a Caribbean ethos in the making of an archive, necessitating the kind of exposure that leaves the researcher completely vulnerable, because that is the nature of the work and the life (and lives) it is intended to preserve. The beating heart understands what the mind is hard-pressed to conceive: We must take our time. To "take our time," as people, as archivists, and as rhetoricians, is to take the past, present, and future into more flexible consideration, to look at the corresponding products—defined, in part, by their forensic, demonstrative, and deliberative qualities—for an approach to life that is far more dynamic than the sum, subtraction, or supposition of its constitutive parts. To possess it and be possessed by it, by that which is ours, which has been left for us to find or to discard. Which, to the unseeing eye, can only seem like sorcery; to the ear that does not hear, will sound like ole talk. In truth, however, it emerges from the conscious understanding of shared values, and the deliberative expression of those values in different situations. Thus, our considerations of rhetoric, rather than a series of purely esoteric inquiries, should always find their practical and situational grounding in the social and spiritual milieux in which their rationales, exigencies, and outcomes emerged and were ultimately executed.

NOTES

1. Caribbean rhetoric is defined as a system of mediated communication, an enduring collective identification with existing forms of knowing that shape the more abstract and supernatural suggestions of the elements that constitute Caribbean knowledge on a rhetorical level. An understanding and analysis of rhetoric enables us—all of us—to put that knowledge to productive use in the construction of provisional identities and to increase the probability that that knowledge will have an impact on the societies of which we are a part.

2. The pervasiveness of globalism notwithstanding, the notion of a broader worldview, from the standpoint of a rhetorical framework, is consequential, a result of the transactions between extant Caribbeanness and the world.

3. This is not a call for bootstrapping, or any suggestion that ignores structural inequalities and their attendant monstrosities; rather, it is a suggestion that vernacular practitioners are best equipped to operate on and in their own terms within (and despite) the constraining contexts of the everyday.

4. I say "prophetic" for two reasons: first, because Kincaid's depiction of Time to "the people of a small place" is an abstraction devised in the context of postcolonial (non)response to the protracted effects of Empire, about which (it may reasonably be assumed) the very audience she refers to would rather not be concerned. This is because the claim attempts a metadiscursive analysis of their everyday lives when they would prefer to live; second, we understand that among dispossessed people, the prophetic functions as the suggestion of a method or series of methods that have either been ignored or have yet to be applied, leading to doom, destruction, or the malaise of everyday life.

5. This is as much an existential problem as it is a rhetorical problem, because the overarching issue—implicit in Kincaid and made more explicit now—is the degree of praxis. In this case, we understand praxis as the point at which theory is demystified by practice, and at which practice is buttressed with theory.

6. In fact, the memory of it may very well increase the likelihood that I will actively remember—or be driven, more accurately, to memorialize—those I have lost. Conversely, each loss is more recent than the death event and forms bridges between them and me, their literal materiality no longer being of direct consequence because of the linear logic that I could easily trace and the nonlinear revisionism I could (less easily) apply.

7. This latitude is further amplified when we consider the events in chronological order, presented here in contrast to their respective roles as archives and objects of visual rhetorical import: 1981 Peter drowns; the Letter is composed; 1986 or 1987 Miss Pearl (Peter's mother) dies; 1988 Newallo ("Daddy," Peter's father) dies; 1991 Noel drowns; 1997 Maureen dies; 2000 I perform "Exposition" using elements of Peter's story to tell the story of Noel's drowning; 2011 the Letter is found, shedding further light on Peter's death.

8. A suburb of San Fernando, located near the old Cross Crossing railroad interchange.

9. Maureen emigrated to Brooklyn in 1962, moving to the Bronx shortly after. She became a naturalized citizen in 1974.

10. The introductory paragraph contrasts public memory with private grief: the death and memorialization of Dr. Eric Williams, the first prime

minister of Trinidad and Tobago. Williams died on March 29, 1981. Marjorie's choice here is a deeply ironic one, since Williams's own death was announced with no fanfare by then-President Sir Ellis Clarke, who in an address to the nation stated simply, "The Prime Minister is dead."

11. Marjorie, recognizing the significance of the moment, announces her intent to create her own vernacular archive from newspapers. There is no evidence the archive was created, however. Marjorie died in 2014 without disclosing this.

12. Comparative transition. Marjorie, having offered an earlier contrast between public and private, now makes an effort to equate the two experiences using their initial "shock" as her driving theme.

13. Peter and his older brother Curtis were the two children produced when Newallo John Wright ("Daddy") married Miss Pearl in 1966. His first wife, my grandmother Muriel Pitt, had died seven years earlier, on January 25, 1959.

14. Vessigny Beach, Southern Trinidad. One of the beaches on the western coast of Trinidad, Vessigny is notorious for its silty sand and murky water.

15. The announcement is a combination of unofficial witness testimony (provided by Peter's brother Curtis and other friends) and official elements (time of death later corroborated by the District Medical Officer when Peter's body was recovered).

16. Daddy lived on Dumfries Road, Bamboo Village, between Duncan Village and La Romaine, a few miles from Les Efforts East.

17. The use of *about* in this way is a peculiar discursive feature, presumably inherited from a colonial British past. In general, its usage is limited to news reports that offer descriptions of physical violence.

18. In terms of arrangement, Marjorie provides separate reports of Daddy's and Miss Pearl's reactions throughout the ordeal. Each period spanned five days—Friday to Tuesday in Daddy's case, and Saturday to Wednesday in Miss Pearl's. It is interesting to note that not even the periods themselves were synchronized, with Daddy's reaction and Miss Pearl's separated by a day. This apparent separation may have been due to two reasons: Marjorie's apparent preference to discuss with Maureen the reactions of their father ahead of those of his second wife and their stepmother; and the fact that Miss Pearl was reported to have gone to locate and retrieve the body when Marjorie arrived at Daddy's. The latter, in my view, is more plausible, while the former can only be speculation and conjecture.

19. Marjorie describes the delayed delivery that we also see in the letter's introduction. By using Williams's memorialization as a foil, she was

able to delay the announcement. There was no way to avoid the inevitable, but we see how the intention (that the "news be delivered gently") superseded the convenience provided by other technologies (telephone and cable-wireless services).

20. Marjorie was sure to mention Maureen's remittance, a common practice among immigrant populations. Also, there is a direct reciprocation of Daddy's efforts—noted in a 1962 letter—to have "remit[ted] to her the sum of Fifty Dollars (US) monthly from my account . . . at the under mentioned address [in Brooklyn, New York] until further notice."

21. This is Marjorie's only explicit reference to her own emotional state. It is, notably, in reference to the letter she has had to write rather than to the drowning and subsequent events. Also notable is the fact that while she describes the family's response to the initial shock, she alludes to situations that demand composure. This is consistent with her role as eldest child and de facto matriarch after her mother Muriel's death in 1959.

22. This was an unfortunate premonition. A decade later, in November 1991, Noel would drown at La Tinta Bay in Northern Trinidad. The news was delivered this time by phone.

23. This appears to be a postscript making reference to Curtis's emotional state and the reason for his guilt.

24. Part of the ongoing work of the Caribbean Memory Project (www.caribbeanmemoryproject.com).

25. Furthermore, as the old die and the young are being killed or killing themselves at an alarming rate, we are witnessing the literal depletion of sources and resources who are able to make, share, and preserve knowledge. The urgency is, therefore, quite clear. It is clarified even further when viewed through a Caribbean rhetorical lens.

26. This is not a look at the past simply for the sake of it—I know where the past is, and it is held in place with a healthy suspicion of the nostalgic impulse. Where I come from no longer exists. It shouldn't exist. And, try as I may to revisit the past—in memory or the rants that punctuate the much longer periods of sobering silence that define my everyday—my longing for times past ends at the precarious edge of texts that outlive their authors, recordings of laughter that find the dead mingling with the living, and expressions that push their implicit ethos forward for the purpose of explicit study.

WORKS CITED

Kincaid, Jamaica. *A Small Place*. Farrar, Straus and Giroux, 2000.

Walcott, Derek. "The Spoiler's Return." *The Poetry of Derek Walcott 1948–2013*. Farrar, Straus and Giroux, 2014. 303–08.

Wright-Smith, Marjorie. Letter to Maureen Wright. 13 Apr. 1981.

Afterword

Victor Villanueva
Washington State University

WHEN I WAS IN GRADUATE SCHOOL, I TOOK an upper-division French theory course to meet one of my language requirements (having already met the other requirement through a test in Spanish). It was there, in that class, that I first heard and read the expression (I seem to remember it was Jacques Lacan) *l'Autre*. What a way to categorize people, I thought then—the Other. But the French theorists became (and remain) important social capital in the US academy (at least in the humanities), so the Other remains in our discourse, with our being quite clear who are the Same and who are the Other. It's a term (more than a word) that can never escape the connotation of less than, or, at the very best, less powerful than. I have decided to change the makeup of that noun to the *Othered,* so to acknowledge the real power dynamics at play. It's not our term. It's a term from the Same to recognize the histories that made us "different." In this hemisphere it's a term that finds its roots in an Italian-Spaniard who discovered a world that was already there (and already known to Africans, according to Columbus's diary of the second voyage) yet still decided it was new, never quite acknowledging ignorance more than novelty. Hard for me, as a Puerto Rican, not to think of that, since Puerto Rico has been a continuous colony since Columbus's second voyage.

What we have just read is a series of autoethnographies, as many of the authors have said—talking back to the stories that the Same had contrived about us. Talking back to the Othering. But this is a tricky thing that we do. We follow the conventions of the Same's rhetorics, assert the Self, and in the process try to tell the Same about our Othering, which we of course all realize (and have realized for most—if not all—of our lives). It's an I'm-no-different difference that we espouse. Tricky business: asserting a legitimacy to the Othering and in so doing maintaining the Othering, even if not accepting our diminishment by the Same. This is the bind we're in, though this collection is the necessary step in another direction.

Consider the word *Latino.* I am Latino (with the -o, a male). The term comes from the region in Italy where Rome was built—Latium. So the Romans must have been the first Latinos. And they built an empire. And their language spread across the empire, the languages of Rome, the Romance languages. The language becomes the marker of the Latino. In this hemisphere, those who speak Spanish or Portuguese are Latinos and Latinas—but not the Francophones? Odd, no? Same history, in terms of Rome and Latium. But while Rome might be the historical word-marker, the Spanish-speakers and the French-speakers of this hemisphere have different imperial histories. No longer Rome but Spain. It's one reason we tend not to care for *Hispanic*—too close for colonial comfort. I grew up when Latinx were Latins (with Latin music, which tended to be Cuban, and in the movies most often "Latin lovers," especially Rudolf Valentino, who actually was Italian, or Al Jolson in blackface singing "She's a Latin from Manhattan"), though New Yorkers just called us Spanish. They still do, I'm told. And I grow old as Latinos y Latinas become Latinx. So you see how difficult it is to escape the imperial roots that bind us. Rome, Spain, and for all that is right about avoiding gender and sexuality biases with Latinx, it's an Anglicization, this empire. Somehow, the Same still dictates our Othering, even our self-identification as Proud Others. The world system is a system of empires and imperialist histories, as the introduction to this collection makes so clear and as each contributor so wonderfully demonstrates. So we are left with the overarching concern of this book: How do we break free, decolonize?

My hope is that we might somehow flip the Othering, recognizing that at least rhetorically (since the political economies at play remain always tied to neocolonialism, someone ruling someone else through money) that we too are the Same-as-Othered. As I try to explain elsewhere ("'I Am Two Parts': Collective Subjectivity and the Leader of Academics and the Othered," *College English*, vol. 75, no. 5, May 2017, pp. 482–94) I look for a time when we can somehow maintain our Self and our Other as a subjective collective, each of us recognizing that we have a common memory, the memory of colonization, that even as we acknowledge our own ancestral memories also recognizes that we all share a memory, the memory of being Othered. This collection is a necessary step in that direction, with its beautifully written stories of our binary relations to the Same and the Othered. The next step, perhaps, will be articulating that we are a collective. And I avoid saying a *collectivity* since that oversimplifies the very richness contained in this collection, nullifies it, keeps us locked into the Othered. My hope is that in collections like this we can realize that "[i]t is the shared memories . . . that [can] help to establish the genre of a movement," a collective subjectivity, one whose history might have been colonized and Othered, but now asserts a collective self, freed from the colony.

INDEX

The letter *p* following a page locator denotes a photograph.

EDITORS

Damián Baca is associate professor of English and Mexican American studies at the University of Arizona and faculty with the Bread Loaf School of English. He is author of *Mestiz@ Scripts, Digital Migrations, and the Territories of Writing* and lead editor of *Rhetorics of the Americas: 3114 BCE to 2012 CE.*

Romeo García is assistant professor of writing and rhetoric studies at the University of Utah. He is author of "On the Cusp of Invisibility" (2017), "Unmaking Gringo-Centers" (2017), "Creating Presence from Absence and Sound from Silence" (2018), and "Corrido-ing State Violence" (2018).

CONTRIBUTORS

Fatima Zahrae Chrifi Alaoui is assistant professor of communication studies at San Francisco State University. She is author of "Redefining Arab Feminism through the #RevolutionaryBody: From the Streets to the Tweets" (2015) and "Morocco from a Colonial to a Post-Colonial Era: The Socio-Political Environment through a Grandmother's Autoethnography" (2018).

Steven Alvarez is assistant professor of English and coordinator of first-year writing at St. John's University. He is the author of *Brokering Tareas: Mexican Immigrant Families Translanguaging Homework Literacies* and *Community Literacies* en Confianza: *Learning from Bilingual After-School Programs.*

Sonia C. Arellano is an assistant professor in the Department of Writing and Rhetoric at the University of Central Florida. Her research focuses on textile projects that address social justice issues, particularly at the intersections of immigration, death, and tactile rhetorics.

Kevin Adonis Browne, of Trinidad and Tobago, is a scholar of contemporary rhetoric and Caribbean culture, photographer, poet, and archivist at the University of the West Indies–St. Augustine. He is the author of *HIGH MAS: Carnival and the Poetics of Caribbean Culture* and *Tropic Tendencies: Rhetoric, Popular Culture, and the Anglophone Caribbean.*

Bernadette Marie Calafell is a professor in the Department of Communication Studies at the University of Denver. She received her PhD from the University of North Carolina. Calafell is author of *Latina/o Communication Studies: Theorizing Performance* and *Monstrosity, Performance, and Race in Contemporary Culture.* and coeditor of *Latina/o Discourse in Vernacular Spaces: Somos de Una Voz?*

Ellen Cushman is a citizen of the Cherokee Nation and serves as associate dean of Academic Affairs, Diversity and Inclusion at Northeastern University. She is the author of *The Cherokee Syllabary: Writing the People's Perseverance* (2012) and coeditor of the 2001 edition of *Literacy: A Critical Sourcebook* (with Eugene R. Kintgen, Barry M. Kroll, and Mike Rose).

Haneen Shafeeq Ghabra is an assistant professor of mass communications at Kuwait University. She is author of *Muslim Women and White Femininity: Reenactment and Resistance* (2018). Her specialization includes rhetoric and cultural studies with a focus on Muslim women and intersectionality.

Iris D. Ruiz is continuing lecturer of writing, rhetoric, and ethnic studies at the University of California, Merced, and California State University, Stanislaus. She is author of *Reclaiming Composition for Chicano/as and Other Ethnic Minorities: A Critical History and Pedagogy* and coeditor of *Decolonizing Rhetoric and Composition Studies: New Latinx Keywords for Theory and Pedagogy.*

Shyam Sharma is associate professor of writing and rhetoric at the State University of New York at Stony Brook. He is author of *Writing Support for International Graduate Students: Enhancing Transition and Success,* as well as a number of articles in prestigious venues in writing studies.

Kate Vieira is an associate professor and the Susan J. Cellmer Distinguished Chair in Literacy in the School of Education at the University of Wisconsin, Madison. She is the author of *American by Paper: How Documents Matter in Immigrant Literacy* (2016) and *Writing for Love and Money* (forthcoming).

Victor Villanueva is Regents Professor and Edward R. Meyer Distinguished Professor of Liberal Arts and Director of the University Writing Program at Washington State University.

BOOKS IN THE CCCC STUDIES IN WRITING & RHETORIC SERIES

Rhetorics Elsewhere and Otherwise: Contested Modernities, Decolonial Visions
Edited by Romeo García and Damián Baca

Black Perspectives in Writing Program Administration: From the Margins to the Center
Edited by Staci M. Perryman-Clark and Collin Lamont Craig

Translanguaging outside the Academy: Negotiating Rhetoric and Healthcare in the Spanish Caribbean
Rachel Bloom-Pojar

Reframing the Relational: A Pedagogical Ethic for Cross-Curricular Literacy Work
Sandra L. Tarabochia

Inside the Subject: A Theory of Identity for the Study of Writing
Raúl Sánchez

Genre of Power: Police Report Writers and Readers in the Justice System
Leslie Seawright

Assembling Composition
edited by Kathleen Blake Yancey and Stephen J. McElroy

Public Pedagogy in Composition Studies
Ashley J. Holmes

From Boys to Men: Rhetorics of Emergent American Masculinity
Leigh Ann Jones

Freedom Writing: African American Civil Rights Literacy Activism, 1955–1967
Rhea Estelle Lathan

The Desire for Literacy: Writing in the Lives of Adult Learners
Lauren Rosenberg

On Multimodality: New Media in Composition Studies
Jonathan Alexander and Jacqueline Rhodes

Toward a New Rhetoric of Difference
Stephanie L. Kerschbaum

Rhetoric of Respect: Recognizing Change at a Community Writing Center
Tiffany Rousculp

After Pedagogy: The Experience of Teaching
Paul Lynch

Redesigning Composition for Multilingual Realities
Jay Jordan

Agency in the Age of Peer Production
Quentin D. Vieregge, Kyle D. Stedman, Taylor Joy Mitchell, and Joseph M. Moxley

Remixing Composition: A History of Multimodal Writing Pedagogy
Jason Palmeri

First Semester: Graduate Students, Teaching Writing, and the Challenge of Middle Ground
Jessica Restaino

Agents of Integration: Understanding Transfer as a Rhetorical Act
Rebecca S. Nowacek

Digital Griots: African American Rhetoric in a Multimedia Age
Adam J. Banks

The Managerial Unconscious in the History of Composition Studies
Donna Strickland

Everyday Genres: Writing Assignments across the Disciplines
Mary Soliday

The Community College Writer: Exceeding Expectations
Howard Tinberg and Jean-Paul Nadeau

A Taste for Language: Literacy, Class, and English Studies
James Ray Watkins

Before Shaughnessy: Basic Writing at Yale and Harvard, 1920–1960
Kelly Ritter

Writer's Block: The Cognitive Dimension
Mike Rose

Teaching/Writing in Thirdspaces: The Studio Approach
Rhonda C. Grego and Nancy S. Thompson

Rural Literacies
Kim Donehower, Charlotte Hogg, and Eileen E. Schell

Writing with Authority: Students' Roles as Writers in Cross-National Perspective
David Foster

Whistlin' and Crowin' Women of Appalachia: Literacy Practices since College
Katherine Kelleher Sohn

Sexuality and the Politics of Ethos in the Writing Classroom
Zan Meyer Gonçalves

African American Literacies Unleashed: Vernacular English and the Composition Classroom
Arnetha F. Ball and Ted Lardner

Revisionary Rhetoric, Feminist Pedagogy, and Multigenre Texts
Julie Jung

Archives of Instruction: Nineteenth-Century Rhetorics, Readers, and Composition Books in the United States
Jean Ferguson Carr, Stephen L. Carr, and Lucille M. Schultz

Response to Reform: Composition and the Professionalization of Teaching
Margaret J. Marshall

Multiliteracies for a Digital Age
Stuart A. Selber

Personally Speaking: Experience as Evidence in Academic Discourse
Candace Spigelman

Self-Development and College Writing
Nick Tingle

Minor Re/Visions: Asian American Literacy Narratives as a Rhetoric of Citizenship
Morris Young

A Communion of Friendship: Literacy, Spiritual Practice, and Women in Recovery
Beth Daniell

Embodied Literacies: Imageword and a Poetics of Teaching
Kristie S. Fleckenstein

Language Diversity in the Classroom: From Intention to Practice
edited by Geneva Smitherman and Victor Villanueva

Rehearsing New Roles: How College Students Develop as Writers
Lee Ann Carroll

Across Property Lines: Textual Ownership in Writing Groups
Candace Spigelman

Mutuality in the Rhetoric and Composition Classroom
David L. Wallace and Helen Rothschild Ewald

The Young Composers: Composition's Beginnings in Nineteenth-Century Schools
Lucille M. Schultz

Technology and Literacy in the Twenty-First Century: The Importance of Paying Attention
Cynthia L. Selfe

Women Writing the Academy: Audience, Authority, and Transformation
Gesa E. Kirsch

Gender Influences: Reading Student Texts
Donnalee Rubin

Something Old, Something New: College Writing Teachers and Classroom Change
Wendy Bishop

Dialogue, Dialectic, and Conversation: A Social Perspective on the Function of Writing
Gregory Clark

Audience Expectations and Teacher Demands
Robert Brooke and John Hendricks

Toward a Grammar of Passages
Richard M. Coe

Rhetoric and Reality: Writing Instruction in American Colleges, 1900–1985
James A. Berlin

Writing Groups: History, Theory, and Implications
Anne Ruggles Gere

Teaching Writing as a Second Language
Alice S. Horning

Invention as a Social Act
Karen Burke LeFevre

The Variables of Composition: Process and Product in a Business Setting
Glenn J. Broadhead and Richard C. Freed

Writing Instruction in Nineteenth-Century American Colleges
James A. Berlin

Computers & Composing: How the New Technologies Are Changing Writing
Jeanne W. Halpern and Sarah Liggett

A New Perspective on Cohesion in Expository Paragraphs
Robin Bell Markels

Evaluating College Writing Programs
Stephen P. Witte and Lester Faigley

This book was typeset in Garamond and Frutiger by Barbara Frazier.
Typefaces used on the cover include Garamond and News Gothic.
The book was printed on 50-lb. White Offset paper
by Seaway Printing Company.